A PLUME BOOK

CLASH!

HAZEL ROSE MARKUS, PH.D., is the Davis-Brack Professor in behavioral sciences at Stanford University. She is also a founder and former director of Stanford's Research Institute for Comparative Studies in Race and Ethnicity.

ALANA CONNER, PH.D., is an experimental cultural psychologist, science communicator, and former senior editor of the *Stanford Social Innovation Review*. Her writing has appeared in the *New York Times Magazine* and many other outlets.

Praise for *Clash!*

"This book is a passkey that opens many doors. Using one simple principle, *Clash!* explains some of the most bedeviling cultural divides in our workplaces and communities. It's mandatory reading for teachers, managers, and parents who want to raise their kids to succeed in a multicultural world."

—Chip Heath, Ph.D., coauthor of *Decisive: How to Make Better Choices in Life and Work* and *Switch: How to Change When Change Is Hard*

"*Clash!* offers deep insights into how our cultures and culture clashes make us who we are, and how that matters for success in the twenty-first century. Everyone should read this book."

—Carol S. Dweck, Ph.D., author of *Mindset*

"If you fear that cultural, political, and class differences are tearing America apart, read this important book to learn how we can turn some of our differences into strengths."

—Jonathan Haidt, Ph.D., author of *The Righteous Mind*

"What a brilliant, eye-opening book! Filled with insight, and based on fascinating original research, *Clash!* offers a way to understand and break through some of the deepest cultural divides of our time. It's a page-turner—fun, witty, engagingly written."

—Amy Chua, author of *Battle Hymn of the Tiger Mother*

"In these days of heedless enthusiasm for gene maps and brain scans *Clash!* reminds us that human beings are, above all, culture-bearing culture-sharing, and culture-shaping animals. This thoroughly engaging book shows that to know a person, one must know a culture."

—Barry Schwartz, Ph.D., author of *The Paradox of Choice* and *Practical Wisdom*

"Better than any book I know, *Clash!* illuminates the cultural influences in our everyday lives and how they underlie the major identity clashes of our times. This delightfully written book also imparts a better understanding of ourselves."

—Claude Steele, Ph.D., author of *Whistling Vivaldi: How Stereotypes Affect Us and What We Can Do*

"A brilliant and highly accessible exposition of new scientific findings about profound cultural differences. As the world grows smaller and flatter, the wisdom of *Clash!* will prove essential for effective functioning."

—Richard E. Nisbett, Ph.D., author of *Intelligence and How to Get It*

"Finally! An entertaining and scientifically rigorous explanation of how our cultures work on us and how we can work on them. *Clash!* is a must-read for crafting effective personal change strategies that work within and across most cultures."

—Philip Zimbardo, Ph.D., author of *The Lucifer Effect*

"In the conflict of cultures lies, paradoxically, the ability to construct a self with integrity, agility, and the potential to grow in ways previously unimagined. Full of good science and sage advice, *Clash!* provides the evidence and strength to approach the hard question, 'Who am I?'"

—Mahzarin Banaji, Ph.D., coauthor of *Blindspot: Hidden Biases of Good People*

CLASH!

How to Thrive in a Multicultural World

Hazel Rose Markus, Ph.D.,
and Alana Conner, Ph.D.

A PLUME BOOK

PLUME

Published by the Penguin Group
Penguin Group (USA) LLC
375 Hudson Street
New York, New York 10014

USA | Canada | UK | Ireland | Australia | New Zealand | India | South Africa | China
penguin.com
A Penguin Random House Company

First published in the United States of America by Hudson Street Press, a member of Penguin Group (USA) Inc., 2013
First Plume Printing 2014

THE LIBRARY OF CONGRESS HAS CATALOGED THE HUDSON STREET PRESS EDITION AS FOLLOWS:
Markus, Hazel Rose.
Clash! : 8 cultural conflicts that make us who we are / Hazel Rose Markus, Ph.D., and Alana Conner, Ph.D.
pages cm
Includes bibliographical references and index.
ISBN 978-1-59463-098-9 (hc.)
ISBN 978-0-14-218093-8 (pbk.)
1. Culture conflict. 2. Culture. 3. Self. I. Conner, Alana. II. Title.
HM1121.M37 2013
306.0973—dc23
2012048469

Printed in the United States of America
10 9 8 7 6 5

Set in Bembo

For the brightest stars in our culture cycles:
Alice, Bob, Krysia, Marilyn, Christian, and Taylor

Contents

Introduction

Culture Trouble

"I am large, I contain multitudes."

—Walt Whitman, "Song of Myself"

No TV. No computer games. No choice of free-time activities. And when noncompliant, no food, no water, no bathroom, and no shelter.

To many people, these rules sound like they came straight out of an American prison on a bad human rights day. In reality, they are a few of the parenting tips Amy Chua offers in her 2011 memoir, *Battle Hymn of the Tiger Mother.*[1] An American-born daughter of Chinese immigrants, Chua reveals the parenting secrets of the Chinese, who are famous the world over for their successful children.

Underlying Chinese and Western[2] differences in bringing up the kids, says Chua, is how parents think about their children's selves—their I's, egos, minds, psyches, or souls, to use the technical terms. Western parents assume that children's budding selves are fragile, and so they empower their youngsters with choices and fortify them with praise. But Chinese parents "assume strength, not fragility," writes Chua.[3] As a result, they set the bar dizzyingly high for their children, and then use tough techniques to help them meet the family's expectations.

If the proof of the parenting is in the offspring, Chua's mothering is so far unassailable. Her elder daughter, Sophia Chua-Rubenfeld, made her Carnegie Hall debut at age fourteen, graduated first in her class from an elite prep school, and is now studying at Harvard University. Chua's younger, "rebellious" daughter is no slouch, either. Louisa, an honor student at the same elite prep school, was a virtuoso violinist in the local symphony's Prodigy Program, until she chose to dedicate more time to tennis, at which she also excels.

Despite the triumphs of her self-styled "Tiger Cubs," Chua has outraged much of the Western world. Critics call her methods manipulative, abusive, and even illegal. They protest not only her means, but also her ends. "[Chua's] kids can't possibly be happy or truly creative," writes columnist David Brooks, summarizing the public's concerns. "They'll grow up skilled and compliant but without the audacity to be great."[4] Consequently, they'll crash into the so-called bamboo ceiling instead of rocketing to the top.[5]

This is not a new line of thought. For several decades, the West has dismissed the genius of the East as one of imitation not innovation. But the East is swiftly catching up with the creativity and audacity—the greatness—of the West. Between 2004 and 2008, Chinese scholars penned 10.2 percent of the scientific research papers published in international journals, second only to scientists in the United States. Those rankings are expected to flip as early as 2013, with China taking the pole position.[6] Applying what these scientists find, Asian companies are dominating the emerging industries of clean energy and alternative transportation.[7]

Science and technology are not the only areas of innovation with tigers at the top. Of the thirty-five living artists who earn seven digits for a single work, seventeen are of Asian heritage.[8] Here in the United States, Asians make up only 5 percent of the population but fill three to nine times that number of undergraduate seats at the nation's top universities.[9]

Stats like these fuel the sales of Chua's book. What if she is right? What if raising successful children requires the rigid enforcement of old-school rules? What if the European-American preoccupation with self-esteem, self-expression, and self-actualization is turning our children into hothouse flowers who will wither in the grip of their Eastern competition? What if the clash of Eastern and Western cultures in American classrooms, and around the world, ends with the East on top?

At the heart of the Tiger Mother hysteria are two deeper questions: What kind of person will not just survive, but thrive in the twenty-first century? And can I be this kind of person?

Our book is an answer to these questions. As cultural psychologists, we study how different cultures help create different ways of being a person—what we call different *selves.* We also study how these selves in turn help create different cultures. We call this process of cultures and selves making each other up the *culture cycle.* As we will reveal, many of the clashes that give us the most grief arise when different selves collide. But by using our culture cycles to summon the right self at the right time, we may not only stop many of these clashes in their tracks, but also harness the power of our diverse strengths.

Playlists of the Soul

Most of us ponder the question "Who am I?" at some point in our lives. The more neurotic among us do so several times before breakfast. But have you ever asked yourself, "What is an I? And why do I have one?"

Your I, your *self,* is your sense of being a more or less enduring, single agent who acts and reacts to the world around you, and to the world within you. Your self is the hero at the center of your life story, which you are constantly writing (whether you know it or not).[10] It is the part of you that perceives, attends, thinks, feels, learns, imagines, remembers, decides, and acts. It connects your present to your past and your future, helping you make meaning out of your experiences and figure out what to do next.

Having a self is a smart human trick. Because humans are not custom-built for any environment, you must be ready to adapt to all environments. And so your brain, like all human brains, is tuned to a broad band of stimuli.

Your world, in turn, is like a radio playing many different stations at once. Your self moves the dial on that radio. It helps you attend to the channels that are relevant to your needs and goals, and tune out the ones that aren't. At a cocktail party, for example, you prick up your ears if someone says your name, even when you are not paying attention to the chatter around you. That's because some part of your brain is looking out for information about your self.[11] Similarly, you are much quicker to respond to ideas and events that are relevant to your self than to ones that are not.[12] And if you want to remember a new fact, one of the surer routes to deep storage is to link that fact directly to something you value or have personally experienced.

Your self not only selects what information you attend to, but also puts it all together into a coherent experience. Your self makes playlists. It switches between the channels on the world's radio, creating soundtracks with distinct feelings and stories. In so doing, your self also directs just which dance you are going to do, which course of behavior you will take. With your hip-hop playlist on, you will probably not do much two-step.

Although we all have an overriding sense of our self as the same across places, times, and situations, when we look more closely at the stories of our lives, we see that we actually have many different selves within our one self.[13] And they all know how to work the radio. Depending on which self is "on," you act very differently. For example, when visiting their mothers, many otherwise calm and reasonable adults are shocked to realize that their inner preteen self has taken over the dial. Likewise, when we gear up for an after-work basketball game, we are pleasantly surprised to find that the burned-out drone who was just whinging in his cubicle has finally relinquished the dial.

Your Two Selves

Yet there is order in the chaos of your many different selves. For all the varieties of self inside you, we find that most of them sort into two basic styles: independent and interdependent. *Independent selves* view themselves as individual, unique, influencing others and their environments, free from constraints, and equal (yet great!). As we will show, this is the sort of self that mainstream American culture overwhelmingly nurtures. Most of the songs on its radio are about independence.

Interdependent selves, by contrast, view themselves as relational, similar to others, adjusting to their situations, rooted in traditions and obligations, and ranked in pecking orders.[14] As we will explain, the radios in many other parts of the world—including the East, from which Amy Chua's family hails—feature mostly interdependent channels.

TWO STYLES OF SELVES

Independent	**Interdependent**
Individual	Relational
Unique	Similar
Influencing	Adjusting
Free	Rooted
Equal (yet great!)	Ranked

With Japanese psychologist Shinobu Kitayama, Hazel Rose Markus, this book's coauthor, first examined independence and interdependence in the United States and Japan. Over the years, their graduate students (including Alana Conner, this book's other coauthor) branched out to explore independence and interdependence in other nations, as well as in gender, racial, and class cultures. Findings from Kitayama and Markus's Culture Lab form the backbone of this book. Across these many studies, we find that independent and interdependent selves are equally thoughtful, emotional, and active, but often have subtly different thoughts, feelings, and actions in response to the same situations.

Like many people with Eastern heritages, Amy Chua is using her interdependent self to raise interdependent children. (But she also uses her independent self to promote her book and to defend her ideas—a point we return to later.) She dedicates thousands of sleep-deprived hours to helping her daughters meet the high expectations of the important people in their lives. She in turn expects her daughters to give pride, comfort, and support to the people who helped them succeed. With so many relationships protecting Sophie and Louisa's interdependent psyches, Chua assumes that her daughters are tough enough to take a little tussling. So she keeps up a steady stream of criticism to push her kids up to scratch.

In contrast, many of Chua's Western critics front their independent selves. When given a child to rear, they help him cultivate his individuality and uniqueness so that he may distinguish his self from that of others. Many independent parents are also sleep-deprived, but not from holding their children's feet to a fire they laid before they even had children. Instead, these parents spend a lot of time, money, and effort giving their children a wide range of choices—soccer or swimming? piano or painting? drama or debate?—so that their young can select activities that click with their allegedly inborn and unique talents. Because their children's developing selves are delicate, Western parents keep up a steady stream of praise to protect and strengthen them.

Steeped in these different worlds, the children of independent and interdependent parents grow up to have different selves. Just ask them. When European-American students describe themselves, they tend to list their stable, internal, unique, and positive qualities, and rarely mention their roles or relationships. They say, "I am free-spirited and unique," "I always try to be optimistic and upbeat," or "I'm self-confident."

In contrast, Japanese students tend to mention other people and relating to them within their first sentences. "I do what I want to do as much as possible, but I never do something that would bother other people," says one participant. Another reports, "I behave in order for people to feel peaceful."[15]

You can also sense the different selves of European-American and Japanese adults in their e-mails and text messages. For Americans, the most common emoticon is :) or the smiley face. The second most common emoticon is :(or the frown. Japanese writers also use smiling and frowning emoticons, but they just as frequently use (^_^;), which depicts cold sweat rolling down a nervous face. Japanese use this emoticon when they are worried that they have done something wrong and disturbed a relationship. When interdependence is the goal, a symbol that says, "I am worried about how you are feeling," is more useful than one that just expresses what the writer is experiencing.[16]

And Who Are You?

Now think about *your* self. Do you tend to use your independent or interdependent side? Or do you use both sides equally?

Take a look at the two images that follow to help you answer. The independent self on the left is surrounded by people. But they all have solid edges, and they do not overlap. This kind of I is individual, unique, and free. And though other people clearly matter to this sort of self, they are not a core feature of the I in the middle.

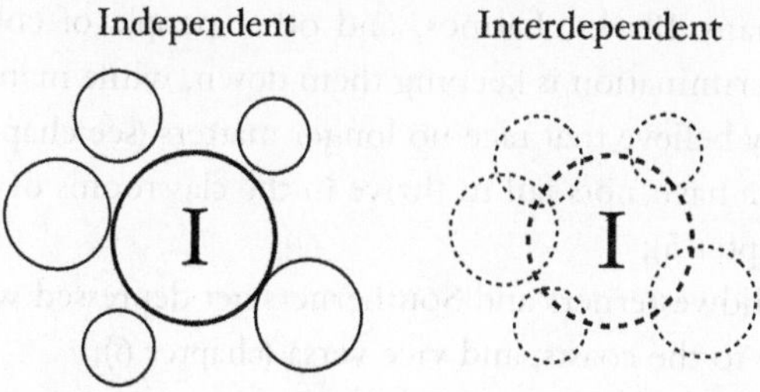

In contrast, the interdependent self on the right has a porous edge, as do all the people surrounding it. They are also all intersecting; this is a self whose relationships with others are essential ingredients. In addition, an interdependent self is made up of not only its relationships with individuals, but also its place in the web of everyone else's relationships. This is a relational, rooted, and ranked self.

In chapter 10, we will give you more tools to discover how you combine independence and interdependence to make your distinct self. We will also show throughout this book that the forms independence and interdependence take vary across cultures and people. But at the heart of independence is a focus on one's own self, while the heart of interdependence is a focus on one's relationships.

Clash of the Selves

Chua's memoir captured the collision of Eastern interdependence and Western independence. It also stoked a clash all its own between its interdependent advocates and independent critics.

Yet the *clash* between independent and interdependent selves is not just an East-West issue. In the following chapters, we show how it ignites a surprising number of other local, national, and global tensions, including:

- Why women are getting stuck on their way up the corporate ladder, while men are falling off the ladder altogether (see chapter 3);

- Why many Blacks, Latinos, and other people of color know that discrimination is keeping them down, while many Whites sincerely believe that race no longer matters (see chapter 4);
- Why the have-nots fail to thrive in the classrooms of the haves (see chapter 5);
- Why Midwesterners and Southerners get depressed when they relocate to the coasts, and vice versa (chapter 6);
- Why the politics of conservative Protestants seem so alien to other religious groups in the United States (see chapter 7);
- Why so many partnerships between businesses, nonprofits, and governments fail (see chapter 8); and
- Why so much of what goes on in the Global South seems irrational, inefficient, and unjust to the Global North (chapter 9).

These culture clashes are becoming more frequent, stressful, and even violent. With new technologies bringing our outsize populations together, we more often interact with people whose ways of being don't jibe with our own, and who therefore leave us baffled. As resources disappear, we must compete even more fiercely with these mysterious people for degrees, jobs, and a decent standard of living. At the same time, we increasingly help people whose intentions and actions we don't fully understand, from neighbors and coworkers of different races, classes, and genders; to people around the world suffering from war and poverty. Meanwhile, climate change, nuclear proliferation, and other global threats demand that we all cooperate more than ever before.

As our planet gets smaller, flatter, and hotter, what sort of self will rise above the fray and flourish?

Chua and the Eastern cultures from which her parents hail would perhaps suggest that interdependence is the way to go. With tight coalitions of people indebted to each other, interdependent selves may better withstand the threats and shocks ahead. After all, there is strength in numbers.

But Western psychologists have overwhelmingly held up independence as the happier and healthier way to be. From Dr. Freud to Dr. Spock to Dr. Phil, psychologists have urged people to realize their authentic selves, actualize their unique strengths, exert control over their environments, free themselves from burdensome obligations, and view themselves as equal to others (who also happen to be great, hence the high levels of self-esteem in these parts). They point out that independent selves don't just sit back and weather the storm; they change the weather altogether. These same psychologists also sternly warn against excessive interdependence, with its bugbears of codependency, inconsistency, and passivity.

Both Sides Now

As twenty-first-century cultural psychologists, however, we are writing a new prescription. To build a more prosperous and peaceful world, everyone must be *both* independent and interdependent. This means that people who tend to be more independent will have to hone their interdependence, while people who tend to be more interdependent will need to polish their independence. Success in love, work, and play will come to those who wisely apply the best self to the situation.

Although many people have a strong tendency toward either independence or interdependence, we all use both kinds of selves. A White male CEO, for example, is a very independent creature until he crawls on the floor with his three-year-old, where he gets in touch with his more interdependent side. Likewise, an otherwise interdependent working-class Latina nurse's aide conjures plenty of independence when she starts a movement to reduce pollution in her neighborhood.

By knowing when and how to use our different selves, we can not only better understand the clashes around us, but also avoid many of them altogether. Both independence and interdependence are legitimate and useful ways to be a person. Yet clashes arise when we channel an independent self for a situation that calls for interdependence, and vice versa.

For instance, let's say you're in the market for a new car. So is your good friend. In the end, you buy exactly the same car as your friend, a few days after he makes his purchase. Have you just offended your friend or cemented your relationship?

As it turns out, the answer depends on your friend's social class. Psychologist Nicole Stephens and her team asked working-class firefighters and middle-class MBA students to imagine just this scenario. They found that the MBA students, with their strongly independent selves, were aghast. "It spoils my point of differentiation," one complained. "Why did he do that?" asked another. "I wanted to be unique."

Yet the more interdependent firefighters weren't the least bit bothered. "I think it's cool," one said. Another offered, "I'd be like, yeah, awesome, let's start a car club." A friend's choosing the same car was hardly an affront to the firefighters' interdependent selves; instead, it was an act of solidarity.[17]

This doesn't mean that you shouldn't spring for that Camaro just because your buddy has. It does mean, however, that if your buddy is a college-educated, middle-class European American with an independent self, copying his ride is likely to trouble your relationship.

By tuning in to other people's selves, you may not only avoid clashes, but also get more of what you want. As we discuss in chapter 3, for example, a woman who wants to earn more must access her independent self to ask for a raise. Likewise, as we demonstrate in chapter 9, an aid worker who wants to prevent famine in a Sudanese village must work within the interdependent traditions, norms, and hierarchies already at play there.

The Tiger Mother herself may agree with our prescription. In the less famous final chapters of her book, Chua admits that she has been too harsh with her second-born and embraces a more independent style. "I did the most Western thing imaginable: I gave *her* the choice," she writes. "I told her that she could quit the violin if she wanted and do what she liked instead, which at the time was to play tennis."[18]

The Culture Cycle

Chua is not alone in her struggles to apply the right self. We all wrestle with the question of which psyche to bring to a given situation. What makes our two-self solution even harder is that you often aren't controlling which of your selves shows up. As Malcolm Gladwell popularized in his bestseller *Blink*, psychologists have long known that most of what actually drives your behavior sails under the radar of your conscious awareness. The same holds true for which self you use: subtle cues in the environment can evoke independence or interdependence *without your even knowing it*. These cues, called *primes*, don't determine how you'll act, but they do raise the odds that certain thoughts, feelings, and behaviors will rise to the surface.

And so changing your I is not simply a matter of making up your mind, all by your lonesome. You must also change the cues in your environment. These cues are part and parcel of what we call culture. By culture, we don't mean the opera, the symphony, or the ballet. Nor do we mean merely the foods, festivals, and clothing that distinguish, say, Mexicans from Indonesians. Instead, *culture* is the ideas, institutions, and interactions that tell a group of people how to think, feel, and act.

Although some primates have the rudiments of culture, no one has culture like *Homo sapiens*. And no one has culture like you. We all have many different cultures crisscrossing through our lives, from major cultures like nations, genders, and social classes; to subcultures like professions, hobbies, and even sports-team fandom. But few people (maybe no one) swims in the exact same cultural mix as you. Your special cocktail of cultures combines with your biology to make you *you*.

No one *makes* culture like you, either. Every day of your life, you make culture without even consciously trying to. That's because your everyday thoughts, feelings, and actions feed into the cultures of which you are a part, just as your cultures shape your thoughts, feelings, and actions.

To help explain how the culture cycle rolls, we've broken it down into four elements: I's, interactions, institutions, and ideas. These elements work together like this:

The Culture Cycle

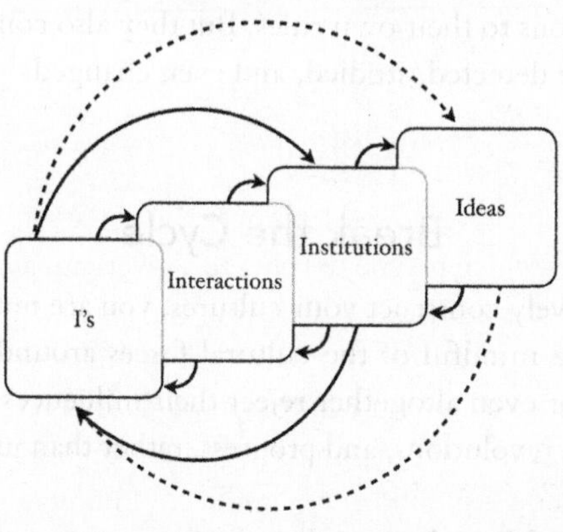

Your I (self, mind, psyche, soul) anchors the left side of the culture cycle with its thoughts, feelings, and actions. The right-hand "culture" side of the cycle includes interactions, institutions, and ideas. You can think about the culture cycle starting from either the left or right side. From the left: your I (or self) creates a culture to which you later adapt. From the right: your culture shapes your I so that you think, feel, and act in ways that perpetuate this culture.

The part of the culture cycle we experience most often is our daily *interactions* with other people and with human-made products (artifacts). These interactions follow seldom-spoken norms about the right ways to behave at home, school, work, worship, play, etc. Guiding these practices are mundane cultural products—stories, songs, advertisements, tools, architecture, etc.—that make some ways to think, feel, and act easier than others.

The next layer of culture is made up of the *institutions* within which everyday interactions take place. Institutions spell out the rules for a society and include legal, government, economic, scientific, philosophical, and religious bodies. No single person knows all the laws, policies, origin stories, or theories at play in their cultures. Nevertheless, institutions exert a formidable force, silently allowing certain practices and products while forbidding others.

The last and most abstract layer of the culture cycle is made up of the central, usually invisible ideas that inform our institutions, interactions, and, ultimately, our I's. Like the unseen forces that hold our planet together, these background ideas hold our cultures together. Because of them, cultures have an overarching pattern. To be sure, cultures harbor plenty of exceptions to their own rules. But they also contain general patterns than can be detected, studied, and even changed.

Break the Cycle

Because you actively construct your cultures, you are not a slave to them. When people are mindful of the cultural forces around them, they can amend, riff on, or even altogether reject their influences. This is why we have technology, revolutions, and progress, rather than just "same species, different century."

Being aware of the culture cycle is the first step to controlling it. Once you know that the environment is full of primes that shape your behavior, you can begin to consciously override these cues, or even replace them with more desirable ones. To give a small example: Anyone who has successfully dieted knows that it takes more than an iron will and clenched jaw to shed the pounds. You also have to make changes in the everyday environments with which you interact. You must liberate your pantry of its chips and your freezer of its ice creams and replace them with fruits and vegetables. You must park your car farther away from your destination so that you get more exercise. You must surround yourself with the friends and family who support you, and figure out something else to do with your drinking buddies.

Yet the idea that an individual can single-handedly alter the course of the culture cycle is a perpetual Hollywood fantasy. Though you are not a slave to your cultures, you are not the lone master of them, either. Because your self and your cultures are so inextricably intertwined, changing your self and your world requires changing your culture cycles. In particular, you must alter the cycle's interactions and institutions, in addition to your I. You cannot directly alter the big ideas that animate the entire culture cycle, because they are so deeply rooted. But over time, as I's, interactions, and institutions shift, big ideas follow suit. And once a new big idea takes hold, a sustainable new culture cycle begins to churn.

To return to the weight-loss example: To keep the pounds off, you should work with the institutions in your community to make maintaining a healthy lifestyle easier. You should ask workplaces to make stairwells safer and easier to take than the elevator. You should encourage markets to offer you more fresh produce and less processed food. You should lobby city governments to set aside plenty of safe, open space for you to exercise. And you should support laws and taxes that protect you from unhealthy foods and food additives.

A more substantial example of what it takes to change culture cycles is the civil rights movement. Tweaking any one part of the culture cycle puts small dents in the problem of racial injustice. Using education to change individual hearts and minds (an individual-level intervention), improving portrayals of minorities in media (a change at the interactions level), and abolishing Jim and Juan Crow[19] laws (an institutional alteration) can move the needle toward greater racial and ethnic equality on their own. But widespread and sustainable change requires ongoing efforts at all three of these levels simultaneously. Over time, these actions in the lower levels of the culture cycle will displace the big idea that some racial and ethnic groups are inherently better than others.

Most of the culture clashes in your daily life will be easier to fix than five hundred plus years of racial injustice. Nevertheless, the same rule holds true: there are no silver bullets. Changing the self or changing the world requires altering the culture cycle that makes them both. Yet as we will demonstrate, a few well-placed nudges can set your culture cycles off in a better direction.

Culture-Blindness

Just because people can change their selves and cultures does not mean that they do so readily. A major obstacle is that many people don't even realize that they have cultures. They think that they are standard-issue humans, that they are normal, natural, and neutral. It's all those *other* annoying people who let cultures bias their ability to perceive the world as it *actually* is.[20]

This line of thinking is especially widespread in middle-class European-American culture, where the independent I is thought to be a self-made self. Consequently, middle-class European Americans often ignore social forces when explaining why people do the things they do, and instead focus on people's internal traits, talents, and preferences. Cultural psychologists call these inside-looking explanations for behavior *dispositional attributions*. In contrast, people in interdependent cultures more often look outside individuals and make more *situational attributions* for their behavior.

Psychologists Michael Morris and Kaiping Peng tracked these two dramatically different styles in English- and Chinese-language newspapers' reporting on two mass murderers: Gang Lu, a Chinese graduate student in physics at the University of Iowa who killed his adviser, several bystanders, and himself after he lost an award competition; and Thomas McIlvane, an Irish-American postal worker who shot his supervisor, several bystanders, and himself after he lost his job in Royal Oak, Michigan. *The New York Times* and the *World Journal* (a Chinese-language newspaper published in New York) covered both tragedies, but told very different stories. American reporters spilled more ink describing Lu as a "darkly disturbed man" with a "bad temper" and a "sinister edge," and attributing McIlvane's crime to his "short fuse," mental instability, and other personal qualities.

In contrast, Chinese reporters dedicated more column inches to situational factors. For Lu, it was the bad relationship with his adviser, the lack of religion in Chinese culture, and the availability of guns in American society that drove him to kill. For McIlvane, tensions with his supervisor, the example of other mass slayings, and the fact that he had recently been fired had led him to homicide.[21]

Because independent selves believe that people's internal qualities drive their actions, they also believe that they react to what's inside people, not to their cultures. As a result, many Americans claim to be color-blind, gender-blind, class-blind, religion-blind, or otherwise culture-blind. We can be forgiven for some of our willed blindness, as some of it reflects the best impulses of the civil rights movement, the feminist movement, the elder rights movement, and other attempts to make the world a fairer place. If people discriminate because of culture, many activists reason, then ignoring culture will help end discrimination. Just treat all people as *individuals*, the thinking goes, and soon, peace will guide the planet and love will steer the stars.

The Other Smart Human Trick

The main problem with this solution is that it's impossible to implement. The culture cycles of nation, gender, race, class, region, and religion have especially deep roots in the world. Even nine-month-olds distinguish between people of different races and genders.[22] This does not mean that people are born racist or sexist, or are otherwise hell-bent on making each other miserable. Instead, it means that having and making cultures is so important to our species that we begin learning cultural categories as soon as we pop into the world.

Making cultures is our other smart human trick. (The first, as you recall, is having a self.) Because of culture, we don't have to wait for genetic mutations or natural selection to give us the biology we need to live in a different terrain, to extract nutrients from new foods, or to cope with a change in climate. Instead, we can invent new shelters, cooking techniques, and climate-appropriate apparel. We can also save ourselves the trouble of reinventing these technologies by learning from our fellow humans how to make them.

Pulling off these nifty innovations requires exquisite social coordination. As British artist Thomas Thwaites recently demonstrated, no human alive today could build a toaster from raw materials all by himself. All the mining, milling, fabricating, assembling, and shipping behind this humble appliance involves thousands of people with highly specialized skills.

For feats ranging from building toasters to launching spaceships, culture helps us sort out who does what, when, where, and how. When a human is born, she is hungry for this cultural information. Her brain has evolved to receive cultural inputs, and so her nature is to seek nurture. Her family, friends, and the many strangers who help keep her culture cycles turning are ready to oblige. With their help, she quickly sees that people of different sexes have different hair, clothes, toys, and friends. With a little experience, she finds that people of different races live in different neighborhoods, hold different jobs, and commit different crimes. She learns that people of different religions have different holidays, places of worship, and values.

These particular cultural divides are not inevitable. We can (and sometimes do) carve up the world differently. We could create Legions of Tall People and Societies of the Short. We could establish separate republics for brown-eyed, blue-eyed, and green-eyed people. (David Bowie would enjoy dual citizenship.)

Yet getting rid of culture altogether is not possible. Millions of years of evolution have wired the need for culture in our brains, and thousands of years of civilization have installed the furniture of culture in our worlds. And so calls for culture-blindness are naïve.

Instead of sweeping culture under the rug, we should embrace it, understand it, and, most important, mobilize it for good. As modern life becomes more complex, and social and environmental problems become more widespread, we must relearn to use our culture cycles and our selves the way nature intended. And that means capitalizing on our diverse strengths. Returning to the radio metaphor: our selves must tune in to more of the world's stations. The more varied playlists that would result would give us more tools with which to meet the challenges of our shrinking planet. At the very least, they would make for more interesting listening.

Chua was on to something. But culture clashes don't have to cause so much suffering. By deftly combining our smart human tricks, we can fit many more selves and their culture cycles into one world.

CLASH!

CHAPTER 1

Hearts and Minds, East and West

"Heejung?"

Hazel cold-called the graduate student at the end of the seminar table.

"Do you have something to add?"

Schooled in South Korea, Heejung Kim was now deep into her Ph.D. studies at Stanford. Hazel was her adviser and expected students to chime in during class discussions.

Yet again, Kim shook her head and whispered, "No."

Slightly peeved, Hazel tried once more: "Heejung, what do you think about this claim that Asian students who sit silently in class and don't contribute to the discussion aren't thinking for themselves?" Hazel was referring to a widely publicized news article by a college professor who criticized Asian and Asian-American students for not participating in class.[1] The professor concluded that the students were "freeloading," and that "to become independent thinkers, they need to learn to express themselves."

The other students waved their hands in the air and fidgeted in their chairs. Finally, Kim looked down and quietly asserted, "You know, talking and thinking are not the same thing."

No one knew what to say, so the class carried on to another point.

Later that day, Kim e-mailed Hazel her response to the weekly class assignment. As usual, her commentary was both deep and succinct. But what really caught Hazel's eye was Kim's new e-mail signature: "The empty carriage rattles the loudest."

For all their interdependence, Asian students don't talk much. At least that's the perception many educators wrestle with, including Gail Davidson. Davidson is the principal of Lynbrook High School in Cupertino, California, which serves more than 1,700 students, 80 percent of whom are of Asian heritage. A public school, Lynbrook High is the envy of its competitors, with one of California's highest academic performance index ratings, a blue ribbon from the U.S. Department of Education, and a gold medal from *Newsweek*'s rankings of the nation's high schools.

"Our students are fantastic and achieve at a high level by all objective standards," Davidson says, "but our teachers are concerned when students don't speak up in class. Students absolutely need to develop their communication skills to succeed in the wider world."[2]

East-West clashes, like the one over how much students should speak, cause ripples of contention through schools around the world, ranging from prekindergarten classrooms to postdoctoral lecture halls. In the United States, for example, many teachers see how Asian interdependence can send a kid to Harvard (as it did Chua's daughter), but they still feel put off by it. "Why do Asian students so seldom talk or get excited?" they ask. "Why do they put their parents' wishes before their own? Why do they work so hard to fit in?" These are not the sorts of hearts and minds most Western teachers were trained to educate.

Western teachers also worry that their students with Eastern backgrounds are not cultivating the skills they will need in the Real World. Some even see how the independence of Westerners can hold Easterners back, both in the classroom and in the workplace.[3] At the same time, many suspect, as did the op-ed writer, that Eastern students' way of being is somehow unfair to their Western classmates.

A closer examination of the selves of people with Eastern and Western heritages can help demystify their different ways of doing school. For many East Asians and their children growing up in the West, listening, following the "right" way, fitting in, and keeping calm are not odd classroom behaviors; they are the very route to being a good person—a good interdependent self, Eastern style.[4] But for their Western classmates and teachers, speaking up, choosing your own way, standing out, and getting excited are also ways of being a good person—but in this case, a good independent self, Western style. Understanding the meanings and intentions behind these ways of being can not only dispel bad feelings in school and at work, but also help us harness the strengths of Eastern and Western selves for the betterment of both groups.

Talk or Listen?

After six years in the United States, Heejung Kim was getting irritated with professors needling her to talk. She had been taught that silent contemplation, not half-baked chattering, paved the path to wisdom. As the great Confucian sage Lao Tzu wrote: "He who knows does not speak. He who speaks does not know."

Kim knew she felt comfortable listening without talking in a way that many of her European-American colleagues did not. And she knew that connecting what she heard with what she already knew was a lot of work. She definitely did not feel she was freeloading.

As a budding cultural psychologist, Kim was learning that irritation was often the bellwether of a good research idea. So she decided to explore why Americans worry so much about silence in the classroom. Hers was a rather revolutionary hypothesis: for European Americans, talking helps thinking, but for Koreans and many other East Asians, talking can actually hinder thinking.

She tested her hunch with Richard, a European-American graduate student from New York. Having logged many hours talking on his high school's debate team, Richard opined, "Talking really helps clarify what you're thinking. Sometimes it's hard to know what you think *without* talking."

Kim then consulted with other East-Asian students. Akiko, a graduate student from Japan, shared Kim's frustration with the American assumption that talking is thinking, and supplied her own set of proverbs: "The mouth is the source of misfortune," "Guard your mouth as though it were a vase," "You have two ears and one mouth, to be used in that proportion," and "The duck that quacks the loudest gets shot."

Armed with these insights, Kim set out to test her ideas. She first devised a survey with statements that reflected both Eastern beliefs about talking and thinking such as "Only in silence can you have clear thoughts and ideas," and Western beliefs such as "An articulate person is usually a good thinker." She then asked people in San Francisco and Seoul how much they agreed with the statements. She found that Americans of many different ages and professions thought that talking is good for thinking. Koreans, in contrast, more readily agreed that talking can impede thinking.

Just because Americans believe that talking helps them think, however, does not mean they are right. Likewise, East Asians may mistakenly believe that talking interferes with thinking. To find out exactly how talking affects thinking for European Americans and East Asians, Kim asked American students who had grown up speaking English to take a nonverbal intelligence test called the Raven Progressive Matrices. Half the students had European backgrounds, and half had East-Asian backgrounds (including Korean, Chinese, Vietnamese, and Japanese). All the students completed half the intelligence test items in silence, and the other half while "thinking out loud," that is, verbalizing their problem-solving process.

Kim found that the European Americans performed better when they were solving the problems while speaking. In contrast, the Asian Americans performed much worse when they solved the problems while thinking aloud. But when the Asian Americans were allowed to solve problems in silence, they performed better than the European Americans.[5]

For Asian Americans, then, silence is not a sign of checking out. Instead, it produces their best thinking. The op-ed writer was wrong.

Choose My Way or Follow the "Right" Way?

Hazel found herself in the middle of an East-West clash of a different sort when one of her star students finished his undergraduate degree. A scholar, musician, and athlete, Bobby Wong[6] had gained admission not only to several top-flight medical schools, but also to a highly competitive work-study program in China. Bobby sorely wanted to take a year off from school and explore his cultural roots. But his father, a Chinese immigrant, had other ideas.

"C'mon," Hazel encouraged Bobby, "you just need to explain to your father in a very calm and respectful way that a trip to Mainland China with people who really know the country is an opportunity of a lifetime.

Medical school will let you defer your admission for a year. What's the problem?"

"I explained everything calmly and respectfully," Bobby replied. "But he just says, 'No, you have to start medical school in the fall.'"

"But you did so well in undergrad, and you got into every med school you applied to," Hazel said. "I'm so proud of you! He must be proud of you, too."

"He is proud," Bobby conceded, "but he says the next step on my path is medical school, not a year abroad."

"Well, I guess he will just have to be angry for a while," Hazel said. "Once he sees what you are doing in China, I'm sure he'll come around."

"He won't be angry," Bobby sighed, "because I'm not going. It's not up to me; it's not my choice." He slumped a bit lower in his seat.

Despite her initial reaction, Hazel knew that Mr. Wong was not being a bully, and that young Bobby had not misplaced his spine. Instead, the Wongs senior and junior were following the logic of interdependence.

Independent European-American parents and teachers say that a student should first choose what she wants to do, and then do it her own way. In the West, choice is perhaps the most important act because it lets people realize all five facets of independence. Choice allows people to express their individuality and unique preferences, influence their environments, exercise their free will, and assert their equality.

But interdependent parents such as Wong and Chua lay out a different agenda: I show my child the *right* thing to do, and then help her do it *the right way.* In the East, following the right way is a central act because it lets people realize all five facets of interdependence: relating to others, discovering your similarities, adjusting yourself to expectations and the environment, rooting yourself into networks and traditions, and understanding your place in the larger whole.

Mother Knows Best

When you have an interdependent self, you aren't blazing new trails on a barren social frontier. Instead, you are finding your place in a web of relationships. Most of these relationships (parent-child, teacher-student, boss-employee) are between levels of a pecking order. Your parents and other family members not only help you hook into the web, but also make sure that your place in it is as comfortable as possible. This demands knowledge of the rules of the web, of *the right way* to be. For their efforts to root and rank their children's selves well, Asian parents receive heaps of *filial piety*: the blend of respect and responsibility that interdependent children feel toward their parents.

If you have an independent self, in contrast, these machinations seem downright unjust. Inherited hierarchies are an affront to independent notions of uniqueness, control, freedom, and equality[7] (although, as we explore throughout this book, independent selves erect plenty of social ladders of their own). And though you know that you should "honor thy mother and father," as the Bible says, you often jettison this commandment when it interferes with what you want to do. You want choices, not instructions.

The power of filial piety to motivate Asian Americans, on the one hand, and the power of personal choice to inspire European Americans, on the other, is already apparent in early elementary school, find psychologists Sheena Iyengar and Mark Lepper. In clever experiments, they first recruited seven- to nine-year-olds whose parents had either emigrated from East Asia or were born in the United States. The researchers then asked all the children to solve as many word-unscrambling puzzles as possible, but under different conditions. One-third of the children got to choose the topic of the puzzles (for example, animals, a party, or food). The second third did not get to choose because the researchers had already chosen the puzzle topic for them. But the third group learned that their own mothers had chosen their topic, just for them.

Which of these conditions would make you feel most driven to solve as many puzzles as quickly and as correctly as possible? Which condition would undermine your motivation?

If you had an independent self, you would probably perform like the European-American kids in this experiment. You would probably thrive when you got to choose the puzzles by yourself, for yourself, but would balk when someone told you which puzzles to work on—especially if that someone was your own mother.

But if you had an interdependent self, you would probably solve the most puzzles in the "mom condition," as did the Asian-American kids in this study. For you, as for these children, your mother's involvement would inspire you. She has shown you the way, and now it's your job to follow it.[8]

Here's a starker demonstration of the importance of parents for Asians and of choice for European Americans: Your house is on fire. Inside, your mother is asleep in one bedroom and your spouse is asleep in another bedroom. You have time to rescue only one of them.

Whom would you save?

Susan Cross, Tsui-Feng Wu, and their colleagues posed this dilemma to hundreds of European-American and Taiwanese students. True to the spirit of filial piety, the interdependent Taiwanese students more frequently chose to save their mother. And true to the power of choice, the independent American students more often chose to save the person they had chosen for themselves: their spouse.[9]

Majority Rules

Even in tight-knit East-Asian cultures, parents aren't always there to show their children the way. What happens then? Do Easterners finally strike out on their own and express their independence? Or do they search for other interdependent cues to guide them?

To find out, Kim and Hazel went to that bastion of confusion and anonymity, the San Francisco International Airport. There, they tapped Asians heading home to Taiwan, Japan, and Korea, as well as European Americans traveling to destinations in East Asia, and asked them to fill out a short questionnaire.

Supposedly as a gift for completing the questionnaire, the researchers next offered participants a pen. And then the *real* experiment began. Half the time, the researcher extended four pens with orange barrels and one pen with a green barrel, and invited the participant to choose one to keep. The other half of the time, the researcher offered four green pens and one orange pen for the participant's choosing.

Using their independent selves, the European-American travelers took this experiment as an opportunity to go their own way. They overwhelmingly picked the unique pen, the one whose color was different from the other four. Yet most Asian participants chose the "majority" pen. In other words, when there was one orange pen and four green pens, European

Americans usually selected the orange pen, but Asians tended to take green one. Absent any other cues of which pen was the right one, Asian defaulted to the more common pen color—the one that the previous an next participant were more likely to choose. Like the firefighters who en joyed the thought of their friend's buying the same car, these participant also wanted to fit in with a group—even in an anonymous three-minut experiment.[10]

Stick Out or Fit In?

Steven Heine witnessed the clash of independence and interdependenc from the other side of the Pacific. As an English teacher at a high schoc in Japan, his students were earnest, diligent, and respectful. Yet they wer not progressing as fast as Heine had hoped.

Eager to distinguish himself as a good teacher, he tried to rouse hi charges to Anglophone greatness. He did what his teachers back in Canad had done. When students answered correctly, he praised them. When the erred, he nevertheless found something to compliment. And when a bi test was on the horizon, he delivered pep talks, assuring them that the could do whatever they wanted, as long as they believed in themselves.

Still, his class's performance trailed, until one day, Heine overheard Japanese colleague lecturing. The teacher expressed grave disappointmen that his students were falling further behind his expectations. He tol them to be very worried that their skills were still so poor. And he warne them that their lessons were going to get even more difficult, so the should expect to spend long hours studying.

Heine winced at the words. But then he saw that, rather than slump- ing in their seats and staring at their shoes, the students were straightenin their backs, squaring their shoulders, and setting their jaws in determina- tion. Words that would have deflated his European-Canadian friends an family spurred these Japanese students into action. Sure enough, when h unleashed a similar tongue-lashing on his own students, they performe much better on their tests.[11]

Years later, Heine was still asking, "Why did the Japanese student respond so well to criticism?" Everything he knew about psychology tol him that people react best to praise. As a newly minted cultural psychologist, he took his question into the laboratory. His team gave European-Canadian and Japanese students the same creativity test. Partway through the experiment, the researchers told half the participants that they were rocking the test, but the other half that they were botching it.

Like many Western researchers before them, Heine and his colleagues showed that the European Canadians persisted longer after the success feedback than after the failure feedback. These participants had found something that they were "good" at—something that would allow them to stand out—and so they stayed with it. But negative feedback deterred them; the test was not an opportunity for them to show their selves in a favorable light.

The Japanese students did just the opposite. They persisted longer when they believed they were flunking the test than when they thought they were acing it. Having learned that they were not yet up to snuff, they doubled down and worked even harder. To them, the test was not a stage on which to strut their stuff or hide their flaws. It was a place to learn what the standard was and then to try their best to meet it.[12]

Westerners set their selves apart in other ways. When Hazel asked her European-American Stanford undergraduates, "What percentage of students in this university are smarter than you?" they estimated that only 30 percent of the other students outshone them. In other words, they saw themselves as smarter than 70 percent of the student body.

But when Shinobu asked his Kyoto University students the same question, they reckoned that about 50 percent of the students were smarter. In other words, they saw themselves as average, in the middle, *normal.* This self-estimation showed both social awareness and statistical savvy: chances are, you *are* average on a given trait in a given population.[13]

Tests of self-esteem similarly reveal the Western drive to individuate and feel great about one's self versus the Eastern drive to relate and adjust one's self to other people. Across several studies, European Canadians clock dramatically higher self-esteem scores than do Japanese students.[14] Americans raised on the belief that psychological health requires high self-esteem might conclude that the Japanese students must be depressed. Yet the opposite seems to be true; Japan has fewer cases of depression than the United States, even when researchers use the most conservative and culturally sensitive measurements.[15]

Stand by Me

If they're so psychologically healthy, why *don't* Japanese have high self-esteem? Once again, Hazel, Shinobu, and their colleagues find that the answer lies in the self. Feeling fantastic about your self can hinder your ability to relate to others. And relating to others is the very route to health and well-being for interdependent selves. Examining the physical and mental health of thousands of Japanese and European-American adults, we discovered that the Japanese respondents with the most harmonious friendships and family relationships had the fewest physical problems, including diabetes, high blood pressure, and back pain. Having good relationships also helped the health of American respondents, but not as much as did having a sense of control.[16]

Psychologist Yukiko Uchida and colleagues have explored health and interdependence from a different angle. The research team showed Japanese and American participants photographs of Olympic athletes who had just won gold medals. In some photos, the athletes were alone; in others, the same athletes were shown with their teammates. Japanese participants who viewed photos of the athletes with their teammates guessed that the medalists were feeling more emotions—more happiness, pride, and joy—than did Japanese participants who viewed photos of the same athletes all by themselves. They applied the interdependent belief that psyches are most alive when they are sharing a moment with others.

Yet the Americans showed the opposite pattern: They estimated that the solo athletes were feeling more emotions than the medalist surrounded by teammates. They applied the independent belief that psyches are most alive when they are alone in the limelight.[17]

Amp Up or Calm Down?

Asians also aren't known for their emotional effusiveness. "Our teachers wish their students wouldn't hold back in expressing their thoughts and feelings," Lynbrook's Davidson says. This lack of expressivity leaves some of the students' European-American teachers and, eventually, employers feeling suspicious and left out. Why are these Asian Americans holding back? *What* are they holding back?

Yet psychologist Jeanne Tsai bristles when you ask her why Asians repress their feelings. "My family is really emotional," she says, speaking of her Taiwanese parents, "and not at all stoic or inscrutable. If anything, my parents always comment on how Americans are difficult to read because they hide their emotions behind smiles."

Growing up in Irvine, California, Tsai also recalls her scientist father admonishing her not to get too excited. But a few miles away, in Anaheim, the crowds at Disneyland routinely indulged an altogether different impulse.

Never been to Disneyland? Let us paint you a picture:

Streaked with purple, green, blue, red, and orange laser lights, the night sky is a riot of color. Bursting out of this backdrop are firecrackers that become hearts, flowers, and rockets, and then—gasp!—the face of Mickey Mouse. Dancing through the park are Mickey, Minnie, Donald, Pluto, and Sleeping Beauty. Cinderella arrives with her horse and carriage wrapped in thousands of sparkling white lights. A loud and perfectly synchronized soundtrack pours in. Floats with live performers complete the scene.

Over it all, a live announcer narrates the incomparable pleasures of the Main Street Electrical Parade. Meanwhile, tens of thousands of people are all expressing themselves. They jump. They dance. They clap. The three-year-olds cry. The six-year-olds scream, "Mommy, look! It's Mickey!" The eleven-year-olds shriek, "Ohmigod, it's sooo awesome!" The adults beam broadly and congratulate themselves; Disneyland is expensive, but you sure get your money's worth.

Halfway around the globe, at Tokyo Disneyland, the scene is both exactly the same and completely different. The lasers, the lights, the music, the Disney characters are in place. The crowd is equally huge.

Yet this scene of mass pleasure is orderly, almost quiet. Children are wide-eyed, pulling and leaning on their parents. The smallest ones are sitting on their parents' shoulders. Some are holding up their fingers in *V* signs. Some are moving gently with the music, and all are carefully tracking the shape-shifting lights. Heads turn in the direction of each explosion. People are attentive and consumed.

But no one is shrieking. Only the youngest children are jumping, dancing, and clapping. The crowd is intent, yet doesn't seem excited or high. Farther around the Pacific Rim, at Disneyland Hong Kong, the emotional reactions are also subdued.

From an American perspective, the low-watt reaction of Japanese and Hong Kong park-goers is curious. Yet judging by the yearly attendance, Disneyland may be even more popular in Japan and Hong Kong than in the United States.

If East Asians aren't repressing their feelings, what exactly *are* they doing? And why are Westerners amping up their feelings so high?

Tsai and her colleagues are answering these questions. They find that which emotions feel good to people varies dramatically with cultural background. East Asians like being calm more than Westerners do. Being interdependent requires paying attention to other people and tracking their thoughts and feelings—activities best performed while calm.

Westerners, in contrast, like being excited more than East Asians do. Being independent means expressing your uniqueness and exerting your freedom. For these ends, excitement is the more useful emotion to muster.[18]

At Disneyland, Hazel witnessed how excitement animates the independent self. Two families were spending the day together. In one family, both parents were Asian American, and in the other, the mom was Asian American and the dad European American.

As the families were getting ready to leave, the European-American dad loudly asked, "How much fun was *that*?"

A school-age boy from the Asian-American family answered quietly, "A lot." The European-American dad shouted, "Did you think so? If you do, then say it with passion! Say, 'a *lot*!' Let me hear it! I need to know how you *feel*! *Express* yourself!!"

Less Bitterness

East and West. Independence and interdependence. These are, of course, messy categories. Japan is not China or Korea or Vietnam or India. The United States is not France or England or Australia. And as we will soon show, the interdependent selves of Midwestern men are not exactly like the interdependent selves of Southern women; the interdependent selves of working-class European Americans are not identical to the interdependent selves of middle-class Japanese; and the independent selves of Protestant businesspeople are not just like the independent selves of agnostic West Coasters. Although each of these groups will have most of the qualities for either independence or interdependence that we listed in the introduction, few will meet all five criteria. In addition, the way they live out the specific details of independence or interdependence will reflect the many other features of their culture cycles.

Yet once you explore how people in different places answer the really big question, "Who am I?" you see patterns in the seeming chaos. You also see patterns in the conflicts that ensue when the two selves bump into each other. As Amy Chua learned the hard way, you can't just plop the practices of one culture into another and expect them to take root. Her younger daughter, Louisa, rejected the very methods that had propelled Chua's elder daughter, Sophia, to stunning success—hence the long subtitle of her book: . . . *This was* supposed *to be a story of how Chinese parents are better at raising kids than Western ones. But instead, it's about a bitter clash of cultures, a fleeting taste of glory, and how I was humbled by a thirteen-year-old.*

You can, however, skillfully apply your independent and interdependent sides to improve your self and your worlds. How can Westerners tap into the power of interdependence to prepare themselves for a more competitive marketplace? How can Easterners plug into independence so that they may better collaborate with their neighbors in the other hemisphere? There are no quick fixes. There is, however, one relatively simple system that explains both where these clashes come from and how to soften them. And that system is the culture cycle—the topic of our next chapter.

CHAPTER 2

A Spin through the Culture Cycle

"What do you want for breakfast, sweetie?" Hazel asked her then-four-year-old daughter, Krysia. "Cheerios? Rice Chex? Special K?"

"Special K," Krysia answered.

"Special K for my special K? Sounds good. And what do you want to drink? Apple juice? Orange juice? Cranapple?"

"Do we have anything purple?"

"No, honey. I'm sorry. How about something orange?"

"Okay. And Mommy, can I have a turkey sandwich today, instead of peanut butter and jelly?"

"Sure, sweetie. And what would you like for breakfast, Shinobu?"

Hazel turned to a jetlagged Shinobu Kitayama, just arrived from Kyoto and staying with Hazel's family while attending a conference.

"Uh . . . I'll have what she's having?"

"Okay. Would you like some coffee with your Special K?"

"Yes, thank you."

"Do you take it with milk?"

"Um. Sure."

"Whole, two-percent, or skim?"

"Uh, whatever you think is best."

A few minutes later, Shinobu politely asked, "Hazel, you gave Krysia and me a lot of choices. Is that an American thing?"

"Well," Hazel started. But then she had to think for a moment. "Everybody likes to choose, right? It gives people a chance to express themselves, to feel in control," she said, reflecting the consensus of her fellow psychologists at the time. "Don't you let Lila choose her breakfast? Don't you want to get your coffee just the way you like it?"

Shinobu considered his own young daughter back in Kyoto. "I guess we think that it's the parents' job to know what the children will like and then make it for them," he said. "We usually give Lila freshly steamed rice, some vegetables, and a bowl of fresh miso soup—you know, what all the kids like. And we give her variety, of course. Sometimes we put an egg on the rice."

Hazel held back a laugh. "But you know the research, Shinobu," she said. "Choice makes kids happier and more creative. And just look at Krysia. She's only in preschool, but she already knows a lot about herself."

It was true. Krysia knew not only what she liked to eat, but also what she liked to wear—soft, not scratchy; purple, not brown. She liked *Good Night, Moon* more than *"I Can't," Said the Ant*. And she knew exactly what kind of cake she wanted at her birthday party: a yellow cake with pink and green buttercream flowers.

"Lila's the same, no? She knows what she likes."

Shinobu thought for a moment, and then sighed. "It's true that Lila has a strong will," he conceded. "But she's getting much better at paying attention to other people. She's only in preschool, but she already trusts that we know what's best for her."

Hazel and Shinobu fell silent for a moment, and then realized they had stumbled into two excellent research questions: What sorts of selves were they trying to raise? And what methods were they applying to this most important of endeavors?

Their breakfast ended more than twenty years ago, but their conversation continues in a collaboration that has produced hundreds of studies exploring different culture cycles and selves.[1] At the beginning of this collaboration, Hazel didn't quite know that she usually used her independent self, the one that strove to be individual, unique, influencing, free, and equal; nor did Shinobu quite understand that he tended to use his interdependent self, the one that aimed to be relational, similar, adjusting, rooted, and ranked. In general, folks don't know their own culture's recipe for being a self. We don't recite the recipe every morning like a scout's pledge or study it in school like a manifesto. Instead we learn our cultures' recipes for how to be an appropriate self simply by living our lives. Those lives we live, in turn, are made up of the many culture cycles rolling through them.

As we discussed in the introduction, the culture cycle looks like this:

The Culture Cycle

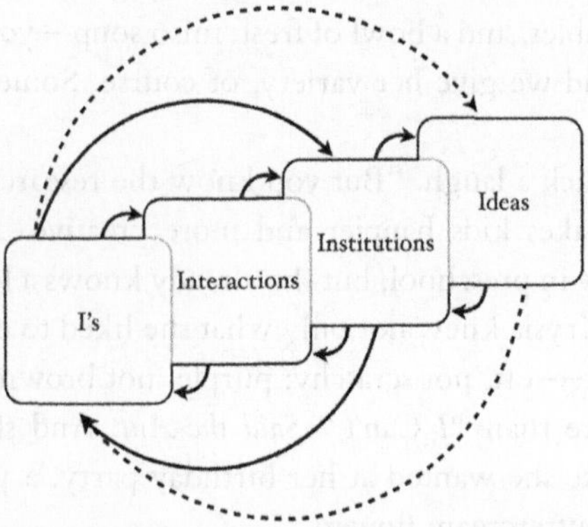

To summarize once more how the culture cycle works: Our I's (or selves) both produce and are produced by cultures out-in-the-world, including the customs and artifacts that give shape to our daily *interactions*, which themselves foster and follow from cultural *institutions*, which in turn reflect and support our cultures' big *ideas*, including ideas about what a person is and should be. Because our I's are embedded in cultures, we cannot survive without them. In this way we are like fish in water.

Also like fish in water, we evolved so that we don't notice culture. Indeed, as we will show throughout this book, culture is powerful precisely because it is usually invisible to the untrained eye. We are born into culturally saturated worlds, and seldom do we see or discuss how other worlds are arranged. Only when we travel to new places or, say, read a book about cultural psychology do we begin to understand how much culture shapes our selves and appreciate how many different forms cultures can take.

In this chapter, we lay bare the culture cycles that drive independence in the West and interdependence in the East. Once you understand how the culture cycle works, you will see it everywhere—in the ads you watch on television, in the policies you follow at work, in the words you say to your own kids. (Ever wonder why you are turning into your parents? Stay tuned.)

You will also have a better way to think about differences between people. Ignorant stereotyping is bad because it results in unfair treatment. But appreciating that people are cultural beings who are exquisitely attuned to their physical and social environments is a first step toward understanding why people with different backgrounds have different selves. It is also the first step to understanding why these different selves so often clash.

By knowing how the culture cycle works, you can also reverse-engineer it to calm the culture clashes that erupt in your own life. Should children choose their own way, as Western parents and teachers such as Hazel often assume, or should they do things the right way, as Eastern parents and teachers such as Shinobu, Amy Chua, and Bobby Wong's dad believe? Should people stand out from the crowd, as Western culture cycles mandate, or should they fit in with others, as Eastern culture cycles teach? Should people openly express their thoughts and feelings through talking and emoting, as is the Western habit, or should they listen and attend to the feelings of others, as is the Eastern practice? More broadly, is the independence of the West the best way to be a self in the twenty-first century, or will the interdependence of the East prove to be the better sort of psyche for the challenges ahead?

As we discussed in the preceding chapters, our answer is that both sorts of selves will need to take pages from each other's playbooks, and then use the culture cycle to apply both selves wisely. For their part, Western independent selves will need to get in touch with their interdependent sides to create institutions that educate everyone for the future, interactions that help students stick to their studies, and individual hearts and minds that make their classmates and colleagues of Eastern heritage feel more welcome. At the same time, Eastern interdependent selves must adopt some of the independent practices of their Western neighbors, including crafting unique ideas and then sharing them verbally. By meeting each other in the middle, Eastern and Western selves will amplify everyone's contributions, for the benefit of all.

What's the Big Idea?

At the highest, most abstract *idea* level of the cycle, cultures have all types of big ideas that answer all types of big questions. Richard Shweder, a pioneer in cultural psychology, has traveled the world and identified the big questions that most cultures answer, including, Where did the world come from? How did things come to be the way they are? Why do things change? And, undergirding all, What is good?[2]

For psychologists of the self, the most important ideas are those that answer these big questions: What, exactly, is a person? What is a *good* person? and, What is her or his relationship to other people, the past, and the environment? As we shall see, the cycles that feed and flow from the big idea that the self is independent are quite distinct from the cycles that feed and flow from the big idea that the self is interdependent.

Built around these big ideas, the cultural worlds outside people's bodies have just as much structure, pattern, and order as do the genes, neurons, and brain regions within their bodies. So understanding what people are and why they do what they do requires mapping not only their brains and genomes, but also their cultures' institutions and interactions. In charting the course of your self, your postal code is just as important as your genetic code.

Interactions for Independence

All selves start small, both in physical size and in the daily interactions that mold them into culturally appropriate people. Parents get the culture cycle rolling. At breakfast, for example, Hazel gave Krysia several chances to assert her independence through choice—a behavior that lets people individuate, express their uniqueness, influence their environments, exercise their freedom, and feel equal to others. But no mother or father can craft an independent self alone. So Krysia's other family members, teachers, and friends—real and virtual—picked up the task, usually without even knowing it.

While eating breakfast, for example, Krysia tuned in to television's *Sesame Street*, where she sang along with her puppet friend Grover. "Yes, I do have pride in me," the two crooned. "I feel so satisfied in me." And why were Grover and Krysia so proud and satisfied? The song's answer hit the "uniqueness" note of the independent self: "Because I am so special." (In Grover's case, a unique pelt was the source of his high self-esteem: "I love every bright blue side of me," he sang.).[3]

Hazel next drove Krysia to preschool in the family's roomy sedan—a cultural product that lets many Americans spend hours alone every day. "It's not just your car, it's your freedom," sang a General Motors radio ad. Krysia's teacher greeted her with a hug. Like parents in many American settings, teachers understand themselves as not only guiding children, but also befriending them, reinforcing the idea that everyone must be treated as equal individuals, no matter their age or role.

To help Krysia practice choosing, the teacher asked her, "What would you like to do this morning?" She then gave the four-year-old a choice of nine activities, from coloring to gardening to playing dress-up. After lunch (Krysia's chosen turkey sandwich and juice packet), Krysia took a nap beneath her favorite poster: a picture of a Dalmatian puppy with red, yellow, and purple spots urging the preschoolers, "Dare to Be Different."

Next came VIP time. A preschooler named Jacob was VIP that week. Like all VIPs, he and his parents had decorated a large poster board to tell the class who he was. He had included drawings of his favorite things and pictures of himself with friends, family, and his cat. Jacob stood in front of the class and presented his poster for a full five minutes. At recess time, Jacob got to be the first out the door.

After recess, Krysia and her classmates voted on which story to hear. They selected "Goldilocks and the Three Bears." In the Western version of this widely told tale, Goldilocks exercises choice several times as she decides which of the bears' chairs, porridges, and beds is just right for her. She then bolts when the bears return to find her sleeping in their home.

As a special treat at the end of the day, the whole class celebrated Anna's birthday, singing "Happy Birthday" and playing her favorite game, musical chairs. Children marched around the chairs until the music stopped and they scrambled to sit in a chair. Because there was always one fewer chair than children, the child without a chair was out of the game, the teacher removed a chair, and the game continued until one of two remaining children snagged the last chair and was pronounced the winner. Although American classrooms foster equality, they also include competition from a very early age, giving children opportunities to individuate and feel great about their selves.

Practicing Interdependence

Meanwhile, half a world away, Lila lived out her preschooler's day in Kyoto and took part in a different culture cycle. Before Lila awoke, her mother prepared breakfast, which she then shared with her daughter. While Lila put on her school uniform, her mother carefully prepared Lila's lunch—a bento box of rice with small pieces of salmon, cooked vegetables, and pickled radish. Every day, Lila's mother prepared a different bento. She never asked Lila what she wanted, but instead selected what she thought would be best for her daughter.

Lila and her mother next walked to preschool with a group of other children and parents. As the children entered the classroom, they greeted the teacher with a bow, signaling their respect and appreciation.

That day, the students drew murals together. Crayons, shiny scissors, and textured paper were close at hand. Notably, there wasn't enough of any one supply for all students to use at the same time. Instead, the students had to share. Whereas Krysia's teacher used scarcity (in musical chairs) to spur competition, Lila's teacher used scarcity to encourage cooperation.

When the children descended into chaos, the teacher brought them back to attention by starting one of their favorite songs. The preschoolers quickly chimed in: "We're all friends. We'll be friends forever, forever," they sang of their connections to each other. "Even when we become adults, we'll be friends," their song continued, polishing the "rooted" facet of the interdependent self. "We've played together, we've fought together, we've laughed together, we've cried together," the tune concluded, emphasizing the children's similarities.[4]

After lunch came nap time. Lila took her place next to the wall where her teacher had posted a beautifully hand-lettered poster with the class's goals: "Let's Cooperate" and "Let's Pool Our Strengths."

Following their naps, the children headed for the playground, first putting on their outside shoes. Changing shoes signaled the transition from student to kid—roles with decidedly different rules. Because it was the first day of the month, recess ended with a parade of all the children who had birthdays that month.

Next came story time. The teacher also read aloud "Goldilocks and the Three Bears." But in the Japanese version, when Goldilocks is caught, she sincerely apologizes to the bears for entering their home uninvited and tasting their porridge. The bears do their part to smooth things over, and then invite her to come again.

Before their parents arrived, the children cleaned up the classroom, as they did every day. In American classrooms, cleaning is either a punishment or a custodian's job. In Japan, cleaning is another opportunity to cooperate and to reinforce the idea that environments shape the mind.

The teacher and students spent the last few moments of the day quietly contemplating how they could improve their performance the next day—a practice known as *hansei*. *Hansei* isn't just kid stuff. In his book *You Gotta Have Wa*, the Japan-based journalist Robert Whiting describes how Japanese professional baseball players pursue *wa* (harmony with the people in your group) by writing essays about their flaws and ways to improve them.[5] The image of Barry Bonds or Mark McGwire taking a self-criticism break is hard to conjure. But from a Japanese perspective, self-criticism helps everyone be part of the whole, no matter who he is or what that whole may be.

The Path Less Traveled

Over the course of Krysia's and Lila's childhoods, friends, family, teachers, employers, and even strangers continued to create everyday interactions that reinforced the kinds of selves they should be. In school, Krysia proves to be exceptionally skilled at the Socratic method, a verbal give-and-take where teachers call on students and require them to answer their questions aloud. Many schools in the West regard the Socratic method as an educational best practice.[6]

To occupy herself after school, Krysia chooses activities for which she has something that the adults call "ability" or "talent": cello, math, and track and field. She attempts to follow the prescription of discovering one's talent, applying effort, and then finding success. But she doesn't like cello, math, or track and field, and so eventually she rejects them all.

In college, Krysia decides to major in film because it reflects her unique interests and her need to create. Yet after graduation, she turns down film jobs, moves to Central America, and opens her own socially responsible business. She eventually returns to the United States to pursue her MBA so she can better compete in the emerging field of social entrepreneurship.

For the rest of her life in the United States, Krysia will have daily opportunities to express her uniqueness, to separate herself from others, to influence her world, to exercise her free will, and to experience herself as equal to others who are as great as she is. Like many middle-class European Americans, she will see and feel the world in terms of individuals. And through her thoughts, feelings, and actions, she will perpetuate the independent culture cycle that helped make her.

Working to Fit In

Meanwhile, back in Kyoto, Lila rounds out her education by attending *juku* ("cram school") several days a week so that she can meet Japan's high educational standards. Following Confucian educational methods, she quietly listens to her teachers, working hard to master what they tell her. As with many East-Asian students, she is following a well-worn path: studying leads to ability, ability leads to success, and success leads to happiness. Education is decidedly not about discovering her unique genius, expressing herself, or having fun.

In high school, she complies with the national mantra "Fail with five, pass with four," sleeping no more than four hours per night so as to avoid academic disaster. Despite her rigorous academic schedule, she takes up volleyball because her friends encourage her to do so. After enduring the hellish rite of passage known as the national college entrance exam, she scores well enough to attend a prestigious university. Following her father's advice, she majors in environmental science.

During the summer, Lila takes an office job. To show her commitment, she arrives early, leaves late, and often goes out with her colleagues after work. Acknowledging their shared commitment, Lila and her coworkers depart with the standard workplace farewell, "*Osaki ni shitsurei shimasu*" ("I'm sorry to leave before you"). The remaining workers reply with "*Otsukaresama deshita*" ("You must be tired").

For the rest of her life in Japan, Lila will have opportunities to discover how she is connected and similar to others, to contemplate how her role and rank should constrain her behavior, and to adjust her self accordingly. Like many middle-class Japanese people, she will see and feel the world in terms of relationships. And through her thoughts, feelings, and actions, she will perpetuate the interdependent culture cycle that helped make her.

Selling Selves

Rustling, humming, and blaring alongside Krysia and Lila is a constant stream of mass media. In a single day, the average person in the United States is exposed to more than five thousand images from magazines, television, websites, and billboards.[7] These cultural products both subtly and blatantly convey the right way to be a person.

In the Tokyo subway, for example, a bright yellow poster with hundreds of red fish swimming in the same direction reminds morning commuters that, when the train comes, do what the fish do: get in line. But in the United States, Madison Avenue serves up seafood with an independent twist: "Only dead fish swim with the current," reads a Templeton Global Investments ad.

Built around the themes of individuality, uniqueness, choice, freedom, and equality, American ads hammer home the culturally appropriate way to be a self. Gerber touts that its baby foods are "a good source of iron, zinc and independence." Gap markets its widely appealing, yet wholly unremarkable clothing with the command "Individualize." Apple sells computers by pairing famous artists, scientists, and activists—Albert Einstein, César Chavez, the Dalai Lama—with the American mantra "Think different." Joe Camel advises herds of impressionable youth to "Choose anything but ordinary."

Suspecting that media in the East sell a different self, Hazel and Heejung Kim analyzed thousands of magazine ads in the United States and Korea. They found, indeed, that the ads in Korean magazines stressed interdependence, with themes of relating, fitting in, adjusting, following tradition, and observing rank. For instance, a Korean grocery store reassures young wives, "With effort, you may one day prepare pork as well as your mother-in-law." Likewise, a red ginseng beverage's main selling point is that it "is produced according to the methods of a 500-year old tradition." Rather than "Ditch the Joneses," as an American Jeep ad urges, Korean ads tend to promote more amicable actions. One university, for example, reassures readers that it "is working toward building a harmonious society."[8]

How to Smile

Media also direct people in the East and West to express their feelings differently. In one study, psychologist Jeanne Tsai and her research team compared the bestselling illustrated children's books in the United States and Taiwan. To test their idea that Easterners like calm emotions more than Westerners do, while Westerners value excited emotions more than Easterners do, Tsai and her colleagues did something simple but completely novel. They measured the width of the characters' smiles.

Tsai's team discovered that the American and Taiwanese characters beam an equal number of smiles at their young readers, but the American smiles are decidedly wider. For a typical American-made expression, think Max in *Where the Wild Things Are.* His grin extends across the page as he bounds through the forest announcing himself and making as much noise as he possibly can. The main character in the Taiwanese book *Xiao en yue de gushi* (*The Story of February*) also smiles, even though her eleven siblings trick her out of getting the thirty or thirty-one days she was due, and leave her with only twenty-eight. (Her father rewards her patience and restraint by giving her an extra day every four years.) But February's smile is narrow and serene.

Women's magazines showed the same pattern. In American glossies, the smiles are usually toothy and huge. Think Julia Roberts. But Asian fashion magazines most often feature small, closed-mouth smiles. Think Zhang Ziyi (of *Crouching Tiger, Hidden Dragon* fame). Of course, there are always exceptions. But as a general rule, Eastern stars have subtler smiles than Western ones.[9]

Even religious self-help books feature different kinds of smiles, as well as different messages about the right way to feel. Joel Osteen, the pastor of a Christian megachurch in Texas that reaches more than seven million people, is the author of *Become a Better You.* On the cover of his book, Osteen sports the signature toothy American smile. In the book's pages, he asserts, "I'm excited about my future," and counsels readers to find their excitement, too.

Another bestselling self-help book is by the Dalai Lama. On the cover of his *Art of Happiness,* His Holiness also smiles, but gently. He urges readers to seek happiness, but advises that the happy life is built on a calm and stable mind.[10]

The Right Stuff or the Right Staff?

Even at international events like the Olympics, the media of different cultures produce, package, and broadcast different models of the self. Cast your memory back to the 2000 Olympics in Sydney, Australia. First stop, the pool. American swimmer Misty Hyman, gasping for breath, drags herself out of the water and realizes that she has captured the gold medal for the women's 200-meter butterfly. The American news cameras zoom in on Hyman's wide smile and shining eyes. A journalist asks, how did she do it?

"I think I just stayed focused," Hyman answers. "I knew I could beat Susie O'Neil, deep down in my heart I believed it, and I know this whole week the doubts keep creeping in, they were with me on the blocks, but I just said, 'No, this is my night.'"

Meanwhile, at the track across town, Japanese running sensation Naoko Takahashi breaks the ribbon to win the gold in the women's marathon. The Japanese video cameras follow Takahashi for half her victory lap. Then they pan to the stands and close in on the man who made her special shoes. Next they find her assistant coaches, and then they follow her main coach for a full twenty seconds as he runs through the track house to meet her. At last coach and victor meet, and the Japanese cameras show the back of Takahashi's head as she cries in the arms of her beloved coach.

At last a journalist catches up with Takahashi and her crew. Instead of talking about herself, the champion says, "Here is the best coach in the world, the best manager in the world, and all of the people who support me. All of these things were getting together and became a gold medal."

The American and Japanese media broadcasted these two different scenes—Misty Hyman's beaming face, Naoko Takahashi and her coach's embrace—over and over again, to millions of viewers, impressing upon them not only the story, but also the right way to tell it.

To bottle exactly what those right ways were, Hazel and her colleagues trained a group of American and Japanese bilingual observers to code hundreds of hours of Japanese and American coverage of the 2000 and 2002 Olympics. The observers systematically analyzed everything the athletes, commentators, and journalists said.

Totting up the observations, the research team first found that American journalists drew on their understanding of the self as independent and talked a lot about the athletes' personal characteristics—the powerful feet of Ian Thorpe, the robotic stride of Mo Green. When athletes won, it was because they had the right stuff. When they failed, it was because their competitors had superior personal attributes.

In contrast, the Japanese commentators drew on their understanding of the self as interdependent and focused on the expectations of important others, now and in the past. Failure was the result of not trying hard enough to do what was expected. Reflecting the Eastern tendency to criticize one's own actions so as to know how to improve, the Japanese athletes and press made nearly twice as many negative comments as did the Americans.[11]

Particles, Protestants, and Politics

Madison Avenue and Hollywood did not write the recipe for the independent self that now pervades the West, nor did the East's redoubtable media moguls dream up the notion of the interdependent self all by themselves. Instead, big ideas about how to be a self formed over millennia. The way people happened to do things became the way they had to do things, and cultures canonized these rules in their institutions.[12] These institutions then informed the interactions and I's downstream in the culture cycle, as well as reinforced the big ideas upstream.

Many institutions now driving and deriving from the Western independent self began in ancient Greece, where philosophers viewed the stuff of this world—trees, tables, and even people—as made up of unchanging particles that determined their qualities. A tree was made of tree particles that gave it tree qualities, just as each person was made of person particles that gave him or her person qualities.[13] As a result of this philosophy, Greeks—and the Western civilizations that followed in their wake—believed that to understand an object or a person, you must first break it, him, or her down into parts.

From this view eventually emerged the Western fascination with the internal and allegedly stable causes of behavior: character, talent, intelligence, cognition, emotions, motivations, brains, frontal lobes, genes, neurotransmitters, molecules, and so on. In Western philosophy and the sciences built on it, these parts come together to make the mind a mechanical device—a switchboard, a set of gears, or a computer. And this machine, in turn, powers behavior.[14]

Competence is also *in* the mind. The Socratic method at which Krysia excelled and against which Heejung Kim rebelled is the Western teacher's way of drawing out the student's knowledge—much of which presumably already resides inside the student's head. Education, Western-style, aims to develop the student's unique mind and increase her independence *from* the world. The student's job, in turn, is to develop unique ideas and then express them through talking and showing enthusiasm.[15]

Alongside this model of the internally steered, autonomous person arose an innovation called democracy—a form of government that allows individuals to govern themselves by making choices in the form of votes. Before democracy, leaders of Greek city-states spoke for their subjects. After democracy, individual citizens could change their worlds merely by casting a vote.

Meanwhile, in a hot and dry corner of the Roman Empire, a radical preacher was honing a different facet of independence. Named Jesus of Nazareth, this teacher not only hewed to the Jewish idea that there is only one God, but also taught that this God cared about each and every person, even the poor and the meek. Christianity's New Testament includes many tales and parables of God's relationship with individuals.

A millennium and a half later, a German cleric named Martin Luther took this idea to the extreme. In 1517 he nailed his Ninety-Five Theses to a church door and proclaimed that all people could have a direct and personal relationship with God without the help of priests or popes. On the heels of the Spanish Inquisition and other Catholic movements to roust out dissenters, Luther's call to do away with the Church hierarchy was revolutionary. So was his argument that God has a special purpose for each individual—a "calling"—which good Protestants should spend their lives discovering and perfecting. The sociologist Max Weber called this set of ideas the Protestant work ethic and argued that it fueled the growth of capitalism in Western Europe and, later, in the United States.[16]

Much of Europe continued to get in deep with independence during the Age of Reason and the Enlightenment. In 1615, René Descartes famously declared, "I think, therefore I am," asserting that his thoughts alone had enough authority to prove his existence. John Locke, the seventeenth-century English philosopher, pushed the authority of the individual one step further by contending that individuals come first, and societies emerge only when individuals form a social contract to protect each one's rights.

As the importance of the individual rose in Western religion, politics, and philosophy, the authority of monarchs and other leaders receded. In its place, equality and individual rights rushed in. By the time Thomas Jefferson sat down to write the U.S. Declaration of Independence in 1776, the balance of power between kings and subjects had been leveled: "We hold these truths to be self-evident, that all men are created equal, that they are endowed by their Creator with certain unalienable rights, that among these are life, liberty, and the pursuit of happiness."

Role and Rank, Yin and Yang

On the other half of the planet, people in the East came up with quite a different answer to the big questions, What is a person? What is a *good* person? And what is his relationship to the world and other people? Their answers weave together strands from Confucianism, Taoism, and Buddhism, and from more local philosophies like Japan's Shintoism.

As cultural psychologist Richard Nisbett eloquently discusses in *The Geography of Thought*, these philosophies view the world as constantly changing and ruled by external forces.[17] Shintoism, for instance, does not spell out a rigid ideology. Instead, this oldest of Japan's philosophies describes how people should relate to gods, ancestors, and nature. Its rituals reinforce the idea that people are but one part of a far larger, interconnected whole.

Indeed, the word *jibun*, which Japanese people often use to refer to themselves, means "my share" or "my portion of the whole."

All over the East, local practices mingled with the ideas of Confucius, who lived in China from 551 to 479 B.C. Confucius held that becoming a person begins in the most important social unit, the family, and requires living up to family obligations and responsibilities. "Of myriad virtues, filial piety is the first," he wrote. Getting right with family, in turn, means respecting parents and other older relatives, minimizing their worries, bringing them honor, and protecting their reputations. Confucianism also intricately defines the ranks and roles of people in society, stressing that knowing one's place takes precedence over expressing individuality and autonomy. People are not in this life for their own advancement or actualization, but for the advancement of their families and maintenance of the social order.

Just as Greek ideas still animate the Socratic method in the West, Confucianism informs the pedagogical techniques of the East. In the Confucian method, the first step is respecting and paying attention to the teacher. Then students must memorize the materials the teacher provides. (American parents and teachers often dismiss these techniques as "drill and kill.") Only during the final steps of instruction are students to question the material or add their own perspectives.[18]

Knowledge thus resides not inside the student's head, but out in the world. And minds, in turn, are not motors that turn and churn. Rather, they are natural phenomena like water, or living organisms like plants. According to these metaphors, the outside—wind and light, sun and soil, teachers and texts—interacts with the inside to develop a person. The self, in other words, is interdependent with its environment.

Taoism is another Chinese philosophy that spices the recipe for the self in the East. Unlike the many ancient Greek philosophies that viewed nature as stable and inherently consistent, Taoism holds that the world is constantly in flux and replete with contradictions. Rather than destroying each other, however, these contradictions require each other—just as the dark yin and the light yang in the Taoist symbol require and contain a drop of each other. Accordingly, understanding people and matter requires looking at their surroundings, rather than peering at the particles that make them up. These basic philosophical beliefs are alive and well in the ways people of Eastern heritage look outside of people, not just inside of them, to explain behavior.

A final major philosophical force that animates the East is Buddhism, which holds that enlightenment comes to people who can transcend the illusion of the self as separate and replace it with an understanding of the self as completely intertwined with other forces. As the Zen Buddhist master Tozan taught, "The blue mountain is the father of the white cloud. The white cloud is the son of the blue mountain. . . . They are quite independent, and yet dependent."[19]

Educate for Everyone's Future

East and West are likewise both independent from and interdependent with each other. But they are growing ever more interdependent as the planet shrinks. Although their distinct culture cycles took thousands of years to form, they can be brought into better alignment with a few thoughtful changes to their institutions, interactions, and I's.

In the West, people of Asian heritage dominate the highest-paying, fastest-growing industries. And with a solid pipeline of successful Asian students feeding the West's best universities, their ranks are likely to swell. What can Westerners do to keep pace with their Eastern brethren?

As Amy Chua learned the hard way, you can't just import Eastern practices wholesale into Western contexts and expect them to work. Yet a few injections of interdependence into the institutions, interactions, and I's of the West could help us do a better job of preparing for the multicultural future.

At the level of institutions, the United States needs better standards and resources for educators and students. The No Child Left Behind Act, which marked the first time in U.S. history that Congress mandated testing at set grade levels (in the past, states established their own testing schedules), was a move in the right direction. But its narrow goals (testing only reading, writing, and math), standardized tests (which assess only low-level skills), and curiously punitive incentives have not only lowered overall student performance, but also widened the gaps between social classes and races.[20]

A more interdependent approach to national standards would educate the whole student with offerings of science, music, and art. This education would prepare students to be well-informed contributors to society, rather than just able competitors in the game of life. A more interdependent education system would also devote more time, money, and people to raising up the lowest-performing schools to a shared standard, rather than weeding them out.

Within classrooms and homes, teachers and parents can use more interdependent interactions to help their kids keep up with the Zhangs. Channeling kids' choices toward jobs that actually exist would go a long way toward preparing them for the twenty-first century. In the depths of the latest recession, 10 percent of Americans were unemployed. Yet more than a million jobs in science, technology, engineering, and math (STEM) went unfilled, because the U.S. education system failed to produce enough qualified graduates.[21] To put this problem in interdependent terms: American schools and students were failing to meet the needs of their nation. Though Asian Americans are overrepresented in STEM, they are not numerous enough to fill in the employment gaps.

The problem, psychologist Judith Harackiewicz finds, is that Western parents are not helping their children connect the dots between studying STEM now and joining their nation's workforce later. Instead, high school students dream about careers that fit their teenage preferences, rather than pursue careers that both satisfy their desires and meet their society's needs. To fix this problem, Harackiewicz and her team devised a novel intervention. They randomly assigned the parents of 181 teens from high schools all over Wisconsin to receive information that linked math and science to the teens' current and future goals. (Parents in a control group did not get these materials.) For example, one brochure coached parents on how to help their teens see the relevance of math and science to video games, cell phone use, and driving.

The remedy was small, comprising only two brochures and a website. Yet it had a big impact. Students whose parents received the materials took one more semester of math or science than did students whose parents did not get the materials. The information had empowered parents to help their children choose a path that would be more difficult in the short term, but more profitable in the long term. Although parents didn't override their children's choices altogether, as would be acceptable in many interdependent contexts, they did direct their children more than is customary in independent worlds.[22]

Grow Some Grit

Another interdependent practice that would benefit Western children and adults alike is to start treating each other, and ourselves, like the dynamic and tough creatures we are. In her bestseller, *Mindset*, psychologist Carol Dweck documents that people who view their minds as constantly growing (like plants) work harder, learn more, take bigger risks, and cope with setbacks better than do people who view their minds as fixed entities (like machines). These two mind-sets map onto the different styles of explaining behavior (situational versus dispositional) we discussed in the introduction. People with a growth mind-set think that situational causes like effort and social support drive achievement, while people with a fixed mind-set think that dispositional causes like talent and intelligence generate success. Perhaps not surprisingly, a growth mind-set is more popular among people of Eastern heritages, while a fixed mind-set is more widespread among people of Western heritages.[23]

It only takes a few daily practices to instill either a growth or a fixed mind-set. Want your child, spouse, or coworker to view himself as limited by his permanent attributes? Then praise him for the abilities that make him "special," judge him for failures that reveal allegedly inherent flaws, and eventually lower your standards to protect his faltering self-esteem. Want your child, spouse, or coworker to grow into his potential? Then praise him for his effort, help him develop a realistic account of his failures, and work with him to meet high standards.[24]

Psychologist Angela Duckworth has similar suggestions. In her many years as an educator, Duckworth noticed that it wasn't the kids with the high IQs who excelled. It was the kids who could throw themselves whole-heartedly and single-mindedly into a personal mission, and achieve it no matter the setbacks. To capture this ability to persevere, she developed a simple twelve-item "Grit Test," which includes items such as "I am a hard worker" and "I have achieved a goal that took years of work." She and her colleagues then found that grit predicts everything from which West Point cadets survive their first year to who wins the National Spelling Bee.[25]

Instilling growth mind-sets and grit takes more interdependence than does ingraining fixed mind-sets and baseless self-esteem. You can't just set a high standard and then walk away; you have to establish and maintain a strong relationship to nurture the other person's efforts. "What Chinese parents understand," writes Chua, "is that nothing is fun until you're good at it. To get good at anything you have to work, and children on their own never want to work, which is why it is crucial to override their preferences."[26] Although taking away choices altogether will not fly for independent selves, helping people identify their weaknesses and work hard to improve them should.

Burn the Bamboo Ceiling

While the West is getting in touch with its interdependent side for the sake of its own competitive advantage, it should also extend some of that interdependence toward the East. In a 2011 study from the Center for Work-Life Policy, Asian-American respondents were the group that felt least comfortable "being themselves" at work. Fewer than half reported that they had a professional mentor, compared to more than half of European Americans. Asian-American respondents also felt that the leadership in their organizations failed to recognize their contributions. For these and other reasons, Asian Americans hit a "bamboo ceiling" on their way up their professional ladders, and are underrepresented in the highest echelons of corporations and governments.[27]

To help Easterners break through the bamboo ceiling, Westerners should take a chance on Asian leaders. Although their footholds may be slipping, people of European heritage still control most of the institutions in the West, and thus have more power to change those institutions than do people of Asian heritage. Extending a little affirmative action and promoting Asians into leadership positions would go a long way toward improving Asian employees' morale, creativity, and productivity. It would also allow Asian leaders to deploy their strengths on a larger scale. And because organizations with diversity at the top tend to perform better than organizations with more homogenous leadership, putting Asians in a higher place would likely redound to the corporate bottom line.[28]

Western organizations should also work harder to accommodate the work styles of their members of Eastern descent. Speaking up in a group is hard for many people, but as we discussed in chapter 1, it is even harder for interdependent selves, who are used to staying quiet so that they can better tune in to other people. Talking in groups is also more physically taxing for Asian Americans. Studies show that Asian Americans have higher levels of cortisol (a stress hormone) when speaking in formal settings than do European Americans. Giving employees the chance to contribute their ideas in writing or in informal settings can let them shine without undue stress.[29]

Daily interactions between people of Eastern and Western heritages could also use a tune-up. Even Asian Americans who were born in the United States feel "forever foreign" because they still field questions such as "Where are you *really* from?" Psychologists Sapna Cheryan and Benoît Monin captured what happens when European Americans make Asian Americans feel as though they aren't yet members of the club. Clipboard in hand, they approached Asian-American students on campus and asked, "Do you speak English?" They then asked the students to recall as many American television shows from the 1980s as possible.

Feeling the need to defend their American-ness, these Asian-American participants spent much more time on the TV task than did Asian-American respondents who were not asked about their English-speaking ability. As we will demonstrate in the following chapters, this time spent defending one's self against threats is time *not* spent on more personally and socially beneficial pursuits. And in the long term, these small assaults on the self can undermine people's performance and motivation, robbing all of us of the contributions they could have made.[30]

Express Yourself

To flourish in Western contexts, the interdependent selves of the East can likewise alter their culture cycles to adopt more independent interactions and I's. Back at Lynbrook High School, Gail Davidson is working with teachers, students, and parents to do just that. Many of the school's Asian-American students and their parents are holding fast to the only model of success they know: an interdependent model in which meeting expectations is the surest route to happiness. Despite their desire to excel and contribute, they do not know that school in the West has very different rules.

The teachers had already tried a variety of strategies to get students to talk more. But you can't just tell students who grew up not talking suddenly to speak up. Sharing opinions requires that you believe you should say something, and that you have something to say. Both take cultivation. Developing your own voice, Western style, begins with preschool show-and-tell and proceeds through a twelve-grade cascade of "me-projects." The independent culture cycle propels this process in millions of other small ways, many of them invisible.

To reveal the inner workings of this culture cycle, Davidson and her staff held a series of meetings with teachers, parents, and students to discuss Western and Eastern cultures' different ideas about education. They invited outside speakers to describe their research on culture and learning. They learned that although talking doesn't necessarily equal thinking, students need to be able to express themselves so they can succeed in the Western world, including at college and in their careers.

Davidson and her staff also developed practices to help students speak up in class. Rather than "cold-calling," per the Socratic method, the teachers now "warm-call" students whom they've told ahead of time to prepare their ideas for sharing. And to reduce the intimidation that comes with thirty pairs of eyes and ears trained on your every move, they also convene their students in carefully composed small groups.

Let's Dare to Be Different and Pool Our Strengths

Global warming and the global financial crisis; epidemics and ethnic conflicts; food shortages and foundering infrastructure—the scariest problems facing modern humans are not local. Indeed, many of them spring from the fact that our world is getting smaller, flatter, and hotter than ever before. Yet when seeking solutions, we often limit ourselves to the wisdom of the village genius (or, occasionally, the folly of the village idiot).

Rather than sticking to the same old knitting and letting our differences get the best of us, the time has come for us humans to harness our diverse culture cycles for the better. Built into our species' DNA is our ability to emulate and perpetuate cultures. Although we tend to favor our own people's ideas, institutions, and ways of interacting, we are clever primates. We can also borrow from other people and push our culture cycles in new directions.

We can also look backward to find our way forward. The father of modern psychology, William James, never made it to Asia, but his extensive travels through the Americas and Europe revealed to him the many ways to be a self, as well as the many strengths of those many ways. "The whole drift of my education," he wrote in his most famous work, *Principles of Psychology*, "goes to persuade me that the world of our present consciousness is only one out of many worlds of consciousnesses that exist, and that those other worlds must contain experiences which have a meaning for our life also."[31]

A contemporary take on James's writings can be found in a mash-up of Krysia and Lila's favorite preschool posters: Let's dare to be different and pool our strengths. In the following chapters, we show how people of different genders, races, classes, regions, religions, workplaces, and halves of the globe are retreading their culture cycles to do just that.

CHAPTER 3

Women Are from Earth, Men Are from Earth

Gender Cultures

Look out, America! Women are taking over the joint. Women now hold more managerial and professional jobs than men,[1] and urban women under thirty now make more money than their unmarried and childless male counterparts.[2] To scale the socioeconomic ladder, the fairer sex is using decidedly American ratchets: education and entrepreneurship. Women now earn more bachelor's, master's, and doctoral degrees than men, and as many or more professional degrees in most fields.[3] On the entrepreneurial front, women own or half-own 47 percent of all U.S. firms.[4]

Meanwhile, American men seem to be languishing. The Great Recession of 2007–2009 hit men harder than women—so much so that bloggers dubbed the economic spinout the "he-cession." As the male-dominated manufacturing, construction, and finance sectors sustained the recession's hardest hits, 5.4 million men lost their jobs, compared to 2.1 million women.[5]

Men now shoulder not only the consequences of the recession, but also the blame. "The aggressive, risk-seeking behavior that has enabled men to entrench their power—the cult of macho—has now proven destructive and unsustainable in a globalized world," political commentator Reihan Salam wrote in *Foreign Policy*.[6] The people of Iceland and Lithuania agree; in the wake of financial collapse, both nations pointedly elected women to head their governments.

The younger members of the XY set are faring poorly, too. In the same years that girls made gains across the academic board, boys dropped out of high school in record numbers. Girls' standardized test scores continued to climb a right-sloping curve, but boys' scores slumped down a left-leaning luge, widening the gender gap in education.[7]

For all their hard-won triumphs, women and girls aren't exactly doing a victory dance in the end zone. Women have always suffered more from depression than have men. But now women are getting sicker, younger, than ever before, psychologist Stephen Hinshaw documents in *The Triple Bind.* Today, self-mutilation, eating disorders, depression, violence, and suicide acutely endanger 25 percent of American teenage girls.[8]

Beneath these upticks in suffering, we detect the clash of independence and interdependence. As we will reveal in this chapter, women's selves, ways, and worlds are more interdependent, while men's selves, ways, and worlds are more independent. Now that men and women are sharing spheres to a degree not seen since before the industrial revolution, their culture cycles are grating against each other.

Take a look at high school girls. During their teenage years, young women are expected to hone their "girl skills," which Hinshaw describes as "making people feel comfortable, figuring out what they need, and then giving it them."[9] Yet they are also under increasing pressure to triumph at all the traditional "boy stuff"—namely, excelling at school, sports, and extracurricular activities so that they can get into good colleges and secure fulfilling careers. This combo puts girls in an impossible situation: they must beat out the competition without hurting anyone's feelings. And they must do so while conforming to increasingly narrow notions of beauty—the third bind that Hinshaw describes. Like the old quip about Ginger Rogers, who danced all the same steps as Fred Astaire, but backward and in high heels, young women must not only shine at independence, but also do so interdependently and while looking effortlessly hot.

Among men, the clash of independence and interdependence likewise forms the core of much anguish. When the base of wealthy nations' economies moved from manufacturing and construction to service and information, labor demands likewise migrated from male to female bailiwicks. "A white-collar economy values raw intellectual horsepower, which men and women have in equal amounts," journalist Hanna Rosin explains. "It also requires communication skills and social intelligence, areas in which women, according to many studies, have a slight edge."[10] Even before they enter the workforce, men begin to lose their footing on the socioeconomic ladder when their budding independent selves fail to thrive in classrooms dominated by the female form of interdependence.[11] As you will see, this way of being interdependent is not identical to the East-Asian interdependence we discussed in the past chapters. Indeed, throughout this book we will show the many shapes that independence and interdependence may take. At their cores, however, independent folks everywhere see their selves as separate from and prior to their relationships, while interdependent selves see their relationships as a fundamental part of who they are.

The integration of men and women is not complete. A few traditionally female professions—nursing, teaching, social work—remain estrogen enclaves, despite the decent salaries they would pay to men willing to jump the gender line. Meanwhile, the very highest levels of government, corporations, and academia remain testosterone zones. Only 17 percent of U.S. representatives and senators are women—the lowest proportion of any industrialized nation[12]—and only 3.6 percent of Fortune 500 CEOs are women.[13] Men still dominate physics and engineering, the most lucrative of the sciences. Partly because they are locked out of these elite ranks, women still earn only seventy-seven cents to a man's dollar.[14] For women, the other side of the glass ceiling remains tantalizingly elusive.

Women are quickly closing the gap, however, and men are slowly wending their way into the female fold. For both to succeed in this increasingly mixed-up, muddled-up, shook-up world, each will have to accommodate the other's self—namely, men will need to extend an interdependent hand, while women will need to wield their independent sides. Mustering your better self for the situation is not as hard as it may seem. Using your newfound understanding of the culture cycle, you can move institutions, interactions, and I's to help bridge the gender divide.[15]

Heterogeneity Is Tough

If asked to list the hotspots of the gender revolution, few people would likely mention the symphony orchestra. Yet that is precisely where psychologists Jutta Allmendinger and J. Richard Hackman went to explore what happens when women enter male-dominated institutions—especially elite institutions whose success depends on individuals working well together.[16]

The researchers' laboratories were seventy-eight professional symphony orchestras in the United States, the United Kingdom, and former East and West Germany. Despite the fantastic talents of their individual members, the symphonies soured when they introduced women to the mix. As the proportion of women in an orchestra crept up, players' attitudes, relationships, and performances all slid down. These unhappy patterns held true regardless of the prestige of the orchestra or the place the orchestra called home.

Yet a funny thing happened when orchestras hired enough women to have a 40-percent-female ensemble: Both men and women started liking their jobs and their colleagues more. They viewed their finances as more abundant and their positions as more stable. They also thought their playing was more musical.

Why did the addition of a few women hobble entire orchestras? And what happened at that 40 percent tipping point to make both men and women feel more content?

Some thirty years of research show that orchestras are not alone. No matter the organization, industry, or sector, when women make serious inroads into organizations, the going gets bumpy.[17] Part of the problem is just human hijinks; ours is a conservative species that likes to keep its social roles clear. In many cultures for the past few millennia, labor was divided so that men won the bread and women made the homes. (Yet as we reveal later in this chapter, many other cultures more equitably divided labor between the sexes, with surprising effects.) Upsetting that well-worn pattern is stressful for everyone.

At an economic level, men rightly perceive the entrance of women into their workplace as a threat to their earnings. Across industries, the rising of the women means the falling of the wage. This is because women command lower wages, so their entrance into a field drives down how much a given industry pays on average.[18]

For the women storming the castle, being the new kid on the block is no fun, either. Pioneering women are greeted with less social support and greater isolation than males.[19] They also face greater pressure to perform, partly to defy the stereotype that women are less competent than men—a stereotype broadcast in cultural artifacts such as Teen Talk Barbie

Push a button on her back, and Barbie ditzily exclaims, "Math class is *tough!*"

Women's attempts to disprove these stereotypes often backfire, psychologists Michael Inzlicht and Avi Ben-Zeev find. These researchers randomly assigned undergraduate women to take a math test in the presence of either two men (a triad that is only 33 percent female) or two women (a triad that is 100 percent female). They discovered that, like the orchestras with less than 40 percent women, the women in the 33-percent-female triads performed worse on the math test than did women in the 100-percent-female triads. The overwhelming male majority threw the ladies off their game, as the women were so anxious about confirming the women-can't-compete stereotype that they choked on the test.[20] Psychologist Claude Steele calls this fear of confirming negative beliefs about one's group "stereotype threat."[21] As we will discuss here and in following chapters, when people are distracted by stereotype threats, they cannot dedicate 100 percent of their brains to actually doing a test. Consequently, their performance suffers, and they ironically wind up validating the stereotype they fought so hard to disprove.

Once the proportion of women in an organization reaches a critical mass, however, things turn around not only for them, but also for the organization as a whole. For instance, psychologists Anita Woolley, Thomas Malone, and their colleagues demonstrated that the more women a group has, the better it performs on a wide variety of tasks—an ability the researchers call *collective intelligence.*[22] In their laboratory experiments, groups with more women crafted better solutions to an architectural design problem, scored more points against a computerized checkers opponent, and more deftly performed other feats of reasoning, negotiation, and creativity.

Organizations may already be taking women's collective intelligence to the bank. Economist Judith Hellerstein and her colleagues find that, among manufacturing plants with considerable market power (that is, they are influential enough to affect the price of products), the more women in the workforce, the more profitable the plant.[23] Sociologist Cedric Herring likewise finds that the more gender-balanced an organization, the greater its sales revenues, customer base, and profits.[24]

Fewer studies examine what happens when men infiltrate traditionally female fields, largely because men so rarely defy the gender divide. Yet as we will discuss, some studies suggest that women get their revenge by discriminating against men. Males in female places also face a peculiar challenge that sociologist Christine Williams calls the glass escalator. Even if these men want to stay on the front line, they get "kicked upstairs" into higher-paying, higher-status, traditionally male positions.[25]

In addition to these organizational obstacles to achieving gender balance, we see a deeper psychological one: the selves of women and men are slightly, but significantly, different. In the next few sections, we explore what these psychological differences are, where they came from, why they collide, and how to commingle them more peacefully.

The Straight Dope on Difference

For the past millennium or so, a popular pastime has been to list the many ways that men and women are not the same. Favorite entries are that women are less intelligent, less mathematical, less logical, less assertive, less rational, more Venusian than men; while men are less caring, less verbal, less emotional, less gentle, less intuitive, more Martian than women. Often built into this game is the assumption that these differences are innate, hard-wired, essential, *biological*.

In the past few years, spoilsports have tried to ruin the game by arguing that these alleged gender differences are *just* stereotypes. Gender differences, they say, are only social constructions, mere figments of the collective imagination. People can choose whether to believe them or not.

Both groups are quite wrong, yet also a little right. Women and men are indeed biologically different, but not as different as the stereotypes about them suggest. And those stereotypes are not wimpy will o' the wisps that we can brush away or summon on a whim. Instead, stereotypes are human-made products that help drive the culture cycle. Over time, as they insinuate themselves in the I's, interactions, institutions, and big ideas of culture cycles, stereotypes exert tremendous force in shaping the lives of men and women.

True, men are bigger and stronger than women, and only women can gestate and nurse offspring. These biological differences may give rise to a few psychological ones. But not many, finds psychologist Janet Shibley Hyde.[26] To survey the dizzying pile of research on sex differences, Hyde reviewed all the existing meta-analyses on the topic. (A meta-analysis is a powerful statistical test that combines the findings of many studies so that researchers can tease out which effects are "really real" and which are flukey one-offs.) She found only two psychological features with very large gender differences: motor performance and sexuality. In particular, men can throw faster and farther, and have stronger grips. They also masturbate more and feel better about casual sex.

Not exactly earth-shattering results.

Of the remaining gender differences, 78 percent were small or close to zero.

Only 21 percent fell in the range of moderate to large differences. In that 21 percent, we see two characteristics that reflect differences in notions of the self. No matter the measure or context, men are more aggressive, and in a way that reflects a more independent self.[27] In contrast, women are more agreeable (more trusting and more "tender-minded"), a quality more indicative of the interdependent self.

The remaining midsize effects point to the oft-reported finding that females have greater verbal prowess while males rule the visual-spatial roost. But as we shall see later, many of these so-called ability differences vanish when testers dispel stereotypes by reassuring women that they are not, in fact, born idiots, and men that they are not, in fact, callous brutes.

Hyde's study did not consider gender differences in independence and interdependence, because meta-analyses on gender and self do not yet exist. Yet a growing body of research suggests that women more often deploy an interdependent self—that is, their relational, similar, adjusted, rooted, and ranked side. Meanwhile, men more frequently front an independent self—that is, an individual, unique, influencing, free, and equal (yet great!) I.

In one of the largest cross-cultural studies of the selves of men and women, for example, Australian psychologist Yoshihisa Kashima and his team found that undergraduate women in Australia, the United States, Japan, and Korea scored higher than men on "relatedness," a construct that reflects ideas such as "I feel like doing something for people in trouble because I can almost feel their pain."[28]

To zoom in on this relational aspect of interdependence, psychologist Susan Cross created the Relational Interdependent Self-Construal (RISC) scale. Closer to the notion of interdependence than many existing scales, the RISC asks respondents how much they agree with items such as

"When I think of myself, I often think of my close friends or family also" and "My close relationships are an important reflection of who I am." Subsequent studies find that women score higher on this scale than men.[29]

Meanwhile, men score higher on measures of independence. And when they describe themselves, they list more unique, internal abilities (e.g., "I am smart"), preferences ("I like basketball"), and traits ("I am tall") than do women, who list more roles and relationships.[30]

Of course, like all people, men are inherently social animals. The project of crafting an independent self requires other people to individuate from, to compare with, and to influence. In addition, individuals must band together to create the interactions, institutions, and ideas that sustain and stem from independence. You can't be a self—even an independent self—by yourself.

Miss Understood

For women, thinking, feeling, and acting reverberate with connections to other people. Recall the Woolley and Malone team's finding that the more women a group has, the higher the group's collective intelligence. Suspecting that what drives collective intelligence is social sensitivity, the researchers gave participants the "Reading the Mind in the Eyes" test. For this test, participants view photographs of the eye regions of different actors. They then choose which of four words best describes what the person in the photograph is thinking or feeling. Developed by psychologist Simon Baron-Cohen—who is, incidentally, a cousin of comedian Sacha Baron-Cohen, of *Borat* infamy—this test reliably distinguishes between people who have autism (and thus are often not very socially sensitive) and people who do not. Malone's team found not only that women scored higher on this test, but also that women's greater social sensitivity was the reason the female-ful groups performed better than the lady-lean ones. In other words, social sensitivity was what made the groups with more women smarter.

These findings are only the latest in a long line of studies showing that women more accurately read other people's thoughts and feelings.[31] In several classic demonstrations, for example, psychologist William Ickes and his colleagues paired strangers (in either same- or mixed-sex dyads) for five minutes of interaction, which researchers surreptitiously videotaped. After the five minutes, the pairs split up so that each participant could watch a video of the conversation. While the tape rolled, participants wrote down what they were thinking and feeling, moment by moment, and their guesses about what their partners were thinking and feeling. The researchers found that the women, compared with the men, more accurately described their partners' thoughts and emotions during the videotaping. This mind-reading ability took effort; women sat closer to their partners and looked at them more than did men. Women also smiled and gestured more.[32]

Memory follows attention. So perhaps not surprisingly, study after study finds that women have better memories for the names, faces, hair, and clothes of both strangers and friends.[33] Within marriages, wives have more vivid memories of important moments in their relationships than do their husbands.[34]

Women's interest in other people is not merely academic. Their hearts and health rise and fall with those of close others. When women's friends or relatives are hurting, women's own well-being takes more of a hit than does men's. Likewise, divorce and other kinds of relational strife take a bigger bite out of women's psyches and bodies than men's, while marriage and new friendships give women a bigger boost.[35] To untangle the kinks in their social networks, women apologize more often than men.[36] And when women face threats, their first instinct is not to fight or flee, as has been the mantra of the mostly male scientists who study conflict. Instead, psychologist Shelley Taylor finds, it is to "tend and befriend"—that is, to seek out alliances and launch a coordinated front.[37]

Because of women's greater interdependence, if you want to know how a woman is doing, you must look at both the height of her self-esteem and the state of her relationships. The smoother her social world, the better her physical and mental health. But if you want to predict a man's well-being, you need look no further than his self-esteem—a measure on which men routinely register higher levels than do women.[38]

When women ascend to the top of the corporate ladder, they don't leave their interdependence behind. Instead, they adopt a more participative, democratic, "transformational" style, as psychologist Alice Eagly calls it. People with this leadership style communicate values, consider new views, and attend to the individual needs of their reports. In contrast, men more often employ a more command-and-control, "transactional" manner, with which they focus on rewarding successes and punishing mistakes.

Eagly and her colleagues' research also suggests that transformational leaders are more effective than transactional ones, inspiring extra effort from their subordinates, eliciting better reviews of their leadership, and driving better results from their teams.[39]

Fighting for Independence

Men, of course, are not robots, staring at their navels and contemplating the awesomeness of their solitary selves. Instead, while the gals are smiling and gesturing and reading other people's minds, the guys are flexing and separating and sizing other people up. In other words, they are tracking and broadcasting cues about their independent selves.

The most obvious way that men individuate and influence others is through aggression. Across cultures, situations, settings, eras, ages, measures, and flavors (physical or verbal, direct or indirect), men are the more aggro half of the species. Their belligerent advantage emerges early, with more rough-and-tumble play starting at age two, and more verbal aggression, such as insults, curses, and taunting, quickly following. (Some theorists have argued that girls are meaner and inflict more indirect aggression, but research has not held up this claim.) Men's violent tendencies reach their zenith between the ages of eighteen and thirty, as a quick survey of your local prison, hockey rink, or civil war will attest. Even when men mellow out at midlife and old age, they never lose their edge over women in the aggression department, and continue to clock higher rates of homicide and other violent crimes until their dotage, when they are more likely than women to commit suicide.[40]

Male humans are not alone in their penchant for pugnacity. In most mammalian species, the males are the scrappier half. This is because baby-making males are a dime a dozen, while fecund females are fewer and farther between. To have a shot at reproduction, males must often physically compete for access to females. Their size and strength assist them in this enterprise.

Unlike other mammals, however, human males have also evolved psychological selves that plan for the future, reflect upon the past, and observe social mores in the present. To do violence in the ways that evolution requires calls for a more independent self that can suspend empathy and value one's own interests over those of others.[41] Laboratory experiments confirm that when men are induced to think of themselves as even more independent than usual, they express even more dominance over other groups.[42] Inside and outside the lab, both experiments and observational studies show that the higher a man's self-esteem, the easier he can be roused to violence. Previously thought to suffer from low self-regard, bullies actually log the highest levels of self-esteem. Mess with the bully, though, and you get the horns, psychologist Roy Baumeister finds. Bullies (whose ranks include more men) most readily react to assaults on their egos.[43]

Every bit as angry as men,[44] women, too, have their witchy ways. Backbiting, rumor-mongering, and ostracizing are the favored weapons of the she-set. Women also throw their fair share of punches in close relationships.[45] Yet when it comes to absolute levels of barefisted bandying, men are far more likely than women to put their bodies on the line.

Men are also more likely to sign up for subtler forms of risk.[46] Teenage boys' risk-taking in drinking, driving, and sex is the stuff of insurance company profit margins. Many boys who survive their adolescence later capitalize on their risk-seeking ways by making bank in high risk, high-pay-off professions such as investing or trading. What risk giveth, however, risk can also taketh away, economists Brad M. Barber and Terrance Odean find. Examining six years' worth of data for some thirty-five thousand households, the researchers discovered that men built riskier stock portfolios than did women. Men's overconfidence in their trading abilities also led them to trade equities 45 percent more often than women. The market rewarded men's risk-seeking and overconfidence with returns that were 0.93 percentage points less than women's.[47]

Having constructed their independence through aggression and risk-taking, American men then add their own special twist: self-serving biases. Compared with people in East-Asian cultures, Americans more often pull the psychic tricks that make their selves seem better, including the self-serving attribution bias (congratulating yourself for your successes but blaming situations for your failures) and the false uniqueness bias (viewing yourself as better than most others).[48] American men, moreover, outdo American women when it comes to seeing themselves as legends in their own eyes. Starting in childhood, boys boast about their abilities more than girls do.[49] In high school, boys systematically rate their math chops higher than do girls with the same grades—a tendency that fully explains why more boys than girls take calculus.[50] In adulthood, women outgrow their self-serving biases, while men maintain their self-kvelling across the lifespan.[51]

From Cradle to Gender

Around the world, high-status groups are perceived as more agentic—that is, more assertive, independent, and masculine—while low-status groups are perceived as more communal—that is, more relational, interdependent, and feminine.[52] Coincidence? We think not. Instead, we see that the different selves of women and men both reflect and support the culture cycles of worlds where men have historically enjoyed higher status than women. In other words, a big reason women more often employ interdependence is because that is what many lower-status people do—namely, support the higher-status people. And a big reason men more often employ independence is because that is what many higher-status people do—namely, control the lower-status people, and earn a higher wage for doing so (stay tuned for more on status and class in our next chapter).

Yet the higher status and independence of men are not biological birthrights. Nor are the lower status and interdependence of women genetic inevitabilities. If you thought that gender differences in selves and statuses arose mostly from biology, you could be forgiven. For the past several hundred years, scientists and philosophers have busied themselves with locating the sources of gender differences inside the body. As each purported site of sex differences disappeared under closer scientific scrutiny, another cropped up to replace it, not unlike a game of anatomical Whack-a-Mole.

This hunt for the biological sources of gender differences continues unabated, recounts psychologist Cordelia Fine in her incisive and witty work *Delusions of Gender.*[53] Replacing the tape measures and scales of yore is a cast of new technologies: functional magnetic resonance imaging, hormonal assays, genetic sequencing, and other shiny tools. For all the big guns of modern biotech, however, many of the "harder" sciences still suffer from wildly biased inferences. The result, Fine argues, is not a new and improved neuroscience of sex differences; instead, it's that old canard of "neurosexism" dressed up in the emperor's new machines.

Meanwhile, the "softer" sciences of social and cultural psychology have amassed their own arsenal of explanations for why women and men differ. Rather than coursing through the veins, leaping across the synapses, or lighting up the cerebral lobes of men and women, the causes reside in the products and practices of men's and women's daily lives. In other words, they're cultural. These everyday interactions not only convey the good and right way to be a man or a woman, but also become self-fulfilling prophecies, at once prescribing and describing the sex differences we see in the world.

Parents' different expectations for boys and girls emerge even before their children are born. Talking with mothers-to-be in their last trimester, sociologist Barbara Rothman noted that women who knew they were having sons described their fetus's movements as "vigorous" and "strong," while the mothers who were having daughters defended the jabs of their unborn daughters as "not violent, not excessively energetic, and not terribly active." Mothers who did not know the sex of their fetuses, in contrast, described the rumblings in their uteruses in similar ways, regardless of the sex of the baby they eventually had.[54]

When newborns greet the outside world, adults are standing by to shape the infants' selves in gendered ways. In their classic study, psychologists (and spouses) John and Sandra Condry asked college students to watch a video of a nine-month-old infant. Half the participants learned that the baby was a boy named "David"; the other half learned that the same baby was a girl named "Dana." In the video, David/Dana startles, cries, and then screams in response to the repeated eruptions of a jack-in-the-box. Undergrads who thought they were watching a boy named "David" viewed him as angrier, more active, and less fearful than did the undergrads who thought they were watching a girl named "Dana."[55]

In a follow-up experiment, the Condrys found that female high school students responded more quickly to a crying sixteen-week-old baby named "Andrea" than they did to the exact same baby when it was named "Jonathan." (Male high school students were equally slow in responding to the allegedly male and female infants, a point we shall return to later.)[56] On the blank slate of these experimental babies, adults were already projecting their belief that boys are more independent and girls are more relational.

Real mothers give their real daughters the interdependence treatment as well. They talk with their daughters more than they do with their sons, even though male infants are just as receptive to speech as female infants.[57] Mothers also discuss emotions with their daughters more than they do with their sons.[58]

The toys that adults put in children's hands likewise send a message about where those children belong and how they should behave. Dolls, kitchen appliances, and other "toys of the home" populate girls' playtime, while vehicles, machines, and other "toys of the world" rove through boys' recreational spaces.[59] Parents then reinforce which toys are gender appropriate—especially to boys, who get considerably more flack for flouting the gender rules.[60]

Media add a tailwind to the teaching of gender. A popular refrain among today's egalitarian-minded parents is "*We* didn't raise our daughter (son) to be a pink princess (bombastic brute). She (he) must have been just *born* a priss (hellion)!" The heartbreaking reality, of course, is that parents are only one part of the culture cycle. As journalist Peggy Orenstein recounts in *Cinderella Ate My Daughter*, media shout loud directions about the "right" way to be a boy or a girl.[61] Ever notice that all Dr. Seuss's main characters are male? Most children's books, television shows, and movies feature male lead characters. Video games also overwhelmingly spotlight boys or men saving the world from mayhem. Even advertisements targeting children depict boys as more knowledgeable, active, and effective than girls. Meanwhile, in these same media, most portrayals of girls and women are either in traditional nurturing roles or as sex objects. These representations of women reinforce the idea that their value lies not in the content of their psyches, but in the contours of their flesh and in the care they give to other people.[62] Note that this is not just the stuff of 1950s sitcoms; most of this research was conducted in the past ten years.

Separate and Unequal

For the past few centuries, Western boys and girls rolled along these parallel tracks relatively peaceably, cultivating and reinforcing their complementary selves. Upon arrival at adulthood, women took their interdependence to the domestic sphere (or, if they worked, into teaching, nursing, or "pink-collar" professions), while men unleashed their independence in the working world. But after several major wars, social movements, and other cultural jolts, women are infiltrating the independent spheres of men and, to a lesser extent, men are wandering into women's worlds. In these places, both genders stumble into culture cycles that do not foster or reflect their selves.

In college, for example, many women find the fields of science, technology, engineering, and math (STEM) decidedly unwelcoming. Women thus feel discouraged from entering STEM fields, which offer some of the most stable and lucrative jobs in the new economy. Part of the problem is that STEM is represented as an independent undertaking—the province of Lone Rangers and cutthroat geniuses who can abstract theories from applications and separate signals from noise. Because women thrive on social connection, default to cooperation, and are rumored (though not proven) to think more practically than abstractly, women and STEM seem to be bad cultural "fits."

Women also allegedly lack the knack for STEM. As we mentioned at the opening of this chapter, one of the larger and more consistent findings in the long tradition of sex differences research is that women excel at verbal tasks while men excel at spatial ones. Yet in the past decade, a host of studies has shown that women perform just as well as men, and often better, when testers take the time to dispel the stereotype that women have little talent for STEM. For instance, when the test directions on the math portion of the Graduate Record Examination (GRE) state that the test has never detected a gender difference, women actually outscore men. But women falter in a condition that arouses stereotype threat by communicating (like many standardized tests) that the GRE is designed to discern why some people are better at math than others.[63]

Even when thoughtful educators cleanse the air of threatening stereotypes, the artifacts of everyday life convey the message that women simply do not belong in STEM. For instance, in an attempt to understand why so few women enter computer science—a field that started out as "women's work"—psychologist Sapna Cheryan and her colleagues took a look at the typical computer science lab. Suspecting that the junk food wrappers, disemboweled electronics, *Star Trek* posters, and technical magazines made a poor welcoming committee for potential female recruits, the researchers created an alternative lab environment, one with healthy snacks, coffee mugs, art posters, and general-interest magazines. They found that female undergraduates who were randomly assigned to complete a career development survey in the alternative lab expressed more interest in computer science than did the women who completed the study in a "geek lab" outfitted with the typical computer science detritus. Indeed, women in the alternative lab were just as interested in computer science as were men in both the alternative and geek labs.[64]

STEM is not the only realm whose artifacts put women off. Entrepreneurship's alleged requirements likewise seem inconsistent with women's more interdependent selves. Popular culture overwhelmingly portrays entrepreneurs as aggressive, risk-taking, and self-promoting men. Yet the evidence that these stereotypically masculine qualities are actually necessary for the successful pursuit of entrepreneurship is lacking. Indeed, generous and self-effacing billionaires such as eBay's Jeff Skoll and Zappos's Tony Hsieh are walking rebukes to the entrepreneur-as-asshole model.

Few women know this, however, says business professor Vishal K. Gupta. So when he and his colleagues randomly assigned female business majors to read an article about entrepreneurship that did not mention gender, these young women showed little interest in starting their own businesses. But when they read an article explicitly arguing that entrepreneurial success requires features that transcend gender (such as being creative, well-informed, and generous), the women's entrepreneurial ambitions rose.[65]

Women aspiring to leadership positions likewise stumble into independent culture cycles that conflict with their interdependent selves. Employers too often fail to promote women into positions of power because the latter are thought not to be assertive, competitive, or confident enough.[66]

Despite these obstacles, some women do reach the top of the corporate ladder. Once there, however, many crash into a subtler, yet stronger glass ceiling, one made of the fact that the very behaviors that get men ahead get women hated. One unsavory manifestation of this hostility is sexual harassment. Fans of the television show *Mad Men* know: it's not the office sweetheart, secretary Joan Harris, who get the most vicious gropes and overtures; it's the office upstart, copywriter Peggy Olson. Psychologist Jennifer Berdahl finds the same pattern in the real world. Men harass women who describe themselves as assertive, dominant, and independent more than they harass women who describe themselves as warm, modest, and deferent. They also harass women in traditionally male occupations more than they harass women in traditionally female occupations.[67]

Words Are for Birds

Although the situation is changing, men still have more status and resources than do women in most realms, and so men have more power to create and maintain a culture's interactions and institutions. Yet the culture cycle spins both ways. When women have more status in a domain, they, too, sometimes create worlds that are hostile to the masculine half of the species. The most pronounced example of this is the classroom, where the mismatches between female teachers' expectations and male students' proclivities leave many boys feeling frustrated, bewildered, and, ultimately, not in it to win it.

Over the past twenty years, the teaching profession has become more feminized than ever, recounts Peg Tyre in her 2008 bestseller, *The Trouble with Boys*.[68] The percentage of male teachers in elementary schools has fallen from 18 percent in 1981 to 9 percent today. In secondary schools, men now comprise only 35 percent of teachers. This spells not only a lack of male role models, but also a dearth of male voices weighing in on the best ways to meet the needs of boys.

With an overwhelming female workforce, schools are becoming increasingly difficult places for men to get jobs. Just as men in STEM and business view women's interdependence as incongruent with the demands of the workplace, women see men's independence as inconsistent with teaching. For instance, in one small experiment Tyre recounts, a mostly female hiring committee evaluated the written interview responses of several male teaching candidates. The committee found the responses to be too confrontational and not sufficiently collaborative, and so did not recommend the candidates for a second round of interviews. Little did the committee members realize that they were evaluating their own district's most talented and beloved male teachers.

Not only the personnel, but also the practices and paraphernalia of today's classrooms disadvantage boys. In part to make girls feel less intimidated, teachers have cracked down on the random acts of exuberance that typify young boys' behavior. At the same time, the no-fun edicts of No Child Left Behind have whittled recess, hands-on learning, and free play down to a few minutes per day. With no way to work off their excess energy, boys now have a harder time paying attention to an increasingly rigid and narrow curriculum.

Reading is no respite. Because girls are ready for language earlier, boys quickly get the message that reading is a girl thing. Female teachers do not help matters when they discourage boys from reading the goofy, action-packed, and sometimes violent comic books and magazines to which they are drawn. As Tyre relates, "It's an awkward moment when a teacher suggests *Little House in the Big Woods*, by Laura Ingalls Wilder, and her little male student opts instead for *The Day My Butt Went Psycho*."[69]

As boys flounder first in reading, and then in writing and other subjects, adults more frequently pathologize them than they do girls. Teachers hold back twice as many boys as girls, and doctors give diagnoses of attention and learning disorders to boys four times as often as they do to girls. Boys are less likely to recover from these early slips on the education ladder, so elementary school setbacks ripple throughout their educational careers. This is bad not only for males, but also for the females who would marry them a few years down the road, legal scholar Richard Banks and journalist Kate Bolick portend. For want of suitably educated and employed husbands, more women are forgoing marriage altogether.[70]

Very little of this gender stratification is intended. Study after study shows that, when asked, most men and women say they like each other and consider themselves equals. But implicit measures and subtle behaviors tell a different story: flying under the radar of conscious awareness, American men and women believe they are different and unequal. And these unconscious beliefs drive our outward behaviors, thereby turning the handle of the culture cycle.[71]

Although ancient and sneaky, these beliefs are neither natural nor inevitable. Indeed, as we shall see next, they are not even universal. Contrary to the bad rap that many developing cultures get, many of them harbor fewer gender differences than their wealthier neighbors.

Hoes in Different Area Codes

Back in the day, our ancestors realized they got to eat more often if they grew their own food, rather than hunting or gathering it. They also discovered that there's more than one way to sow a cereal. People who lived in places with rocky, sloped, or shallow soils tended to use hoes and digging sticks, while people who lived in places with smooth, flat, and deep soils tended to use ploughs drawn by livestock.

Which tool did your ancestors use? We'll give you a hint: if you have a favorite maize, millet, or cassava dish and you think that women have just as much right to work as men, your ancestors probably farmed with a hoe or stick. But if you hanker for one of your mother's wheat, barley, or rice specialties and/or you're not totally jazzed about women working outside the home, chances are your people walked behind a plough. That's because your forebears' choice of farm implement ultimately shaped not only which grains they grew and ate, but also whether your mother and sisters work outside the home today. And because people are not rational creatures, but rationalizing ones, your attitudes toward gender equality both stem from and sustain how your people have been dividing labor through the ages.

It all comes down to strength, economist Alberto Alesina and his colleagues argue.[72] Ploughs are heavy and unwieldy, as are the animals that pull them. So cultures that adopted the plough delegated the work of the field to men and the work of the home to women. Alesina's team shows that this pattern persists to this day: even in areas where no one has farmed for generations—say, much of Europe and the Middle East—the progeny of ploughmen tend to send fewer women into the workforce. Mirroring and remaking this division of labor, both men and women in these regions agree more with statements such as "On the whole, men make better political leaders than women do" and "When jobs are scarce, men should have more right to a job than women."

Hoes and digging sticks, on the other hand, are sufficiently lightweight and maneuverable that a woman can use them. Hoes also cannot break free and trample a small child. So cultures that stuck with sticks and hoes sent the entire family to the field. Thousands of years later, these regions—sub-Saharan Africa, parts of Central and South America, Central Asia, and Siberia—still support greater gender equality in both word and deed.

So accidents of agriculture planted the seed, so to speak, for more or less gendered ways of working and, ultimately, larger or smaller differences between the selves of men and women. Over time, other institutions then joined the culture cycle to reinforce patterns of greater or lesser inequality, including laws that forbade women from working outside the home, going to school, owning property, or voting. Once again, these institutions seldom resulted from people scheming in single-sex cabals about how to make life miserable for the other half of humanity. Instead, they usually arose from shifts in culture cycles that set histories, and psychologies, on a different course.

Independent Women

Make no mistake: men are biologically stronger than women, and women are biologically better at having babies than men. These differences mattered a lot when economies relied on physical strength and when infant mortality was high. But economics and epidemiology have changed. Now what counts isn't muscles and skeletons, or wombs and breasts. It's brains. And as women's success in academics and business attests, they have brains aplenty.

To meet the challenges of the twenty-first century, communities must harness the talents of all their people, including women. This will require changes at every level of the culture cycle—its institutions, interactions, individual I's, and, eventually, its big ideas. At the institutional level, men still hold disproportionate sway; so the onus is on them to alter their culture cycles to accommodate the selves of women. The prescription is straightforward: get in touch with the better side of chivalry, open the door, and let the women in. Research suggests that the best tool for getting and keeping women in the workplace is affirmative action.[73] In their systematic evaluation of diversity programs, sociologist Alexandra Kalev and her colleagues compared the diversity-promotion practices of 708 randomly selected medium-size U.S. companies. They found that diversity training and mentoring programs did little to increase the number of women (and minorities) in these workplaces over a thirty-one-year period. In fact, diversity training programs seemed to slow the tide of integration, perhaps because they inspired backlash against the very people they were designed to help. In contrast, organizations that made a human being or committee responsible for setting and monitoring diversity goals retained more women.

To keep women on their rosters, organizations must also adjust the interactions in their culture cycles. As Cheryan's research shows, a little mindfulness goes a long way. Thinking twice about which posters to put on the walls, which knickknacks to display on the shelves, and which snacks to stock in the break room helps make spaces that are more welcoming to women. It goes without saying that zero-tolerance sexual harassment policies are de rigueur for a female-friendly culture. Adjusting work expectations to accommodate the fact that women still provide the overwhelming majority of child and kin care in the United States would also help keep women happy and productive at work.

An even better intervention would be for men to become domestic gods in their own right. At every level of income, women do more housekeeping than do men. But a chilling thing happens when women make more money than their spouses: the women start putting in even more hours at home. Sociologists explain that women are trying to make up for violating the man-brings-home-the-bacon norm by zealously following the woman-fries-it-up norm. We humbly submit that this isn't fair. If women are going to pull more weight in the public sphere, men should pick up more slack at home.[74]

Although the bulk of the responsibility for achieving gender equality should not fall to the less powerful half of the population, women can adopt a few tricks of independence to help steer their culture cycles in a more equitable direction. As both Hinshaw and Fine document, women must already master many aspects of independence and interdependence to succeed academically and professionally, which results in bewildering paradoxes and exhausting double binds.

The part of independence that women do not sufficiently exercise, however, is asserting their needs. As the title of their book *Women Don't Ask* suggests, economists Linda Babcock and Sara Laschever find that women initiate negotiations 25 percent as often as do men. When women do knock on the door for more, they typically ask for and get less than do men—about 30 percent less, in fact. So the gender gaps in starting salaries, raises, and ranks are not just because men discriminate. They're also because women underestimate, and then poorly negotiate.[75]

Women's wariness at the negotiation table is not unfounded. In experimental settings, public policy professor Hannah Riley Bowles and colleagues show that men perceive women who ask for higher pay as less nice and more demanding than women who accept salary offers as is.[76] There *is* a social cost to asking. But women can walk the line between the independence they are seeking and the interdependence others are expecting by framing their requests in terms of what's best for the organization. This tactic communicates that although the woman intends to get ahead, she also cares about her relationships at work.

Another bargaining tactic that is useful for women is imagining they are negotiating on someone else's behalf. When the haggling gets hairy, women who recruit their interdependence for independent ends persist longer than women who rely solely on their independent drives.[77]

A final act of independence that individual women can use to smooth their entry into independent domains is to fight the hype. Ben-Zeev arms college students with potent antidotes on the first day of class: "I tell them, you cannot say, 'I'm bad at math,' in my class. You can say, 'I have had bad experiences in math.'" Otherwise, Ben-Zeev half-jokes, "I will kick you out of my class and give you an F."[78]

The New New-Age Men

Just as men need to help pave the way for women to enter traditionally independent domains, so, too, must women support the boys and men who would dwell in their realms. This meeting in the middle should start in nursery school, where boys' ways are increasingly clashing with girl-friendlier products and practices. Giving boys more time and room for rough-and-tumble play and hands-on experimentation helps take some of the wild out of the Y chromosome.

When it comes time to hit the books, Tyre recommends offering stories with a little less conversation and a lot more action. Putting male volunteers in front of the classroom can also help boys understand that school isn't just for girls.

What isn't necessary, argues psychologist Diana Halpern and colleagues, is all-boys or all-girls schools.[79] Many advocates of single-sex education contend that schools must cater to the hardwired biological differences between boys and girls. Once again, however, the science supporting the existence of these differences is shaky at best. Moreover, high-quality studies fail to find any stable advantages to single-sex schooling.[80]

Well-controlled studies with random assignment *do* show, however, that dividing children by sex reinforces gender stereotypes and robs children of daily opportunities to learn how to work together.[81] These deficiencies can cast cold shadows into adulthood; one large-scale study in the United Kingdom, for instance, showed that men in their early forties who had attended all-boy schools were more likely to be divorced than were men who had spent their formative years mixing it up with the lassies.[82]

Likewise, rather than dividing and not conquering, women and men can work together to support men seeking work in traditionally female jobs. Women's transition to more masculine fields has left many so-called nurturing careers understaffed. These careers include not only nursing and teaching, but also the hardest and least glorious job of all: stay-at-home parenting. Yet as sociologist Jennifer Sherman recounts in her ethnography *Those Who Work, Those Who Don't*, a few working-class men are dipping their toes into this hazardous occupation. To make peace with their new roles, these pioneers reframe their newly interdependent behaviors as manifestations of an older strain of independence.

Sherman's book documents her year spent in a rural Northern California community after federal legislation to protect the spotted owl shut down local logging and milling operations. This move left many men without work and forced many women to work outside the home. Sherman found that the families suffering the least strife were the ones who revised their notion of masculinity from meaning "sole breadwinner" to "active father"—a role replete with changing diapers, helping with homework, and attending sports matches. To make childcare more palatable to their independent selves, the men framed it as teaching the kids to hunt, fish, and camp. And rather than seeing themselves as at the forefront of the liberal feminist agenda, these men saw their new roles as extensions of the older male mandate to work hard and take care of one's family.

Female-leaning institutions that want to lure more men into their ranks could learn a lot from these loggers turned full-time fathers. Few men want to be the forward scouts of the sex role revolution. Yet many men can get behind the idea of supporting their families with hard work. Spreading this idea through the culture cycles of nursing, teaching, and childcare could make these fields more appealing to men.

Same as the Old Boss?

As unappealing as it may be to people who yearn for the good old days when men were men and women knew their place, the gender-blending genie will probably not go back in its bottle. Western women are likely to continue climbing up the chain of command and spreading out into traditionally male fields. Meanwhile, Western men's best hope may be to leap the gender fence and occupy the traditionally female jobs that women are abandoning.

These trends lead to a new topic for parlor game speculation: Will putting women in charge make the world a better place?

Probably not, says Deb Gruenfeld, a psychologist who studies how power shapes people's thoughts and feelings. Her research shows that when people of either sex are randomly assigned to positions of power, they act more impulsively, feel more optimistic, and have more trouble taking other people's perspectives, relative to people randomly assigned to positions without power.[83] "It's the power, not the gender" that makes men act in assertive, risk-taking, and slightly antisocial ways, Gruenfeld says. Once women get power, they will likely follow suit. It's like The Who once sang: "Meet the new boss / Same as the old boss."

Other research suggests, however, that the day when women are as assertive, competitive, and self-enhancing as men is in the distant future. A major check on power's corrupting sway is women's habitual interdependence, several millennia in the making. In one set of experiments, psychologist Serena Chen and colleagues found that power amplifies people's habitual states and traits. If women are habitually interdependent—and the need to gestate, feed, and rear children will likely preserve that interdependence for many women—then power may actually enhance their relationality, which may in turn improve their leadership.[84] Early results on the leadership capabilities of women are promising enough to warrant a larger experiment. For instance, one study shows that when firms add at least one woman to their top tier, they generate $40 million more in economic value.[85]

The Real Sputnik

This odd time in the history of gender relations could be our nation's true *Sputnik* moment. Children of the space age will recall that *Sputnik* was the name of the Russian satellite whose launch kicked off the U.S.-Soviet space race. President Obama later resurrected the phrase to inspire more investment in innovation so that Americans do not fall even farther behind their competitors. In both cases, *Sputnik* came to symbolize "the fear of slipping behind in a dangerous world," as security analyst Frank Kaplan put it.[86]

In reality, though, the word *sputnik* has nothing to do with fear, or competition, or danger. To the contrary: in Russian it means "traveling companion"—a rather sweet moniker for the Earth's first satellite. As men and women embark upon a fragile future plagued with economic, ecological, and political uncertainties, they, too, could become traveling companions, rather than adversaries. With a few repairs to their culture cycles, men and women can make their worlds more comfortable for each other.

CHAPTER 4

Color Lines

Cultures of Race and Ethnicity

"I am so sick of this," said the man, hastily clicking through the slides of a PowerPoint presentation. "I mean, we have a Black president, for Christ's sake! Why do I have to waste my time on *these*?"

Hazel looked up to see what was irritating the passenger on her left. She recognized the bullet points of a diversity training course. She also noticed that the man's face was reddening above his button-down collar. A vein at his temple had begun to throb.

"You know, I treat everyone at work exactly the same, no matter what color they are. I don't even see color. Do you? Does anyone anymore?"

He turned to Hazel, but before she could answer, he plunged onward.

"I respect everyone equally, and I'll bet you do, too. But people are still in such a twist over race. When are they going to realize that *race just doesn't matter*?"

Just then, the passenger to Hazel's right, a middle-aged Black[1] male professional, returned to his seat. Her left seatmate fell silent and turned his attention back to his laptop.

The angry White passenger had a point. All over the world, racial and ethnic[2] divides aren't what they used to be. In the United States, for example, people of color are now leaders in government, media, and sports. Just in the past ten years, we have witnessed the election of President Barack

Obama and the appointment of Secretary of State Condoleezza Rice, Secretary of State Colin Powell, and Supreme Court justice Sonia Sotomayor. We have also watched as Oprah Winfrey, Denzel Washington, Jennifer Lopez, and many other entertainers of color have become the richest people in America. The names of Blacks who dominate many major sports are too numerous to list, as is the case with Latinos in baseball.

Hazel's aggrieved seatmate is not alone in his opinion that race no longer matters. Studies show a majority of Whites believe that discrimination against Blacks is not a major problem, and more than two-thirds believe that Blacks have equal opportunities in employment, education, and housing.[3] Some Whites feel that the tables have turned so much that they are now the primary targets of discrimination.[4] "When is *White* History Month, anyway?" complained a student in one of Hazel's classes.

Yet not everyone thinks that race and ethnicity have dropped off the nation's issue list. In particular, most people who are not White—Blacks, Latinos,[5] Asian Americans, Native Americans, and other people of color—believe that race and ethnicity matter very much, for better and for worse.[6] Some of their evidence is hard to dispute. Racial inequality persists. Blacks indeed have the worst education and health outcomes, the shortest life spans, and the highest violence and incarceration rates in America.[7] Latinos, Asian Americans, and Native Americans also suffer poor outcomes in many areas, including housing and health.[8]

Other signs that race still shapes people's lives are maddeningly ambiguous. Was it just the Black teenager's imagination, or was that store manager really tailing him? Is it okay when a Latina's coworker inquires, "So, what do you Latinos think about Barack Obama?" How should the third-generation Asian American feel when a White American asks him, "Where are you *really* from?"

In the clash between people who think that race is *so* twentieth century and those who think that it tops the national agenda, we see two different sorts of selves at work. On the one hand are the independence-minded Whites, who view themselves and other people as largely self-made and self-propelled. As we discussed in chapter 2, Americans of European heritage are heirs to a long tradition of separating from their groups, doing things differently, controlling their environments, freeing themselves from obligations, taking advantage of equal opportunities, and feeling *great* about themselves. As members of the mainstream majority, White Americans indeed have considerable power to create and perpetuate culture cycles that let them be independent of other people. Consequently, Whites are apt to think of themselves as without color—the default, natural, *neutral* humans. Remember the "flesh" crayon? It was a pinkish peach, as if this were the only color of human flesh. Likewise, until recently, *nude* pantyhose came in only this shade, as did adhesive bandages.[9]

On the other hand are the many interdependent people of color who view their races and ethnicities as central to who they are. These selves are heirs to the more collectivistic traditions of Asia, Africa, and South America—places where people are viewed as relational, similar, adjusting, rooted, and ranked. The culture cycles with which racial and ethnic minorities interact in the United States—cycles whose I's hold stereotypes, whose interactions reveal prejudices, and whose institutions discriminate (sometimes unintentionally) against people of color—further foster an interdependent self. After all, it's hard to pretend that race or ethnicity don't matter if your culture cycles keep reminding you that they do.

Very soon, the tensions between independent selves who don't see race and interdependent selves who do are likely to intensify. The nursery foretells the future. As of 2011, slightly more than half the children in the United States under one year of age were not White. By 2050, people of color will outnumber Whites in the United States.[10]

In California, this majority-minority crossover has already happened. Many people who grew up thinking they were just plain ol' *people* are now finding that they are a particular kind of people: White people. Meanwhile, their neighbors of color are pointing out that White selves, interactions, institutions, and ideas are not the only way a culture cycle can roll. As Whites recede into the minority, all groups will need to work together to construct culture cycles that accommodate their competing needs and aspirations.

To soften the impact of these collisions, we suggest that White independent selves learn from interdependent people of color. This means recognizing that the United States has not become a postracial society, as many proclaim, but is still a highly color-coded nation. Embracing our diversity can lessen racial and ethnic tensions, while pretending that race and ethnicity don't matter may actually deepen culture divides. In one study, for example, psychologist Jacquie Vorauer and her colleagues studied conversations between White college students and students of color. The researchers told half the White participants, "at our core, we are really all the same," and told the other half, "different cultural groups bring different perspectives to life." In a subsequent conversation with partners of color, White participants who received the "we're all the same" message focused more on themselves, made fewer positive comments to their partners, and felt worse during the interaction than those who received the "difference is good" message.[11]

For their part, people of color must more skillfully deploy both their independent and interdependent sides. As we will discuss, many American minorities have already developed robustly independent selves that travel alongside their interdependent selves. So their challenge will be not to cultivate more of one self than the other, but to conjure more readily the self that best fits the situation. With their ability to switch seamlessly between independence and interdependence, they may hold the secret for how to be a successful self on our smaller planet.

The clash between people of color and people presumably without pigment also varies by gender and social class, as we explore in chapters 5 and 10. Moreover, the clash is not a uniquely American tension. People around the world struggle with racial and ethnic divides, with the people who have more power and resources usually claiming the "White" label, and those with less getting names such as Blacks, Darkies, or Brownies. As they say in Brazil, "money whitens." So although we focus mostly on the Black-White divide in the United States, many of the ideas and suggestions we present in this chapter apply to racial and ethnic clashes all over the world.[12]

Tense Times

Of all cultural categories, race and ethnicity make Americans the most nervous. For several decades, social psychologists have captured this anxiety. A recent example comes from psychologists Nicole Shelton and Jennifer Richeson.[13] In their experiment, White college students were randomly assigned to have a conversation with either a Black or a White stranger. They then had to complete a classic cognitive task called the Stroop test, which requires people to name the color of the ink a word is written in. Sounds easy, right? The trick is, the word *red*, for instance, is written in blue or green ink, while the word *blue* might be written in purple or orange ink. In other words, the color the letters spell out is never the same as the color of the word's ink. When people are distracted, they have difficulty reading the words quickly and accurately.

Sure enough, Shelton and Richeson found that White participants who had chatted with a Black partner later made more errors on the Stroop task than did White participants who had chatted with a White partner. The researchers surmised that the cross-race interactions were so taxing that the White participants could not perform the Stroop task well.[14] Other laboratory studies show that White participants fidget, blink, avert their eyes, and sit farther away when paired with a stranger of color than when paired with a White stranger.[15]

Blacks likewise fumble when dealing with White people. A recent statistical review (a meta-analysis) of hundreds of studies of interracial interactions reveals that most people perform poorly, are less friendly, and feel worse about themselves during cross-race interactions.[16]

Interracial encounters are also hard on a body, finds psychologist Jim Blascovich and his colleagues. When talking with another White person, White participants' heart rates pick up and their peripheral blood vessels open; their bodies are turning "on" in response to the challenge of chatting with another human being. But when talking with a Black person, their hearts pound, but their peripheral blood vessels constrict—a less healthy response that is consistent with fending off a threat rather than rising to a challenge.[17]

Selves in Black and White

Before you begin reading this section, jot down a few answers to this simple question, "Who am I?" Don't think about it too much. Just write down the first ideas that come to your mind.

Now read these responses from two university students:

> I am 21 years old, African American, a woman, a student, a teacher, a daughter, a sister, a granddaughter, a best friend,

> and a girlfriend. I am a poet, a dancer. I am creative, an optimist/realist who seeks to find love. I am a child of God.

> I am unique, a student, a musician and a singer, a huge nut for pop culture, a protector of my friends, a giving individual, can be brilliant when motivated, a son and a brother, a person with "good toys," somewhat lazy, overly emotional, worried about exams.

Both selves show telltale signs of their middle-class American backgrounds. Both are focused on their individual selves. Both are unique. Yet these two selves are also different in a remarkable way. The first person mentions her race, while the second person, a White person, does not. Multiple studies show that this is the usual pattern: people in the minority usually include their race or ethnicity in their self-descriptions, while those in the majority hardly ever do.[18] A recent survey of a representative sample of Americans similarly finds that while 50 percent of Whites never think about their race, only 12 percent of Blacks report that their race never crosses their mind.[19]

One White American who never thinks about race is comedian Stephen Colbert. The only reason he knows that he is White, he quips, is that he has his own show, and other people call him "sir."[20]

When most people don't share your race or your identity, you stick out. And by sticking out, you become aware of what everyone else thinks of you. Descartes famously declared, "I think, therefore I am." Yet when you are in the minority, you quickly realize that your existence is pegged to other people's views. Over time, Blacks and other minorities incorporate the apprising minds of others into their views of themselves, which heightens their sense of interdependence. Rather than Descartes's declaration of existence, many minorities live a declaration of interdependence: "You think, therefore I am."

Psychologist Denise Sekaquaptewa and her colleagues captured this way of thinking in an alleged group problem-solving study. Upon arrival to the laboratory, Black and White students learned that they would join three other study participants online. Their goal was to work together on a novel task. By seeing photographs of their teammates and reading their bios, half the students learned that they were joining a racially balanced group made up of two Whites and two Blacks. The other half learned they were joining an unbalanced group, of which they were the sole Black or White member. In reality, all the students were participating alone, but the researchers had programmed the computer to give everyone the same feedback as if it came from other participants.

Following the task, participants answered questions about their thoughts and feelings. The researchers found that the racial composition of their group affected Black participants' answers, but not White participants' answers. When Blacks were in the minority, they were more anxious about their performance and other group members' opinions of them. They also viewed race as more central to their selves and felt more like representatives of their race than when they were in the balanced group.[21] A lifetime's worth of minority status had sensitized Blacks to their place in any given social web, even a fictitious one. In contrast, Whites felt and thought the same regardless of the composition of their group. With few experiences as minorities, they were indeed independent of their contexts.

Represent

Independence isn't the exclusive province of Whites. Perhaps more than any other culture we examine in this book, Blacks pair their interdependence with a healthy side of independence. In the pen experiment described in chapter 1, for instance, Blacks are even more likely than Whites to choose a unique pen over a common one as a reward for participating in a study.[22] Blacks' self-esteem is also routinely higher than that of Whites.[23] And demonstrating the tendency to individuate and feel great, Blacks often score themselves as better than their peers across a wide range of competencies.[24]

Yet "the ineluctably oversized Black ego is not self-indulgence," writes the journalist Touré. "It's self-preservation—it's armor against a world that seems to have a nefarious, well-funded multimedia campaign working against it round the clock."[25]

Is there a well-funded multimedia campaign working against Blacks? This is a matter of considerable debate. What is clear is that representations of Blacks and other people of color on the screens, on the airwaves, and in the pages of mainstream American culture are decidedly more homogenous and negative than are representations of White Americans.

Television and film have come a long way from when racial slurs and blackfaced buffoons were common. Disney's 1941 classic, *Dumbo*, for example, depicted teams of Black workers singing about how they never learned to read or write and "can't wait to spend our pay away."[26] And who can forget *The Jungle Book*'s King Louie, a jazz-singing orangutan, pleading with Mowgli to help him be more human?[27] Or Looney Tunes' Speedy Gonzales, who called himself "the fastest mouse in Mexico" but who was consistently hobbled by a posse that was slow and often drunk.[28] In these and other animations, artists used stereotypes of minorities as lazy, dumb, and primitive to entertain their audiences.

Movies and prime-time TV shows now feature far fewer negative racial caricatures and many more characters of color. Yet the quality of the representations has yet to catch up with the quantity; the most common roles for Blacks, for example, are as entertainers, athletes, delinquents, criminals, devoted sidekicks, and victims who are saved by a White person.[29]

Even when Black characters are doctors and lawyers, their portrayals do not invite much sympathy or admiration. In one chilling study, for example, psychologist Nalini Ambady and her colleagues selected eleven prime-time television shows that featured a diverse cast with Blacks in prominent roles. Their sample included favorites such as *Grey's Anatomy* and *House*. From each show, the researchers chose several ten-second clips of interactions between White characters and either a Black or White costar. The researchers then muted the soundtrack and edited the clips so that only the White character's silent reactions remained. For example, one clip from *CSI: Miami* featured a White character's responses to the Black character Alexx (removed from the scene). Ambady's team then asked undergraduates and adults unfamiliar with the shows to rate how friendly, sociable, or hostile the target White character was.

Across these shows, participants judged that White actors were less friendly, less sociable, and more hostile when they were interacting with Black characters than with White characters. This was true even though pretests showed that audiences found the Black and White characters equally attractive. Follow-up studies further uncovered that these television shows actually *increased* viewers' racial biases; viewers seemed to be mimicking the White actors' negative reactions to Black costars. Rather than helping audiences see Blacks as uniquely positive individuals, the shows stoked negative attitudes toward the group as a whole.[30]

Old School

Stereotypes claiming that Blacks and other minorities are different from, and worse than, Whites are alive and well, not only on celluloid but also throughout many culture cycles. In the classroom, these stereotypes undercut the performance of Black students. As we saw in chapter 3, when women are reminded of the stereotype that they are bad at math and science, they indeed perform poorly on tests of math and science. Likewise, invidious stereotypes of Blacks as slow and less able are among the everyday artifacts that hinder Blacks' chances in school and on the job.

In a pioneering study, for example, psychologists Claude Steele and Josh Aronson recruited Black and White students with equally high SAT scores. To activate the stereotype that Blacks have less academic ability than Whites, the team told half the participants that an upcoming test (a difficult section of the GRE) was a measure of verbal ability. To the other half of participants (the control group) they did not mention ability, and instead framed the test as an exploration of how students solve problems.

When students thought the test could reveal their academic ability, the Black students scored worse than the White students. But when there was no stereotype in the air—no stereotype threat—and their identities weren't on the line, Black students scored the same as White students. Hundreds of studies have since replicated the finding that subtly evoking the stereotype that Blacks are intellectually inferior harms the performance of even the most prepared, most talented, and most motivated Black students.[31]

What's more, Blacks need not even *believe* the stereotype. Just the threat that negative beliefs might be at play raises their anxiety levels. Instead of concentrating on the test, Black students fear that they will be judged according to the stereotype of their group or, worse, that they will confirm the stereotype. Much of this happens outside their conscious awareness, so they don't even see the phantoms they are fighting with. Eventually, many of the most gifted Black students simply choke, but not from the pressure of the test. They choke from the pressure of the stereotype threat.

Eleanor Roosevelt famously claimed that no one can make you feel inferior without your consent. So why can't people of color just ignore the opinions of others, unleash their independent sides, and slay the test? As it turns out, tuning out the dull roar of stereotypes is incredibly difficult—even for White people. In one experiment, for example, psychologist Jeff Stone and his coauthors showed that White participants who were told that a laboratory golf course was a test of *natural* athletic ability (athleticism is allegedly not White people's strong suit) putted worse than did White participants who learned that the course was merely a sports psychology task.[32]

No matter your skin color, when the air is thick with the idea that your group is inferior, it's difficult to be only an independent self. Instead, you feel that you must either launch a defense on behalf of your entire race or attempt to disavow your association with your race altogether. In either case, you have race on your mind. Because they more often use their interdependent selves, many Blacks, Latinos, Asian Americans, Native Americans, and other racial and ethnic groups also worry about how their performance will reflect on their families, their schools, and racial and ethnic groups in general. These layers of anxiety distract people and impair performance.

Daily Discriminations

Images in the ether and threats in the air are not the only daily interactions that reinforce the interdependence of Americans of color. More tangible products and processes of the culture cycle likewise drive home the message that racial and ethnic minorities are members of their group first, and individuals second or not at all. As we will show, these daily interactions help maintain the lower status of Blacks and other people of color and reinforce the interdependent sides of their complex selves.

The differences that make a difference start early, with many schools offering fewer opportunities to children of color than they do to White children. For example, Black and Latino students with high grades and test scores are less often tracked into honors or Advanced Placement classes than their White classmates with similar credentials. Moreover, school with a higher percentage of students of color offer fewer college prepara tory classes than schools with mainly White students. Minority student are thus less likely to gain admission to college.[33]

After completing their education, Blacks and Latinos face a steepe road to getting a job than do Whites. In one experiment, for example researchers created two polished résumés, one for a man and one for a woman. They then manipulated the names at the tops of the résumés with half the documents headed with White-sounding names like Emily Walsh or Greg Baker, and the other half fronting Black-sounding name like Lakeisha Washington or Jamal Jones. After mailing the résumés to dozens of potential employers, the researchers discovered that the ersat applicants with the White-sounding names were 50 percent more likely to receive a callback than those with the Black-sounding names, even though their qualifications were identical.[34]

Racial bias also pervades blue-collar workplaces. In another experiment researchers trained White, Black, and Latino workers with equivalent cre-dentials to act the same way in an interview. Even with this preparation the researchers found that White interviewees received more callbacks than Blacks or Latinos.[35]

Despite these obstacles, people of color are making their way into many professions. Yet the highest echelons of leadership and full-scale professional respect remain elusive. For example, although prestigious law firms are increasingly hiring Black lawyers, they rarely grant Blacks the rank of partner. The same is true in finance and advertising.[36]

The marketplace is also rife with discriminatory practices. When Blacks phone rental agencies to inquire about an advertised apartment they are more frequently told that the unit is no longer available than are White callers who follow the same script.[37] Car salesmen routinely charge Blacks more than Whites for the same cars.[38] And to patients with the same ages and symptoms, physicians are more likely to recommend life-saving treatments such as blood-clot-busting drugs for Whites than for Blacks.[39]

Public servants are likewise less kind to their Black constituents. City councils more frequently locate dumps and toxic waste sites in Black neigh-borhoods than in other districts.[40] Law enforcement officers stop, interro-gate, arrest, and prosecute Blacks far more than Whites. And judges and juries mete out harsher penalties (including the death penalty) to Blacks than to Whites, for exactly the same crimes.[41]

Even on the basketball court, Blacks get a worse deal than Whites. A study of the National Basketball Association scrutinized six hundred thousand foul calls made in games across thirteen seasons. It uncovered that referees called fouls against Black players more frequently than against White players.[42]

Many consider these subtler forms of discrimination to be lesser evils than the blatant "Archie Bunker" racism of the past. But covert racism has an insidious side effect: because it is harder to see, more people underestimate "the degree to which discrimination contributes to the poor social and economic outcomes of minority groups," sociologists Devah Pager and Hana Shepherd write.[43] Consequently, half-reformed culture cycles continue to roll along unchallenged.

Shared Strength

To stay strong and sane in the face of these many injustices, Blacks have developed daily interactions and cultural institutions all their own. Many of these foster and flow from interdependence: church, family, and community are steadfast supports for many Blacks. Yet other institutions and interactions drive and derive from independence. As their high levels of self-esteem, self-reliance, and self-confidence attest, many Blacks resonate with the label that former presidential hopeful Herman Cain gave to himself: "The CEO of the Self."[44]

One source of interdependence are the culture cycles that survived the African diaspora. Although the peoples of Africa are highly diverse, many share the view that all living things (and some nonliving ones) are interrelated.[45] Indeed, before contact with Europeans, some African languages did not have a word for "alone."[46] When Blacks were enslaved and transported to the New World, "their interdependence helped them survive the harsh new reality," recounts psychologist James Jackson.[47]

Black churches have long helped maintain that interdependence, serving as trusted community centers. Blacks spend more time in places of worship than do Whites. Blacks also espouse stronger religious beliefs and more frequently turn to their fellow worshippers to cope with hardship, especially the hardships brought on by discrimination.[48]

Within families, Blacks draw on their interdependence to face racial hostilities. Compared to White parents, Black parents are three times as likely to discuss race with their children.[49] Some of these conversations are pride-inducing explorations of Black history and culture. Rather than stoking defiance, these conversations inspire good behavior, psychologist Margaret Caughy and her colleagues find. In their studies, Black preschoolers whose parents discuss their heritage with them have fewer behavior problems.[50] Other talks are more difficult dialogues about the hurdles that await a Black person in America. Although few people relish telling their children just how unfair the world can be, studies show that these conversations help Black children cope with prejudice and discrimination.[51]

Our colleague recently had to begin these difficult discussions with her three school-aged sons, ages eight, ten, and fourteen. The family joined another Black professor and her two sons to see a movie at the local Cineplex. Emerging from the theater, the five children chatted excitedly among themselves, arms around each other, as their mothers trailed a few feet behind. The boys were not shouting. They were not running. They were not roughhousing. They were not blocking the hallway.

Yet our colleague watched as a security guard called out and strode toward the children. She quickened her pace to put herself between the boys and the guard, and then caught his eye to halt his approach. She sadly realized that the time had come to teach her boys what to do when a guard or police officer stops them, even when they're doing nothing wrong.

When the Rain Comes Down

For all their emphasis on solidarity, similarity, and coping, culture cycles also push Blacks to be unique, separate, equal, and in control. Black churches stress the idea that each person is a child of God, with unique God-given gifts. Sermons and songs emphasize that each congregant is worthy of love and respect, regardless of his material success or social status. Sunday school classes teach children that Blacks and Whites are equal in God's eyes.[52] These teachings seem to work; when explaining why they have such high self-esteem, many Blacks cite God's love. (Whites seldom mention God when unpacking the sources of their self-esteem.)[53]

Another independence-inducing cultural product in Black culture cycles is music. For instance, hip-hop encourages Blacks to step up, fight back, and speak out—especially when others do not. Indeed, this is a major function of the art form, argues linguists Marcyliena Morgan and Dawn-Elissa Fischer.[54] In his rap "Rain," for example, the artist Akrobatik reminds his listeners that even "when the rain comes down," even when events beyond their control dog them at every turn, they still have a choice: "You can fold your hand and let your world crumble, or fight back and keep it on the humble."[55]

In many Black culture cycles, historically Black colleges and universities (HBCU) are institutions that further reinforce and reflect independent selves. About 25 percent of college-educated Blacks in the United States earned their degrees at one of these 107 colleges, which include Howard, Spelman, and Morehouse. HBCUs have also conferred more than 75 percent of the doctorates that Blacks currently hold. Compared to Blacks who attend predominantly White institutions, HBCU students report better nutrition and healthier lifestyles.[56]

The R-Word

While many Blacks are constructing culture cycles around race and how to deal with it, most Whites are avoiding the *r*-word altogether. A study of seventeen thousand families with kindergarteners revealed that 75 percent of White parents never or almost never talk about race. Instead, they argue that we should ignore race, and that people should just be "color-blind."[57] By their own lights, they succeed. A recent Gallup poll finds that 77 percent of Whites say they rarely or never experience unpleasant thoughts or emotions when they encounter people from different races.[58]

Yet their unconscious minds tell a different story, psychologist Mahzarin Banaji and her colleagues find. In response to survey after survey showing that Whites harbor no explicit animus toward Blacks, Banaji adapted a test to probe their implicit, automatic, and unconscious attitudes. That test, called the Implicit Association Test (IAT), revealed that at a primal, basic level, "white" means "good" and "black" means "bad" for Americans of all races, but especially for Whites.[59]

The IAT is a simple task. Participants must only respond to pictures or words on a screen by hitting a button on a keyboard as fast as they can. But in their reaction times lies a world of information. When asked to use one hand to respond to words that have to do with "black" or "bad" and the other hand to respond to words that have do with "white" or "good," participants have quick reflexes. After millions of exposures and years of practice, people automatically connect "black" to "bad" and "white" to "good." Participants' reactions are fast because they don't have to think about them. Other studies find that people also readily connect "black" with "crime," "animal," and "ape."[60]

But when "black" and "good" are assigned to one hand, while "white" and "bad" are assigned to the other, reaction times hit the skids. Our cultural worlds less frequently tell us that black is beautiful and white is evil, and our unconscious minds reflect this reality. Thus the mental links between "black" and "good" are rather weak, as are the ones between "white" and "bad."

Asymmetries in reaction times aren't just laboratory oddities; they drive behavior in the real world. Some people show more racial bias on the IAT than others, with faster reflexes for black/bad and white/good pairs and slower responses for black/good and white/bad pairs. These small delays may mean the difference between life and death in the emergency room, where the more biased a doctor is on the IAT, the more likely she is to misdiagnose and mistreat heart disease in Black patients. Implicit attitudes likewise drive explicit decisions in the voting booth, where more bias meant a vote for McCain over Obama in the 2008 presidential election. On college campuses, the more implicit racism an undergraduate reveals on the IAT, the farther away she will sit from a Black stranger and the more readily she will cut funding for Black student groups at her university.[61]

Although subtle instruments such as the IAT may be required to detect racial bias with adults, straightforward surveys work well with children. That's because children have not yet learned the party line that race and ethnicity do not matter. For all their parents' politically correct rhetoric, children are not blind. They soak in the products and practices around them, and blithely report that Black people are not nice, pretty, curious, or honest (but White people are).[62]

Uncovering results such as these, psychologist Birgitte Vittrup and her colleagues designed an intervention. They asked families first to watch videos with multicultural storylines, like a *Sesame Street* sequence where the characters visit a Black family, or an episode of *Little Bill* where all the people in a racially diverse neighborhood pitch in to clean up their park. They then randomly assigned half the families to discuss race and interracial friendships after viewing the videos.

But her intervention ground to a standstill because many parents refused to follow the study's instructions.[63] Echoing the frustrated plane passenger, they objected to talking about race, mounting defenses such as "We are all equal" and "God made all of us." They also worried that if they did talk about race with their children, they might say the wrong thing.

The Race for Blindness

Why would a full-grown White adult refuse to acknowledge what is plain as day for her five-year-old son—not to mention for a swiftly growing portion of her fellow Americans? To answer this question, we must jump up a level in the culture cycle to institutions. From this vista, we see that many institutions, including science, religion, economics, and government, have helped drive not only the White independent self, but also many Whites' insistence that race and ethnicity do not shape people's psyches.

During the fifteenth century, Europeans began to explore other continents and encounter other civilizations with different-looking beings. Were they animals or people? And if the latter, were they free or slaves? To these questions, the Europeans applied both religion and science. Religion told them that their God-given duty was to Christianize the newly discovered heathens. Later, science told them that what made these dark people different was a biological quality called *race*. True to their notion of the person as an independent entity, they came to view race as a stable, internal property that determined not only appearance, but also behavior. Swedish naturalist Carolus Linnaeus "discovered," for example, that the "red" Native Americans were obstinate, negligent, and governed by caprice; the "yellow" Asians were avaricious, haughty, and governed by opinions; but the "white" Europeans were acute, inventive, and governed by laws.[64] Many other scientists of European hertiage likewise found that their own race, Whites, possessed the best characteristics.

As White Europeans traveled farther afield, these racial measuring sticks came in handy. They justified seizing territory, plundering resources, and enslaving people who were *scientifically proven* to be inferior. With so many social and material benefits tied to the belief that nature, not people, created the racial hierarchy, few Whites felt the need to question the science behind it.[65]

Even Thomas Jefferson, the American founding father who prided himself on being a man of science, seemed unperturbed to begin the Declaration of Independence with "We hold these truths to be self-evident, that all men are created equal," and then later to pen the Three-Fifths Compromise, which counted Black slaves as only three-fifths of a person.[66] "Their inferiority is not the effect merely of their condition of life," he explained in another document. It is also the effect of "nature, which has produced the distinction."[67]

Two centuries plus later, people of European heritage are undertaking fewer colonial adventures, slavery is officially outlawed, and most scientists agree that biology does not drive the behavioral differences that people perceive between racial and ethnic groups. People did not make up the notion of race out of whole cloth. Genes do drive the physical traits (e.g., skin color and hair texture) that vary across human groups. Yet these genetic differences do not explain differences in behaviors, capacities, or achievements. For example, academic achievement has far more to do with socioeconomic status, parental support, and effort than with what is called race. When race does predict academic success, it is because it stands in for other social, cultural, and economic factors.[68]

In other words, the scientific community now largely agrees that race and ethnicity are so-called social constructions—that is, things that people make. But just because something is a social construction does not mean it isn't real. To the contrary: as our examinations of culture cycles show, social constructions strongly shape and reflect people's thoughts, feelings, and actions. Our ability to make and re-create these constructions, moreover, is an adaptive, naturally selected, biologically based ability. As we said in the introduction, it is our smart human trick.

Race Cards

Now many Whites are eager to bury their racist and ethnocentric past. Although their impulse is laudable, their strategy is not. Pretending that race and ethnicity do not exist, or that we now live in a postracial society, does a disservice to the many people of color whose culture cycles are built around race and ethnicity. For these more interdependent selves, race and ethnicity help answer the big questions "Who am I?" and "Who are we?"

People of color are not alone in looking to their groups to help define their selves. All humans need to feel connected with others. We yearn to belong. Our groups, in turn, tell us how to think, feel, act, and make sense of the world.

White people are no exception. But rather than creating selves around the groups they are given (such as race, ethnicity, and gender), Whites more frequently construct their selves around the groups they choose: the places they move, the professions they join, the hobbies they pick up, and the sports teams they follow. Indeed, the idea that people may have no choice in which groups make them up—the reality for many people of color—can be threatening to independent selves. When people of color point out that race and ethnicity may have something to do with their harder lives, many Whites protest, "Stop playing the race card!"

Yet there is nothing wrong with recognizing other people's races and ethnicities (or claiming your own) because there is nothing inherently negative about racial or ethnic groupings. In fact, race and ethnicity are often forces for excellence. In one study, for instance, Tiffany Brannon and Hazel showed Black and White students either positive Black icons (e.g., a banner for Howard University, the cover of Alice Walker's book *The Color Purple*, the logo for Black Entertainment Television) or positive mainstream American icons (e.g., a banner for Harvard university, the cover of Ernest Hemingway's *The Old Man and the Sea*, the logo for MTV). Among the Black students, those who viewed the positive Black icons performed better on tests of math and creativity than those who viewed the positive mainstream American icons. (Whites performed equally well regardless of which icons they saw.)[69]

The Long Roots of Racism

What *is* wrong is using race and ethnicity to assign unequal levels of value, power, and privilege to different groups. Once discrimination gets into a culture cycle's institutions, getting it out is difficult, especially when the dominant culture is an independent one (which is often the case, as we will explain in the next chapter). Independent selves can have a tough time grasping the idea that institutions can be racist or ethnocentric. Their culture cycles focus them on individual causes for behavior (such as talent, motivation, or evil) and not on situational factors (such as opportunity, discrimination, or history). A Pew Research Center study finds that two-thirds of Americans believe that personal factors, rather than institutional, historical, or economic ones, explain why some people have difficulty getting ahead in life.[70]

"I was taught to see racism only in individual acts of meanness, not in invisible systems conferring dominance on my group," confesses activist Peggy McIntosh in her article "White Privilege: Unpacking the Invisible Knapsack." She then lists fifty white-skin "privileges" her Black coworkers, friends, and acquaintances do not share. Among her privileges: "My chief worries about my children do not concern others' attitudes toward my children's race" and "If I declare there is a racial issue at hand, or isn't a racial issue at hand, my race will lend me more credibility for either position than a person of color."[71]

Feeding and flowing from racist institutions are interactions and individuals that perpetuate the idea that people of color are less competent and deserving than Whites.[72] When a predominantly Black or Latino high school has no AP classes, many people conclude that the students must not need or want them. When Blacks receive the death penalty more than Whites, the media portray Blacks' crimes as more heinous. And when advertising firms have few Black partners, industry groups assume it must be because Black people can't hack—or don't like—the work.

Open the Door

Softening the collisions between the independent selves who think that race and ethnicity are relics, and the interdependent selves who think that race and ethnicity have never been more important, requires changes at every level of the culture cycle. Because Whites are still the more powerful group in most multicultural societies, they should take the first step and instill more interdependence in their institutions, interactions, and I's. People of color, in turn, can draw on both their independence and their interdependence to create culture cycles that better meet their needs and draw on their strengths.

First on the to-do list for mainstream institutions is to diversify their ranks. Although the term has become a dirty word among many Americans, *affirmative action* is one proven-effective way to get more people of color into institutions. Affirmative action merely means explicitly considering race and ethnicity in hiring, admissions, and promotions. Studies show that affirmative action not only gives Blacks and other minorities the opportunities they need to succeed, but also helps Whites develop the skills they will need to compete in a multicultural world. For example, in one of the largest studies of affirmative action in higher education, educators William Bowen and Derek Bok checked up on some four thousand Black students who attended twenty-eight elite colleges from the late 1970s through the early 1990s. Students who were admitted to these selective schools under affirmative action were more likely to go on to graduate and professional schools than Black students who graduated from less demanding institutions. Also, Black college graduates of elite universities were more likely than their White counterparts to lead or participate in professional, arts, and environmental organizations.[73]

White students likewise benefit from a more diverse educational experience. In a major study spanning ten universities, for instance, racially diverse groups of students took a semester-long weekly seminar in which they explored their commonalities and differences. The goal of the course was for students "to build an in-depth understanding of each other's situation," says psychologist Patricia Gurin, the study's lead. The intervention succeeded, and then some. Compared with students who were on a waiting list to take the course, seminar attendees (including Whites) became more empathic with people who differed from them and showed greater understanding of how their own social groups shaped their thoughts, feelings, and actions. They also developed a more sophisticated understanding of how culture cycles can propel people forward or hold people back.[74]

The justice system could also benefit from recruiting more diverse juries, psychologist Sam Sommers and his colleagues find. The research team created either all-White or racially mixed (four Whites and two Blacks) mock juries, which then deliberated on an actual case with a Black defendant. Compared to the all-White juries, the racially mixed groups exchanged more information, cited more case facts, made fewer errors, and were more lenient toward the Black defendant. It wasn't just the Black participants who drove these differences, either; White participants in the racially mixed juries showed the same superior performance.[75]

Make the Place Safe

The corporate world is conducting its own experiments with diversity, inspired by research showing that employees in multicultural workplaces have higher morale.[76] Just getting people of color in the door and showing them to their desks is not enough to harness the power of diversity, however. Institutions must alter their interactions to make everyone feel welcome and comfortable. This means putting an end to legends of color-blindness and acknowledging that race and ethnicity matter. For example, in one study, psychologist Valerie Purdie-Vaughns and her team asked Black professionals to read a brochure about a (fictitious) workplace and to imagine working there. One brochure featured racially balanced photographs and quotes such as "We believe that embracing our diversity enriches our culture." The other brochure featured photographs of White people and quotes such as "Focusing on similarities creates a more unified, exciting, and collaborative work environment." The researchers found that Black professionals preferred and trusted the firms with the multicultural brochures more than the firms with color-blind swag.[77]

Adopting a multicultural ethos may build not only trust, but also profits. In a study of nearly four thousand employees from seventeen different companies, psychologist Victoria Plaut and her team compared work groups that hewed to a policy of color-blindness with work groups that recognized and celebrated racial and ethnic differences. They discovered that minority employees were more enthusiastic about and committed to their jobs when their White coworkers embraced racial and ethnic differences and when organizational policies supported multiculturalism.

Because committed employees produce more and create less employee turnover, a multicultural mind-set might mean bigger profits.[78]

Because White people have feelings, too, crafters of multicultural messages should make sure to appeal to their White audiences. In another set of studies, Plaut showed that many Whites who react negatively to diversity initiatives do so because they feel excluded.[79] They ask, "What about me?" By including Whites in their images and language, and by reminding people that Whites also have cultures, workplaces may avoid alienating their mainstream employees.

Some schools are working overtime to create what educator Dorothy Steele and her colleagues call identity-safe spaces. These are classrooms where students trust one another and do not fear that they will be viewed through the lenses of stereotypes. In identity-safe classrooms, teachers set high expectations for all students, develop good relationships with each child, and talk openly about race and ethnicity. Rather than shying away from racially charged topics when they arise, teachers encourage students to share and understand their different perspectives. These discussions help both hearts and minds flourish. In a study of eighteen racially diverse elementary schools, for instance, Steele and her colleagues found that students in identity-safe classrooms liked school better and scored higher on year-end standardized tests than did students in standard classrooms.[80]

Find the Right Words

Improving interactions outside school and work can ease the tensions between Whites and people of color. Television, film, and other mass media need to realize that just putting Black or Latino or Asian characters in front of the camera is no longer enough. Directors could also carefully attend to how those characters are represented and how their White counterparts react to them. Cameras can catch and perpetuate even the subtlest hints of racism.

And when they do, White families should be standing by to help their younger members make sense of the color-coded world beaming into their living rooms. If parents do not initiate conversations about race, their children often assume that the topic is too taboo to air. Kids then rely on media, friends, and other less-than-ideal sources for their information. Rather than ducking the discussion, parents can use media representations as entrees to conversations about race and ethnicity, and racism and ethnocentrism.

While talking about race, both Whites and Blacks may find themselves struggling for the right words. What the heck is race, anyway? Where did it come from? And why won't it just go away? Playwright Lorraine Hansberry has some answers. In her play *Les Blancs,* a Black and a White American discuss race as "a device," "an invention to justify the rule of some men over others," which "once invented, takes on a life, a reality of its own." This single metaphor counters the two dueling, yet wrong ideas that race is *either* essential and biological *or* superficial.[81]

Finding the right words for race may inspire better behaviors about race. To demonstrate this idea, psychologists Melissa Williams and Jennifer Eberhardt crafted two very similar newspaper articles. The first portrayed race as a biological category, and the second portrayed it as a social process. Undergraduates of all races who were randomly assigned to read the social-process article later reported that they were more likely to befriend someone of another race than were undergraduates who read the race-as-biology article.[82]

Get Friendly

Making a friend of another race, in turn, is a great way for individuals to break down racial and ethnic barriers. "If you looked and looked at all the solutions proposed by scientists over the years to combat prejudice and racism," writes psychologist Rudy Mendoza-Denton, "you'd be hard pressed to find a more effective antidote than intergroup friendship."[83]

In one study, for example, psychologist Elizabeth Page-Gould and her colleagues randomly assigned White and Latino college students (some highly prejudiced, some less so) to pair up with a person of either the same ethnicity or a different ethnicity. The pairs of participants then met several times to complete a series of friendship-building tasks, such as in-depth discussions of their backgrounds and a game of Jenga (which requires players to build a tower out of wooden blocks together). After this friendship-building phase, participants then filled in an online diary every day for ten days. In these diaries, the researchers found a surprising trend: Prejudiced participants who had made a new cross-race friend subsequently initiated more daily interactions with people of other races. Once they got over the hump of making a cross-race friend, it seems, these participants were inspired to seek out more.[84]

For many people, however, that first conversation across a racial divide is nerve-wracking. How do you not come off as a racist? For starters, you should worry less about coming off like a racist and more about paying attention to your potential new friend. Not only will you enjoy your first conversation more, but you will make your partner feel more comfortable.[85] You should also keep in mind that what you want out of the conversation is not necessarily what your partner wants. Observing social interactions in the laboratory, psychologist Hilary Bergsieker and her coauthors find that while Whites want to be liked, Blacks and Latinos want to be respected.[86]

Educating ourselves about race, ethnicity, and discrimination is another way to keep the conversation flowing. Studies show that people who have taken a course on prejudice or intergroup conflict later post lower scores on measures of both explicit and implicit prejudice.[87]

Fix It

"Racism is really not my problem to solve," says performance artist damali ayo. "It's really up to White people." She jokes that Whites should be able to deliver on this mission because, "White people are—I hear—pretty smart."[88]

Nevertheless, ayo and many other people of color are drawing on both their independent and interdependent selves to push mainstream culture cycles in more just and peaceful directions. Working at the level of interactions, for instance, ayo has created a free pamphlet titled, "I Can Fix It! Vol. 1: Racism." Noting that Americans have a third-grade understanding of race, ayo includes plenty of pictures and diagrams in the pamphlet. Her playful project stems from a more serious endeavor: a survey of two thousand people asked to list five things that individuals can do to end racism. She separates their answers into instructions for White folks and those for people of color, mixing both independent and interdependent practices.

One of ayo's independent recommendations for people of color, for example, is to speak out about race and racism, especially when a racist comment or joke comes their way. "Your silence indicates you find their racism appropriate." On a more interdependent note, she advises people of color to "build ties" across racial divides. "Join together as people of color," she writes. "Do you know which Asian American woman held the hand of Malcolm X when he was dying?"[89]

(Among her recommendations to White people, ayo urges, "Be White. . . . Admit that white is a color and a race. Acknowledge that a very real present-day racism arose from social and institutionalized racist practices. . . . Notice where those practices continue and where you participate in them."[90])

In California, an Oakland-based company is putting some of ayo's directives into practice. Named dangerousNEGRO—the U.S. Federal Bureau of Investigations once called Martin Luther King Jr. "the most dangerous Negro in America"[91]—the company fashions T-shirts, hats, and other apparel "to promote African culture and the Black Empowerment Movement through positive propaganda," according to its website. To counter the stereotype of Black women as gold diggers or models, for instance, a female shopper can sport a T-shirt that labels her a "Goal Digger" or "America's Top *Role* Model." Men can front their brains instead of their brawn in T-shirts proclaiming "Smart Is the New Gangsta," for example, or protest the shooting death of Florida high-schooler Trayvon Martin in a hoodie with "Don't Shoot" written across the back.[92]

Connect the Dots

Schools can leverage both independence and interdependence to help Black students succeed. In one simple yet highly effective intervention, psychologist Geoff Cohen and his colleagues asked Black and White middle school students to spend twenty minutes at the beginning of the school year writing about something they personally valued. Some students described their unique strengths and talents; others wrote about their families, friends, or other relationships. The researchers discovered that, compared with Black students who did not write about their values, Black students who *did* do so had earned better grades at the end of the term. A follow-up study showed that these academic gains were still in place two years later.[93] By offering this simple writing exercise, schools communicated that they valued their students' selves, independent or interdependent, which in turn helped the students trust their schools and feel they belonged there.[94] (The intervention neither harmed nor helped White students' grades, presumably because most White students already felt welcome in school.)

Linking Black students' independent and interdependent selves is another way to boost their performance in school. In one set of studies, psychologist Daphna Oyserman and her colleagues gave Black junior high school students lessons communicating that an important part of being Black is excelling academically. Compared with students who received a different set of lessons, students whose lessons connected the dots between personal achievement and Black identity had higher grades and fewer absences.[95]

A final recommendation for how individual people of color can help construct culture cycles that don't clash as much is a wholly interdependent one: make a White friend. This will require patience on your part, advises Baratunde Thurston in his book *How to Be Black*. "You are going to get a lot of questions," he writes.

> Many of them will be dumb. Maintain your cool, and focus on listening to your friends. When they ask, "Why don't more Black people work hard like immigrants?" don't assume bad intentions on their part. Stop. Breathe. Think. This is not automatically racist. They're asking you because they trust you, because they need you to help them understand. If you scare them away, you encourage a troubling alternative. They will continue to live with ignorance, which will eventually find its way into the news segments they produce at their television network jobs or into legislation they pass. A healthy amount of patience as The Black Friend can go a long way toward helping all Black people in unseen ways.[96]

Making a White friend can also help people of color in more visible ways. In a three-year longitudinal study, Mendoza-Denton and colleagues found that the more White friends Black university students had, the more satisfied they were with their university experience.[97]

Friends in High Places

On that long flight from San Francisco to New York, Hazel watched out of the corner of her eye as the angry White professional finished reading his diversity training PowerPoint slides and turned his attention to a legal document. She noticed that the Black professional to her right was also engrossed in a legal document. She wondered what the two men might say to each other about race and racism. She even toyed with the idea of brokering a conversation herself.

Meanwhile, thirty-five thousand feet below, discussions about race and ethnicity were growing quieter. In April of 2010 the Arizona state legislature banned the teaching of ethnic studies. Explaining the decision, state superintendent Tom Horne said, "Traditionally, the American public school system has brought together students from different backgrounds and taught them to be Americans and to treat each other as individuals, and not on the basis of their ethnic backgrounds."[98] Supreme Court justice John Roberts was likewise quoted as saying, "The way to end discrimination on the basis of race is to stop discriminating on the basis of race."[99]

We disagree, and instead side with another Supreme Court justice. In 1978, Harry Blackmun wrote, "In order to get beyond racism, we must first take account of race."[100] To his insight, we add that we must take account of race at all levels of the culture cycle, and how it matters to our selves and to the interactions, institutions, and ideas that make and mirror our selves. We must also adapt to the selves of others by applying our independent and interdependent sides more wisely.

CHAPTER 5

Class Acts

Socioeconomic Cultures

On September 17, 2011, some one thousand people convened in Lower Manhattan's Zuccotti Park to protest . . . well, a lot of things: the failure of the government to take banks to task for the global financial crisis, high unemployment, bad health care, runaway income inequality, and corporate interference in politics, to name a few. Despite their disparate grievances, the protestors united under one slogan, "We Are the 99 Percent," and directed their fury at the richest 1 percent of Americans, who own some 43 percent of the nation's wealth.[1]

Despite its hazy agenda, the Occupy Wall Street movement traveled far and fast, sparking hundreds of protests around the world. One year later, many of these protests were still simmering.

The broad appeal of the Occupy movement demonstrates that the clash between the haves and the have-nots is growing ever louder. Yet in the United States, the deepest divide isn't between the 99 and the 1; it's between the 70 and the 30—that is, the 70 percent of Americans who don't have a college degree versus the 30 percent who do.[2] College-educated Americans have better jobs, earn more money, enjoy more free time, suffer from fewer physical and mental illnesses, and live longer lives than do Americans without a college degree.[3]

Your level of education shapes your life in many other ways, both large and small. Will you marry? If so, when? Will you get divorced? How many kids will you have? Will you fight in a war? How will you vote in the next election? Where will you go for vacation? What music will you listen to tomorrow morning? What will you eat for dinner tomorrow night? The answers to these questions hinge heavily on whether you earned a bachelor's degree.[4]

The same is true in many other industrialized countries, where the number of diplomas on your wall is the most powerful predictor of your place in the pecking order. Income and occupation are also measures of socioeconomic status. But education packs the largest punch in determining just how your life is going to turn out.[5] In particular, a college education has become the tipping point that separates those who thrive from those who struggle just to survive.[6]

Many scholars dice socioeconomic status into finer divisions such as the underclass, working poor, professional class, capitalist class, and so on. In this chapter, we focus on just one distinction: people without a college degree (whom we call *working class*) and people with a college degree (whom we call *middle class*). Of course, some people without a college degree consider themselves middle or even upper class, while the ranks of the college-educated include people who call themselves all sorts of names. But because a college education has become so crucial, we use it as our main dividing line.

A bachelor's degree has not always been so important. In 1979, college graduates earned only 40 percent more than Americans with just a high school diploma; they now earn 74 percent more.[7] As the economy shifted from manufacturing and construction to service and information, people without a college education saw their jobs go overseas or simply disappear. Those with a bachelor's degree, in contrast, had the skills that paid the bills. College-educated Americans now bring home $56,665 per year on average, compared to $30,627 for high school graduates.[8]

In previous chapters, we noted that population growth and technological innovations are forcing people from different cultures to interact more than ever. But the story for social class is different: the worlds of people with and without college degrees are becoming ever more balkanized. The United States is now the fourth most unequal nation among members of the Organisation for Economic Co-operation and Development (OECD), a consortium of the world's thirty-four wealthiest democracies. Only Turkey, Mexico, and Chile have greater inequality.[9] Getting ahead in the United States has also gotten harder. Once known as the land of opportunity, the United States is now the third *least* socially mobile of the OECD nations, topped only by Italy and Great Britain.[10] The United States has also lost its lead as a country that sends its kids to college; the nation now ranks number sixteen in the OECD when it comes to the percentage of twenty-five to thirty-four-year-olds who have completed a college degree.[11]

The widening gap between people with and without a college education is a problem not just for the have-nots. Inequality hurts everyone. The larger the spread between a society's rich and poor, the more dysfunction—including crime, depression, anxiety, drug use, school dropouts, and early deaths—its denizens of all social classes suffer.[12] A study spanning the years 1972 to 2008 similarly finds that Americans are less happy and trustful when there is more income inequality.[13] Liberal academics are not the only people worrying about inequality. No less a libertarian than Charles Murray (of *The Bell Curve* fame) recently released a book documenting how social class divides are tearing the United States in two.[14]

One proven way to reduce inequality is to produce more college graduates.[15] This would help not just the have-nots, but the nation as a whole. More than 70 percent of the nation's jobs require specialized skills that high schools do not teach.[16] With a dearth of qualified workers, many companies must now import workers to the United States or move their operations abroad.[17] This situation is likely to worsen. By 2025 the United States will need twenty million more college-educated workers than it is on track to produce.[18]

Class in the Classroom

Yet educating more people requires softening another culture clash, this time between the selves of the people delivering education and the selves of the people in greatest need of it. Educators are far from our nation's wealthiest people. But with a college education under their belts, and the cultural knowledge, connections, and income that come with it, they tend to see themselves as separate, unique, controlling, free, and equal. In other words, college-educated teachers and professors tend to use independent selves.

Their students hailing from working-class backgrounds, by contrast, tend to use interdependent selves. For working-class Americans, interdependence is not just an interesting philosophical stance; it's a useful strategy for surviving when there are too few resources to go around. Relating to and fitting in with other people helps build networks that can deliver not only emotional support, but also material assistance, when necessary. Adjusting to situations makes good sense when changing them is above your pay grade. Rooting yourself in tradition and location is likewise a good way to weather a relatively chaotic world. And when you're on the lower ranks of the social ladder, it behooves you to pay attention to who's above and below. Consequently, working-class people tend to see their selves as more relational, similar, adjusting, rooted, and ranked.

Working-class interdependence is not identical to East-Asian, female, or other forms of interdependence, nor is a working-class European-American woman's way of being interdependent the same as a working-class man's. Indeed, even though female teachers can make classrooms uncomfortably interdependent for boys as we discussed in chapter 3, teachers' middle-class independence often clashes with the interdependence of their working-class charges. When independence and interdependence collide in the classroom, many working-class students conclude that school is not for them.[19]

Some educators come to agree with them, viewing their working-class students as unmotivated, uncooperative, or just plain dumb. This is a failure not only of education, but also of the American Dream—"a simple but powerful one," as President Bill Clinton described it, that "if you work hard and play by the rules you should be given a chance to go as far as your God-given ability will take you."[20]

Now that dream must be amended: you must not only work hard and play by the rules, but also get a college education. And though there are exceptions—Steve Jobs, for example, was adopted into a working-class family, dropped out of college because it was too expensive, and then grew up to establish and run a computer company you might have heard of—they are so rare that they prove the rule.

To bring more people into the academic fold and create more prosperity for all, educators must tune in to the interdependent selves of their working-class students. At the same time, to take advantage of educational opportunities and make a better rank for themselves, working-class students must cultivate more independent selves. This meeting in the middle will require changes throughout the culture cycle: institutions, interactions, and I's, and then, ultimately, our big ideas about how to divide money, education, and opportunity.

Although we draw primarily from American research and examples, our prescription applies to many other contexts. Over the past three decades, governments around the world have cut programs aimed at helping less affluent people climb the social ladder. The Great Recession only exacerbated that trend. Now education alone must do much of the heavy lifting of social mobility. To narrow the wedge of inequality, nations around the world will have to grapple with class in the classroom like never before.

The University of Independence

"So, why are you taking this course?" Hazel asked on the first day of her psychology seminar. She looked out at the ring of undergraduates and called on John Hopper.[21] Like all the other students, he was sporting the West Coast collegiate uniform of jeans, T-shirt, and flip-flops.

"My adviser said I should take a freshman seminar, and this one fit my schedule," Hopper told his hands, which were splayed on the conference table.

Next Hazel called on Matthew Reynolds,[22] another tanned freshman in full university regalia.

"I chose this class because it has always seemed to me that the mind and the body work in unison," he began, looking Hazel in the eye and then meeting the gaze of his fellow students. "So it seems that they should be analyzed together, not separately. This is my philosophy, and now I want to find out if I'm right."

A few weeks into the seminar, John Hopper knocked on Hazel's office door for his one required meeting. He came prepared to talk about an upcoming paper assignment, but as the conversation warmed, he ventured what was clearly a difficult question. "All those students who talk all the time," he asked. "How do they do it? How do they already have so many ideas and opinions?"

It was the best question Hazel had heard all year, so she tried to get to know her students even better than usual. She learned, for instance, that Hopper was the first in his family to go to college. His father had been a skilled electrician (he abandoned the family when John was still an infant), and his mother was an administrative assistant at a small business. Hopper worked hard in high school, earning great grades, nearly acing his SATs, lettering in two varsity sports, and gaining proficiency in Spanish.

Reynolds also had an impressive résumé, with excellent grades and scores and a national science fair award. All his siblings and cousins were attending or had already graduated from college. His father was an attorney, and his mother was a hospital administrator. An accomplished swimmer, Reynolds also sang and played guitar in a band that was forming in his dorm.

Over the quarter, Hazel observed that Reynolds always asked questions and made comments, some of them quite insightful. Even when his remarks weren't particularly trenchant, he spoke confidently. During Hazel's weekly office hours, which Reynolds regularly attended, he confessed that he had a strong desire to distinguish himself from "the crowd," and asked for Hazel's help in doing so. He inquired about a summer internship in her lab. His actions echoed decades of research findings: people at the tops of hierarchies are more likely to express their attitudes and opinions, to take risks, to formulate long-term goals, and to break social norms in pursuit of those goals.[23]

In contrast, Hopper talked only if called upon. Hazel learned that he also had many interesting ideas, but he didn't yet know which ones were good, and until he did, he didn't want to make a fool of himself. The advice of his grandmother rang in his ears: "It's better to sit quietly and look stupid than to open your mouth and remove all doubt."

Hazel knew, however, that by graduation Hopper would get much better at expressing his unique ideas, not only because he was a bright young man, but also because it is the job of colleges to impart an independent self. In addition to large doses of information about the human genome, the laws of economics, and the Holy Roman Empire, colleges also dispense a lot of time to stew over that very special project: the I inside. Who are you? What are your interests and talents? What do you believe and why? After four years with few obligations to others and so much attention on their selves, college students cultivate the view that life is mostly about their thoughts, feelings, achievements, and choices.[24]

Tell Us about Your Self

In interviews with thousands of North American adults, we hear the familiar refrain of independence among middle-class Americans and the echoes of interdependence among working-class Americans. For instance, when asked to describe himself, a college-educated forty-five-year-old man had this to say: "I'm smart, maybe not brilliant, but well-organized, a good sport. I plan for the future and I make choices about what I want, feel, and want to be." Notice his emphasis on uniqueness, control, and choice—all facets of the independent self.[25]

Now consider this self-description from a forty-seven-year-old working-class man: "I know what is right and wrong. I'm kind to people. I never talk down to anyone and I never talk behind their backs."[26] Notice his emphasis on rooting himself in morality, relating to others, and (dis)regarding rank[27]—all aspects of the interdependent self. A thirty-eight-year-old construction worker likewise stresses the importance of relating and adjusting: "What matters is endurance, not giving up, just being in there, sticking with your friends when the going is not so good, hanging tough."[28] In working-class worlds, family and friends are often a higher priority than individual achievement.[29]

The different selves of working-class and middle-class Americans are apparent not only in their words, but also in their deeds. As we discussed in previous chapters, independent selves cherish choosing because it allows them to shine all five facets of their independent selves. Indeed, thousands of studies show that when middle-class people get to make choices, they are happier and healthier, produce more, persist longer, and perform better than when they do not get to make choices.[30]

But working-class Americans have a different take on choice, as Alana and Hazel discovered. Their research team invited shoppers at strip malls to participate in an alleged marketing study on pens, for which they would receive a pen as compensation. Half the participants chose which of five different pens they would evaluate and take home; the other half rated and received a pen that the researcher chose. As studies with college students had already found, middle-class participants who chose their own pen liked it more than did middle-class participants who were simply given a pen. But working-class participants (who are seldom included in social science experiments) liked their pens equally well no matter who had chosen it. They were just delighted to get a free pen.[31]

Middle-class Americans not only value the act of choosing more than do working-class Americans, they also see more of their actions as chosen. Hazel and her colleagues Nicole Stephens and Stephanie Fryberg asked college students from working- and middle-class backgrounds to list all the choices they made from the moment they got up in the morning. Even though the details of their daily lives seemed quite similar, the middle-class students made twice as many entries as the working-class students. For the middle-class students, "getting out of bed," "taking a shower," and "putting on clothes" are not just steps in a morning routine; they are chosen acts to be undertaken or not depending on the druthers of an independent self.[32] Studies in Hazel's lab also show that working-class participants are less upset when they don't get to choose, are less likely to pursue opportunities for choice, and have more negative associations with choosing than do middle-class participants.[33]

Keeping an I on Others

Because the people taking the bus can't be in the driver's seat, working-class Americans master skills other than choosing and controlling, including adjusting and relating. People without college degrees agree with statements such as "Once something has happened, I try to adjust myself to it because it is difficult to change it myself" more than do people with college degrees.[34] Working-class Americans also work hard to relate to the people around them. Compared to middle-class adults, for example, working-class adults chatting with a stranger more frequently nod their heads in agreement, raise their eyebrows, and look at their conversation partner's face. In contrast, those with higher social status spend more time grooming themselves, doodling, and checking their phones.[35] Working-class adults are also better at guessing the feelings of both strangers and friends.[36]

Perhaps because their own emotional lives are so closely tied to those of other people, working-class Americans invest more in the happiness of others. For instance, in 2001, Americans with household earnings of $75,000 or more contributed 2.7 percent of their income to charity, while those making $25,000 or less donated 4.2 percent of their income.[37] To get a close-up view of this generosity in action, psychologists Paul Piff, Dacher Keltner, and their team gave college students a gift they could share with an anonymous partner in a laboratory experiment. Participants who considered themselves to be lower in social rank gave 44 percent more to the partner than did participants of higher rank.[38] Keltner's lab also finds that lower-status participants make more ethical decisions, negotiate more honestly, and compete more fairly than higher-status participants.[39]

Paying close attention to the thoughts, feelings, and actions of other people is a smart strategy when people of higher rank control your fate. Yet interdependence can take a toll on both body and mind. When other people are demanding, rejecting, or disrespectful, and you are in a subordinate position, you feel the sting more deeply than do people in higher positions. In one study, for example, psychologists Edith Chen and Karen Matthews read to working- and middle-class children a set of humiliating situations, such as hearing a classmate laugh at your comment in class (much as Hazel's student John Hopper feared). The researchers found that the working-class kids literally took the insults to heart, registering a greater change in blood pressure than did the middle-class kids.

Keeping an "I" on other people can also impede interdependent selves from scaling the social ladder. For example, across several studies, psychologist Joe Magee and his colleagues asked half their sample of MBA students to think of a time when they had power over someone (the high-status condition), and the other half of their sample to think of a time when someone else had power over them (the low-status condition). The participants assigned to the low-status condition negotiated worse deals, took fewer risks, and generally acted more "beta" than their randomly assigned "alpha" colleagues. Meanwhile, the arbitrarily alpha participants were quicker to pull the trigger across a variety of business situations—a readiness that helps maintain and ultimately widen the gap between higher- and lower-status folks.[40]

Learning Your Place

Crafting class-appropriate selves starts early, anthropologist Adrie Kusserow finds. She observed the daily interactions of mothers and their toddlers on the tony Upper East Side of Manhattan and in two working-class communities in Queens.[41] To help their children thrive in these very different worlds, parents aim to rear very different selves.

In Queens, that world is a rough place that requires an interdependent self. To protect their children from the corruption around them, parents' first order of business is to root their children in traditional morals. "You have to give them a very strong background," said one mother, "principles that you have to rely on, and . . . you draw the line for them."[42] Working-class parents also make sure that kids know their place. To reinforce who is in charge, they more often use teasing, yelling, spanking, and direct commands than do middle-class parents. These practices help prepare children for working-class jobs, which often require conforming and carefully following orders under close supervision.[43] Parents also give their children more unstructured time with other children to learn how to negotiate status on their own. "I hate it when they don't stand up for themselves," said one mother. "I have one child who whines. I don't want her to come running. I'm like, 'defend yourself and fight it out.'"[44]

But on the wealthy and educated Upper East Side, the world is safe, welcoming, and full of possibilities. Here, parents' main task is to coax their children's independent selves into full bloom. Parents are affectionate and warm, offering their children opportunities to discover what they like and what they're good at. As was the case with Hazel and her daughter in chapter 2, life proceeds as a series of questions: Do you want to read a story before putting on pajamas or after? Which book do you want to read? What did you like about that book? Even discipline comes in the form of a question: Do you have to jump on that chair now? Don't you think you should stop hitting your brother?

Middle-class parents also meet tall tales with a question mark, psychologist Peggy Miller and her colleagues find. A child who contends that, say, Santa Claus comes at Easter, will be asked, "Really, does he? Tell me about it? How does that work?" With a safety net in place, middle-class parents can encourage risk-taking and questioning the status quo. In sharp contrast, working-class parents tend to challenge the same confabulations with a simple, "No, he doesn't. Don't be stupid," conveying that reality is not theirs for their making.[45]

Throughout their exchanges, many middle-class parents bend down to their children's level and look into their eyes, communicating, "We are equals." Working-class parents, in contrast, don't stoop to conquer.

"Upper-middle class parents consciously and unconsciously teach their children how to communicate with teachers and other adults in power," writes Kusserow. "As a result, when [the children] show up for their first day of school, they have already mastered a large, albeit implicit, portion of the curriculum. These behaviors then in turn get called 'talent,' 'sensitivity,' 'intelligence,' 'imagination' and other traits that are supposedly inborn and supposedly necessary for scholastic success—rather than class-based knowledge."[46]

Wealthier parents confer another advantage by immersing their children in what sociologist Annette Lareau calls "a steady stream of speech." In a single hour, middle-class children hear their parents speak almost twice as many words (2,153 words) as do working-class children (1,251 words) and more than three times as many words as poor children (616 words). Middle-class parents also read more to their children and encourage them to share what they're thinking and learning.[47] As a result, by the time middle-class children enter preschool, they already have bigger vocabularies and better comprehension than their less affluent classmates.[48]

You Are Your Media

The daily interactions of working- and middle-class adults likewise drive and derive from different notions of the self. Advertisements in magazines targeted at readers with a high-school education (e.g., *Reader's Digest*), for example, paint a picture of a very different ideal self than do ads in magazines for college-educated readers (e.g., *Time*). In one working-class magazine, for instance, a wife tempts her husband with a thick piece of chocolate cake over the slogan, "Mama said there'd be cake like this." A careful analysis of hundreds of other working-class magazine ads reveals a prominent theme of enjoying comfortable times with family. But in middle-class magazines, the theme of expressing uniqueness sells the wares. An ad for a music player, for example, features a thin woman lounging on a leather couch with the tag line, "You are your play list."[49]

Popular music also pumps out different messages about how to be a self. Musical genres have strong associations with social class. The more education you have, the more likely you are to like rock music, and the less education you have, the more likely you are to like country music—regardless of what region of the country you live in. In a systematic comparison of the bestselling rock and country songs of the last forty years, we found that more rock songs hollered about expressing uniqueness and controlling one's world, while more country songs twanged about maintaining integrity and controlling one's self. The rock band Steppenwolf is "lookin' for adventure" because they're "born to be wild," but country singer Johnny Cash is just keeping "a close watch on this heart of mine." Led Zeppelin is buying the stairway to heaven while Tammy Wynette is standing by her man.[50]

The Catch-22

After eighteen years of daily interactions with distinct practices and products, college students such as John Hopper and Matthew Reynolds emerge with distinct selves. Their different selves, in turn, react differently to the institutions, interactions, and I's they meet in college.

For instance, before taking their places at Stanford, both men were accepted at the University of California at Berkeley. This is the letter that arrived in the big envelope:

> There is truly no place like Berkeley. Anywhere. And you've earned a place here. We think you can take this excitement and make it your own. Take the world's ideas and forge new ones. Learn. Imagine. Experiment. Create. Change the world. You can do it and you can do it here. We know you can. Choose Berkeley.[51]

For Reynolds, the words were reassuring. They said to him, "Keep on expressing your uniqueness, separating from your family, making choices, and otherwise realizing your independent self, just as you have been doing for the past eighteen years."

But for Hopper, the message was bewildering. "What kind of person must I become to succeed in a place like this?" he thought. The interdependent themes of fitting in, relating, and adjusting were nowhere to be found.

The swag Hopper receives from other universities does little to comfort him. One college brochure boasts that its students have "the freedom to select and combine majors from more than 60 areas of study."[52] Another claims, "It is not the task of an academic advisor to tell you what to do . . . your advisor should be seen as a compass, not as a roadmap."[53]

The mismatch between the interdependent selves of working-class students and the independent culture cycles of universities presents a catch-22: To ascend to the middle-class, you must have a college degree. Yet to succeed in college, you must already know how to play by middle-class rules.

What's worse, universities do little to share the rulebook. Many colleges now recognize that people of color can feel alienated, and so design programs to support them. But "if you're white and you come from a poor or working-class background, you show up on these campuses and you are having your mind blown hundreds of times a day, and your reality is never noticed or validated by anyone," noted the late activist Felice Yeskel.[54]

Why First-Gens Flounder

Getting a college education is thus a decidedly more challenging task for a working-class student such as Hopper than for a middle-class student such as Reynolds. For Reynolds, college is simply the next stage in the plan he has been following since birth. Like 82 percent of students who have at least one parent with a college degree or more, Reynolds went to college immediately after high school.[55] To this end, his parents copiloted his Internet searches and college visits, edited his application essays, consulted with friends and family, lined up $200,000, and helped their son select, shop for, and move into his new home. He is now poised to develop his voice, follow his passions, stand out, make good choices, and change the world. He even has a philosophy to test and a growing network of professors on his side.

In contrast, Hopper is like an athlete without a coach. His mother is bursting with pride for her son and would do anything to help him, but she doesn't really know how. As she is not close to many college graduates, she has few people to ask for advice, and the counselors at Hopper's large public high school are too burdened to be of much help. On his own, Hopper figured out how to apply to the schools near his town in Northern California. Like many working-class Americans, he didn't want to go too far from home. As sociologist Michèle Lamont observes, working-class people tend to be "immersed in tight networks of sociability, in part because their extended family often resides within a few miles."[56] On his own, Hopper also applied for loans and scholarships, and earned extra money cleaning pools during vacations. He then went to college directly out of high school, bucking a long-standing trend: less than half of students whose parents do not have a college education enroll in college immediately after high school.[57]

Like many working-class students, one of Hopper's main motivations for going to college was ultimately to give back to his family and his community.[58] But in his first weeks at Stanford, he meets no one who shares his goals. He struggles to find the words to explain why he feels so out of step. But aware of the stereotype that working-class Americans are not as smart as middle-class ones, he is afraid to ask for help, lest he confirm the stereotype. He begins to question whether he is in the right place.

Hopper is not alone. One out of every six students at four-year colleges are the first in their family to pursue higher education. These students routinely trail behind those with at least one college-educated parent. So-called first-gen students receive lower grades, take fewer credits, and have higher drop-out rates. They report that professors and other students respond to them as different, passive, or even slow. And they are less likely to participate in student organizations or to develop close relationships with their peers and faculty.[59]

Working-class students' interdependence conflicts with higher education in other ways. Some of these students worry that going to college will sever their ties to their family and friends back home. "I will become different from my mom and my friends, and what is the point of that?" one first-gen student told Hazel as part of a study. Others feel uncomfortable with all the attention they are getting. "I feel so selfish here with all this fuss about me and what I want to do with my life," confided another student.[60]

The Other Invisible Hand

As education becomes more expensive and less welcoming to working-class Americans, the class structure becomes even more entrenched. This loss of social mobility bodes ill for the country as a whole. The many challenges of the twenty-first century demand an educated and united citizenry. Yet the United States, like many other nations, is dividing along class lines for lack of access to a good education.

Some social inequality may be inevitable.[61] Like our primate brethren, we humans spontaneously arrange ourselves into hierarchies. Put a group of people in a room and, fairly soon, they will establish a pecking order.[62] Even Americans, who famously deny the existence of social class, can readily report on their social standing. In several studies, for example, health psychologist Nancy Adler and her colleagues show participants a simple line drawing of a ladder, and then ask them to mark the rung that represents where they stand relative to other people. The researchers find not only that people can complete this task reliably, but also that their simple mark reveals a wealth of information. The higher the rung a person selects, the better his or her health across a host of measures.[63]

Some of this inequality has its basis in biology. After all, to the larger, stronger, and smarter often go the spoils. Yet many humans create cultures that amp up the consequences of these hierarchies. The culture cycle then works so deftly that it hides the human minds and hands that created these distinctions in the first place. People wind up viewing status, class, caste, and their consequences as natural and inevitable, rather than as human-made and changeable.

Throw Money Better

Unlike our hairier primate counterparts, we humans can also use culture cycles to flatten the slopes and shorten the distances between the rungs of our social ladders. One straightforward approach to leveling hierarchies and bettering lives is to make a solid education available and appealing to everyone. Many countries, including Japan and Denmark, have used this institutional lever to lessen inequality and improve their citizens' health and well-being.[64]

But in the United States, a good education is increasingly reserved for families at the top of the socioeconomic heap. The problem begins long before college. Because funding for primary and secondary public schools is usually tied to local property taxes, U.S. school districts with wealthier residents can spend up to $40,000 per student annually, while districts with poorer residents can spend as little as $4,000 per student.[65] Such larg discrepancies in funding are odd for an industrialized nation. In Canada for example, provinces give each school the same amount of money. As result, children in poor Canadian neighborhoods often have the sam quality teachers, curricula, and materials as do children in wealthy neighborhoods.[66]

In the United States, however, unequal wealth often means unequa educations. Because working-class areas pay their teachers less than do mor affluent districts, working-class neighborhoods cannot attract and retai the most qualified teachers. Students of less qualified teachers, in turn drop out at a higher rate than do students of better teachers. Poor schoo also lack the enriched curriculum, multimedia libraries, and science laboratories that their richer counterparts enjoy. With so little to hold them i the classroom, working-class students are more likely to join the mass exodus that is now plaguing U.S. secondary education. In the nation's fift largest cities, more than half the students do not complete high school.[67]

"How can we sustain an economy in the twenty-first century wit these kinds of graduation rates?" asks educator Linda Darling-Hammond.[6

The state of Connecticut has one answer: fund public schools sufficiently and equitably. With its 1986 Education Enhancement Act, th state increased and equalized teacher salaries, raised standards for teache education, and invested more in teachers' professional development. B 1998, Connecticut's fourth-graders surpassed their competition in a other states in reading and math, and the state's eighth-graders score among the nation's best in math, science, and writing.[69]

As educator W. Norton Grubb recounts in *The Money Myth*, throwin money at the education problem may not be a quick fix. The relationshi between how much funding a school receives and how well its student perform is often weak.[70] Although money alone may not be sufficient t immediately close the gaps between working- and middle-class students it can help buy the things that do make a difference, including early childhood education and government-sponsored, low-interest college loa programs (such as Pell Grants). Money also attracts the skilled teachers sage principals, and stimulating curricula that Grubb cites as the heav lifters in education. In short, at the institutional level of the culture cycle an infusion of cash, smartly distributed, is one nudge that could set u working-class students for success.

Put the Pieces Together

Once in front of their classrooms, better-paid, better-trained teachers should enlist the interdependence of working-class students to boost their entire class's performance. One of the best techniques for leveraging interdependence in schools is called the *jigsaw classroom*, which was created by psychologist Elliot Aronson in Texas in the early 1970s. At the time, school desegregation was fanning hostilities in schools across the South. Reasoning that the competitive techniques many teachers use were actually fueling the tensions, Aronson and his team asked, why not try cooperation instead?

Working with teachers, the researchers split classrooms into groups of five to six children, making sure that each group included plenty of gender, racial, and socioeconomic diversity. Teachers then divided their lessons into five or six interlocking parts, assigning one part to each student in each group. For example, for a lesson on World War II, one student researched Hitler's rise to power, another student covered concentration camps, another handled Japan's entry into the war, and so on. After researching their segments and conferring with the kids assigned the same topic in the other groups, students returned to their home groups and presented their reports. The entire group was later tested on its knowledge of all topics.

At first, students chided the "slower" students for their less polished reports and speaking styles. Once they figured out that their grades depended on everyone's performance, however, the students banded together to shore up one another's weaknesses and capitalize on their strengths. By the end of the eight-week intervention, students randomly assigned to jigsaw classrooms scored higher on their exams, liked school more, and held less racial prejudice than did students randomly assigned to a no-treatment control condition.[71]

To further unleash the power of interdependence, educators should gear their materials (readings, videos, letters, etc.) to the selves of their working-class students. In one laboratory study, for instance, psychologist Nicole Stephens and colleagues invited first-generation college students to evaluate their university's new welcoming materials for freshman. Half the participants viewed materials with an independent slant: the letter from the president, brochure, and flyers portrayed the university as a place to explore one's personal interests. The other half viewed a package with an interdependent angle, presenting the university as a place where students can collaborate with others and become part of a community. First-gens in the independent condition later performed worse on spatial and verbal tasks than did first-gens in the interdependent condition.[72] A second study suggests why: Working-class students in the independent condition underwent a sharp increase in cortisol levels, indicating that they were stressed out while completing the tasks. Middle-class students, on the other hand, remained unruffled in both conditions.[73]

Universities can use the working-class emphasis on community not only to welcome students to college, but also to keep them there. The Posse Foundation, a New York City–based nonprofit with sites in nine U.S. cities, identifies low-income high school students with strong academic and leadership potential, groups them in teams of ten, gives them eight months of precollege training, and then grants them full-tuition scholarships to attend an elite university *together.* Once at college, Posse Scholars help one another navigate the foreign, sometimes hostile terrain of college life.

Educator Deborah Bial helped create the organization after a promising inner-city student told her, "I never would have dropped out of college if I had my posse with me." Since the program's inception in 1989, it has sent 4,245 students to some three dozen partner universities, including Vanderbilt University, the University of Pennsylvania, and Northwestern. The program works; 90 percent of Posse Scholars leave college with a bachelor's degree in hand.[74]

Educators at all grades and stages can help their working-class students by lifting the stereotype threat under which the latter labor. Two psychologists, Jean-Claude Croizet and Theresa Claire, found that when working-class participants were told that a test was designed to assess intellectual ability, they performed worse than when they were told that the test was a measure of readiness to concentrate on a task. The reason? In the ability version of the test, working-class students were anxious about confirming the stereotype that their group was stupid and lazy. This anxiety distracted them from the task at hand, and made them perform worse than when the test was not allegedly assessing some deep, fixed quality. As we have seen in the previous chapters, stereotype threat undermines many people in lower-status positions, including Blacks and women. Yet as this study also shows, alleviating stereotype threat is sometimes just a matter of tweaking directions.[75]

Add Some Independence

To succeed academically takes more than interdependence, however. Working-class students must also cultivate an independent streak. The story of the KIPP (Knowledge Is Power Program) Academies illustrates why interdependence is not enough to thrive in mainstream middle-class worlds.

KIPP is a 20-state network of 109 charter schools that serve primarily low-income African-American and Latino students. Most KIPP Academies are middle schools. Launched in 1994, the program has placed an astounding 84 percent of its thirty-three thousand graduates in four-year universities. But unlike the Posse Foundation, it hasn't kept them there: although their students beat the averages for low-income students, only 36 percent of KIPP alumni graduate from college within six years of leaving high school. This is only slightly higher than the national average of 31 percent for Americans between the ages of twenty-five and twenty-nine.[76]

Stalling these students' meteoric climb is KIPP's almost exclusive focus on interdependent skills. At the heart of the KIPP curriculum is a protocol called SLANT—an acronym that stands for Sit up straight, Listen, Ask and answer questions, Nod your head, and Track the speaker with your eyes. SLANT defuses many of the behavioral issues that plague low-income schools, and helps KIPP students and teachers endure nearly nine-hour school days and compulsory summer school—many hours of which are dedicated to practicing standardized tests.[77]

Yet most colleges want students who can do more than act nice and rock the SAT. They demand that their scholars identify problems, challenge doctrine, dream up solutions, communicate ideas, and refine creations based on the feedback of peers. To these ends, the Posse Foundation spends months training its scholars to cultivate and share their opinions with people from different class, gender, and ethnic backgrounds. In other words, Posse meets the interdependent needs of working-class students, and then helps them hone the independence they will need to excel in college.

Comparing the Posse Foundation and KIPP Academies is not altogether fair. Posse carefully selects its participants; KIPP takes all comers whose parents sign a commitment contract. Posse nurtures its scholars in small batches; KIPP operates full-fledged public charter schools. Yet

KIPP's founders, Dave Levin and Mike Feinberg, agree that its graduation rates need to grow. "We aspire for our students to earn four-year degrees at the same rate as students from the nation's highest-income families, giving them the same opportunity for self-sufficiency," they wrote in a 2011 report.[78] That same report features a photo of KIPP's earliest class of forty-seven students and a sign that reads, "Team Always Beats Individual." Perhaps fortifying those individuals with a healthy dose of independence would help KIPP students succeed in middle-class worlds, where many believe the individual should sometimes try to trump the team.

Psychologist Daphna Oyserman and her team developed one such independence-inducing tactic. Noting that many working-class students have big dreams but no clear idea how to realize them, the research team created an eleven-week School-to-Jobs program to help students develop a sense of themselves as making choices, controlling their futures, and pursuing their unique paths. To test the program, the researchers randomly divided 280 low-income middle-school students into either a school-as-usual class or a *possible selves* class that met twice a week.[79] The students in the possible selves class first found photographs depicting visions of the kinds of adults they wanted to grow up to be. The students then plotted time lines from their current selves to their possible selves, replete with likely setbacks and how to deal with them. Leveraging their interdependence, the students also met with family and community members to discuss their desired futures and to enlist support.

Two years later, Oyserman and her coauthors found that the students who had charted their futures had higher standardized test scores, better grades, fewer absences, and less depression than did students in the control group. A strengthened independent self seems to be at the heart of the program's success. "Students begin to see choices that were invisible before, and to see themselves as the architects of their own futures," says Oyserman.[80]

To build some independence at the university level, psychologists Nicole Stephens and MarYam Hamedani developed an intervention for working-class students. The researchers assigned half their sample of first-generation freshmen to hear first-gen upperclassmen describe how their interdependent ways (for example, fear of asking questions in class) initially caused them difficulties, but how they eventually learned more effective independent strategies (for example, speaking up in class, or asking for help). The other half of the sample heard the same upperclassmen discuss general study skills. Stephens and Hamedani found that first-gen students who learned about how to be independent felt less stress and anxiety and earned higher grades in their first year of college than did first-gens in the study-skills control group.[81]

Cop to Class

Individuals can also help change their culture cycles to bridge social classes. To start, middle-class folks can extend an interdependent hand to their working-class brethren and acknowledge the power of social class. Americans are particularly slow to recognize the socioeconomic structuring of their own culture, even though the United States has long been one of the most stratified industrialized countries. The belief that the United States is a land of level playing fields is an independent one, allowing the better-off to believe that they succeed solely because of their own hard work and brilliance, rather than because thousands of cultural quirks paved the path to their affluence.

Many middle-class individuals who have taken a dose of interdependence see that their own education, income, and occupation have more to do with their parents' education, income, and occupation;[82] with tax laws; with their excellent rapport with their eighth-grade science teacher; and with other institutions and interactions than with their own native awesomeness. They also understand that with this status comes a particular way of seeing the self, an independent way, that is no more natural, right, or inevitable than is their position in society. Many of these cross-class pioneers then set out to understand more interdependent ways of being—which, rather than being slow or weak, are actually the way most people in the United States, not to mention the world, live their lives.

To get a clearer glimpse of interdependence, psychologist Barbara Jensen recommends that middle-class Americans take a trip to the other side of the class divide. Working-class worlds have "an integrity all their own," she notes, "which means you just have to go and experience them for yourself." And who knows? You might like what you find; working-class cultures have much to recommend them. Compared to the middle-class pressures to individuate, choose, control, and plan, working-class worlds can offer "an unearned sense of oneself as part of other people, part of the world we live in, part of life—a foundational sense of belonging," she writes.[83]

Within your own world, take the time to talk to the working-class people you encounter every day, recommends activist and author Betsy Leondar-Wright in her book *Class Matters*. At work, for example, she suggests asking the lowest-ranking people "how they see the organization." You will likely find that things look quite different from below. "Keep asking and listening, as the first answer may not be their whole story," she adds.[84]

Working-class individuals can also get into the class-crossing act by sharpening their independence. A first target is to recognize that you have more options than you may initially perceive. While working-class communities and jobs objectively offer fewer opportunities for choice and control than do middle-class worlds, middle-class worlds probably do not proffer as many choices as their inhabitants perceive. Yet thinking that you are in control, even when you are not, is one of the tricks that more powerful people use to stay optimistic, healthy, and action-oriented.[85] Although delusions of control are likely not good for anyone, a few more illusions of control may give you the extra independence you need to thrive in middle-class worlds.

Close the Chasm

The achievement gap between low- and high-income families is now double the Black-White gap—a complete reversal of the pattern of fifty years ago.[86] Reducing the racial disparities of the 1950s and '60s required changes at every level of the culture cycle. Closing the growing chasm between social classes will likewise require overhauling our institutions, interactions, I's, and, ultimately, our ideas about how to divide our planet's diminishing resources.

One particularly troublesome idea is that the wealthy should have more of society's spoils because they earned them. The French sociologist Pierre Bourdieu calls this way of thinking "the social alchemy that turns class privilege into merit."[87] Bourdieu was among the first social scientists to track how culture cycles—especially their educational institutions and interactions—erect and echo class divides. He documents that higher social status is less a matter of money and more a matter of having the right thoughts, feelings, and actions—in our words, the right self—showing that you belong in the upper echelons.[88]

Judging their young charges against this yardstick, schools inadvertently channel working-class kids into the same dead-end jobs their parents had, rather than giving them the selves they need to make a better life. This is as true in the United States as it is in France: You need an independent self to succeed in school, but your parents needed a solid education to give you that independent self in the first place. In both nations, and in many others around the world, schools thus perpetuate the myth that the rich are rich because they deserve it.

Yet education need not be the obstacle that keeps poor people in their place. To quote Bourdieu, "Enlightenment is on the side of those who turn their spotlight on our blinkers."[89] By training our spotlights on the quiet clashes between independence and interdependence at every level of the culture cycle, we can turn schools into the engines of social mobility that most people want them to be.

CHAPTER 6

States of Mind

U.S. Regional Cultures

Watching Lisa Radloff sprint across a marathon finish line, or vanquish her competition on the racquetball court, you would never guess that just four years ago she weighed 281 pounds. "That's like a linebacker," she points out.

A few years after moving to the San Francisco Bay Area, the native of Palatine, Illinois, saw the writing on the wall: "I was surrounded by athletic girls who all wore a size 2. If I wanted to be successful here, I had to lose weight."

So, over the course of eleven months, the six-foot, one-inch information technology manager dropped 110 pounds. Unlike the vast majority of dieters, she has managed to keep the weight off, mostly because her California home has allowed her to unleash her long-dormant athletic side.

Radloff's rotund husband, however, was a different story. "He didn't even try to get healthy," she says. Instead, he brought home cheesecakes, pizzas, and beer to tempt his shrinking bride. When three years of unemployment packed on another fifty pounds, he could no longer join Radloff in exploring Northern California's mountains and beaches. The couple slowly drifted apart until last year, after twenty years of marriage, Radloff asked for a divorce. Her husband promptly packed up his car and moved back to his hometown of Peoria, Illinois.

The shimmering lure of relocation is a staple of America, a nation of people from somewhere else. Roughly 20 percent of Americans live in a region other than the one where they were born. This year alone, between 5 and 6 percent of Americans will move across a county line.[1]

Some of these internal migrants will discover, as Radloff did, that they prefer using the selves their new homes require. Yet many others will find, as did Radloff's husband, that their new worlds and old selves just don't jibe. These mismatches take a toll. Rates of schizophrenia and substance abuse are higher among more mobile Americans.[2] And Americans who move frequently in childhood have more alcoholism, depression, and suicide attempts in adulthood.[3]

Many migrants can't put a finger on why their selves aren't meshing with their new homes. But in the woes of the wandering, we see a common problem: the clash of interdependent selves with independent places, and vice versa. Within the United States, these collisions follow a pattern. The culture cycles of the South and Midwest support and reflect interdependent I's that strive to relate, fit in, adjust, stay rooted in traditions, and know their rank in the larger social world. In contrast, the culture cycles of the West and Northeast drive and derive from independent I's that aim to individuate, express uniqueness, exert influence, and feel free, equal, and great.[4] Anecdotal evidence suggests that when people transfer to a region whose culture cycle fosters a different sort of self, they experience more malaise than when they relocate to a region with a similar sort of self.

Although Americans aren't as migratory as they were thirty years ago, they are still among the most mobile people in the world.[5] The rise of telecommuting means that Americans are spending even more of their time working with people in different regions. And as more people than ever immigrate to the United States, they are discovering that settling in Tacoma, Washington, is quite a different proposition from settling in Tuscaloosa, Alabama.

Understanding the regional patterning of U.S. cultures can help these present-day pilgrims. Should you find yourself contemplating a move, you can select a U.S. region that best complements your present self or the self you want to cultivate. Or, if you don't have any choice in your destination, you can at least prepare yourself for the culture shock ahead. By knowing what kind of world you're headed to and what kind of self you have (a question we help you answer in chapter 10), you can use the culture cycle to carve a comfier niche for yourself. And if you're staying put, you can also use the culture cycle to make your world more welcoming for other transplants.

The United States is not alone in its regional clashes. The histories of many nations are stained with bloody civil wars. Although many of these conflicts have calmed, some tensions still rear their ugly heads. Quite a few of these collisions take place across the independence-interdependence divide. Understanding this divide and then adjusting culture cycles to build bridges between different regions can help heal the rifts within borders.

Go West or Go Home

Although Radloff is proud of her lean body, she dislikes some of the pressures that drove her to it. "Californians are sort of superficial," she says. In addition to judging people because of their appearances, "they have an annoying habit of making dates and then not showing up. In the Midwest," she adds, "that's a punishable offense."

At first Radloff took the flakiness personally. But after a while, she blamed the weather, and the culture that it encourages.

"I know this sounds like stereotyping," she says, "but in the Midwest, it's too cold to go outside for much of the year. And so you stay inside, watch football together, drink beer, and bond. But out here, you can meet people year round out surfing, and running, and biking. And so you don't have to make close friends, because you can always find new ones." But when you're constantly in the market for friends, "you feel more pressure to look good," she notes.

What Radloff has experienced in her own life, psychologist Victoria Plaut and colleagues see in their research: people who have more potential friends, such as people in more densely populated areas or with more money, value physical attractiveness more than do people with fewer social options, such as folks in rural areas or with less money.[6]

"When you have more choices in friends," Plaut explains, "you need a sorting mechanism. A common sorting mechanism is attractiveness. But when you have fewer choices, your friends tend to be the people you're already connected to—the people you grew up with or you go to church with. And so attractiveness doesn't matter as much."

Accordingly, Plaut and her team show that urban women with high waist-to-hip ratios, and thus more around the middle, are less satisfied and socially connected than their apple-shaped sisters in rural areas. She also finds, as Radloff suspected, that even moderately chunky women suffer more in "free market" social worlds than in more traditional and rooted settings.

As she morphed from apple to hourglass, Radloff discovered that all the choosing, individuating, mastering, and freeing that the West[7] requires not only shrink a body, but also make and mirror an independent self. She also understood that all the accepting, relating, adjusting, and rooting back in the Midwest not only had generated warmth on cold nights, but also had required and reproduced an interdependent self.

With some regret, Radloff realized that the longer she stayed in California, the more her interdependent self receded: "Out here, people think and talk about themselves *all the time*. I never wanted to be that person. I wanted to be the person who asked you about yourself first, because that's what it means to be a decent, good human being. But then you absorb that 'Me! Me! Me!' mentality. And that's been an interesting change. I think about myself first now."

The West and the Rest

Although the differences between the West and the rest of the country are less studied than the North-South differences we discuss later in this chapter, they are no less stark. The region that brought you "Hollyweird," Las Vegas, Silicon Valley, the Silicon Forest, the personal computer, and the self-esteem movement hosts some of the most independent selves in the country. In national surveys, for instance, Westerners describe themselves as more open to new experiences, autonomous, and self-focused, as well as less friendly, agreeable, and other-focused, than do Midwesterners and Southerners.[8]

Even compared to the Northeast—another open-minded, self-focused, and not-so-agreeable region[9]—the West is more independent on some measures. In one study, for example, Plaut and her colleagues explored how residents of San Francisco and Boston get their sense of self-worth. Both cities are refuges for the "tax-hiking, government-expanding, latte-drinking, sushi-eating, Volvo-driving, *New York Times*–reading" liberal elite.[10] Nevertheless, what feeds the selves of their denizens differs. Bostonians' self-worth rises and falls with the circumstances of their families, communities, finances, education, and work. In contrast, the self-worth of San Franciscans is tied mostly to their work.[11]

"This doesn't mean that people in the West aren't nice to each other," explains Plaut. "It doesn't mean that they don't make good friends and colleagues. It just means that they put less weight on social norms than do people in the Northeast."

One big difference between the two cities, explains Plaut, is their ages. Although Boston and its environs hosted the Puritans' arrival, the American Revolution, and other great moments in independence, the area has had many more years to grow roots, nurture relationships, and establish hierarchies than cities in the West. Many Northeasterners now struggle to reconcile their independence with the constraints of an older culture. New and shiny San Francisco, in contrast, is relatively lacking in entrenched traditions, communities, and status systems. And so its selves feel freer to rush headlong toward their individual goals.

On the Move

Some rush so fast that observers ask, is the United States tilted so that all the nuts roll toward the Pacific? Or does the wild, wild West turn its residents into wild, wild people? The answer is yes. Both forces are at work. Across cultures, people who migrate are the ones who are willing to abandon everything they know to pursue something they have never seen or felt. These pioneers then establish culture cycles of ideas, institutions, and interactions that continue to feed and follow from an independent self.

Rob Goldhor is one Yankee who answered the call of the West. In his own words, he "just wasn't feeling it" as a college student in his hometown of Boston. Instead of taking classes in the close confines of a city he already knew, he wanted to be riding his motorcycle in the wide-open spaces of a totally unknown place. On a ski trip back in 1997, he passed through Colorado, liked what he saw, and moved to Boulder two years later.

Now a machinist in Golden, Colorado, Goldhor spends his free time hiking, skiing, and piloting his "rock crawler," a pickup that he customized to navigate the treacherous terrain. "I live more in my skin," he says. "I'm more of who I am, rather than who I thought I was supposed to be when I was growing up in a family of Ph.D.s, with all that pomp and circumstance."

The United States isn't the only country with a wilderness that attracts independent selves.[12] In an intriguing set of studies, psychologist Shinobu Kitayama and his team compared Japanese college students at Kyoto University, an elite university on Japan's main island of Honshu, to those at Hokkaido University, an elite university on the island of Hokkaido, Japan's sparsely populated northern frontier. As we saw in chapters 1 and 2, mainstream Japanese culture cycles sustain and stem from interdependent selves. Yet Shinobu and his colleagues found not only that the Hokkaido-born Japanese showed more independent tendencies—a desire for personal achievement, a need to justify their personal choices, a tendency to look for the causes of events in individuals rather than in situations—but also that students who had relocated to rugged Hokkaido were just as independent as the island's native-born students. In other words, wild people seek out wild places.

Even if you don't start out wild at heart, the mere act of moving makes you more independent. Psychologist Shigehiro Oishi and his colleagues established this fact among American college students. In one study, for instance, they discovered that the more often college students had moved, the less often they mentioned sports teams, churches, or other groups when describing themselves. Instead, these more mobile students more often described themselves in terms of abstract personality traits, such as "hardworking" or "intelligent."[13]

"If you change soccer teams every year," explains Oishi, "the position you play becomes more important than the team you belong to. Likewise, when you move around, *you* are the constant, and the groups you belong to become less meaningful."

Strong Weak Ties

The American West is still a region on the go. Between 1995 and 2000, the five states whose residents moved the most—Nevada, Colorado, Arizona,

Alaska, and Oregon—were all in the West. Reports from the 2000 U.S. Census likewise show that the West is the region with the most people transferring in, out, and around.[14] This constant relocation gives rise to daily interactions that propel a more independent culture cycle.

As Westerners shift and resettle, for instance, they do not shrink their webs of relationships. Instead, these people have *more* friends than their more sessile counterparts. To do this, Westerners make the classic trade-off between quality and quantity: "They throw a wider net instead of having a few deep relationships," says Oishi.

The knots that form these big, shallow nets are not the ties that bind, but they are the connections that inspire innovation. As the sociologist Mark Granovetter demonstrates in a classic paper, the more people in a network and the looser their connections, the more quickly and easily they circulate ideas. Because breakthroughs usually spring from the bumping, churning, and recombining of ideas from all directions, and not from the heads of lone geniuses, weak ties are the superhighways of creativity.[15]

Accordingly, the loosely tied West is the home of some of the most innovative industries of the past century, including motion pictures, semiconductors, software, and the Internet. Three of the top five patent-applying regions are in the West, namely the San Francisco Bay Area, the San Jose area, and Los Angeles regions. Four of the top eight biotech centers also skirt the Pacific, even though the industry is historically rooted in the Northeast.[16] And as author Richard Florida recounts in *Who's Your City?*, more than 50 percent of all venture capital goes to just three regions (Silicon Valley, San Diego, and greater Boston), with two-thirds of that amount going to Silicon Valley alone.[17]

Meanwhile, the folks back east move around a lot less. Four of the five most stable states are in the Northeast: Pennsylvania, New York, New Jersey, and Maine. (West Virginia is the fifth.) These regions are hardly creative backwaters, though; Boston and New York log their fair shares of patents and, along with Philadelphia, are among the biotech giants. New York remains the center of fashion, media, and finance (an industry where many Americans now crave less creativity). Other cities have their niches of genius.

But as Plaut and her team highlight, the way that people practice independence in the Northeast is different from the way they do it in the

West. For example, in their analysis of the websites of venture capital firms (the funders of invention), the researchers discovered that Boston firms stress status and experience more than do San Francisco firms, which instead emphasize egalitarianism and creativity. Boston firms also more frequently mention teams, companies, and other kinds of groups, while the San Francisco VCs focus more on individuals. Even in the highly independent field of venture capital, the Northeast is a shade more interdependent than the West.[18]

The Loss of Depth

Stability may not be the hottest engine of innovation. But it yields different benefits: cooperation, trust, and cohesion within a community. These are the strengths that deep ties bring. They are also the strengths that are diminishing in contemporary America, argues sociologist Robert Putnam in his book *Bowling Alone*. Putnam demonstrates that changes in work, family, and technology are eroding the nation's store of social capital—the networks, norms, and trust that allow people to work together. He also finds that these changes are not affecting all segments of the nation equally. In particular, the right-hand side of the Midwest—Iowa, Kansas, Minnesota, Missouri, Nebraska, North Dakota, and South Dakota—consistently clocks the highest levels of social capital.[19]

Oishi similarly documents that the less peripatetic corners of the country are kinder and gentler. In one study, for instance, he and his colleagues uncovered that people living in more stable ZIP codes are more likely to purchase a license plate whose proceeds support conservation than are people living in less settled communities.[20] To probe further whether and why mobility undercuts altruism, Oishi's research team then randomly assigned college students to either a stable community scenario (groups that worked on four tasks together) or a mobile community condition (groups that reshuffled their members for every task). For the final stage of the experiment, the participants competed against one another in a trivia game for a ten-dollar prize.

The researchers discovered that, compared to participants in the mobile community condition, stable community members offered more help to a struggling coed (actually, an actor planted by the researchers), even though doing so undercut their chances of winning the ten dollars. The researchers also revealed *why* the stable group members acted more generously: these community members felt a stronger sense of belonging to and empathy for their group. Although the researchers did not directly measure independence or interdependence, their results suggest that people in the stable groups felt more interdependent with their new communities, and therefore acted more empathically toward their members than did people in the mobile groups.

Big Box versus Mom and Pop

Oishi himself is a global migrant. A native of Japan, he moved to the United States to pursue his graduate studies, whereupon he made a curious observation: "Individual Americans love uniqueness. But if you look at American suburbs, they are amazingly uniform. You see cookie-cutter developments everywhere, and all the shopping malls have exactly the same stores." In stark contrast, the hamlets of interdependent Japan are all distinct.

"Why, does the U.S. look the same in so many places?" Oishi asked. He sensed that the answer had to do with Americans' wanderlust. Although moving brings the separation and uniqueness that independent selves crave, relocation is hard on a psyche. "You become a stranger in a strange land," he says.

When faced with the stress of strangeness, Oishi reasoned, perhaps Americans do as infants everywhere do: cling to the familiar. But instead of security blankets, mobile Americans turn to Barnes and Noble, Best Buy, Starbucks, and other national chain stores.

"Americans want to pursue their own individual goals," Oishi explains, "and so they've created this landscape where it's easy to move around." Oishi and his coauthors indeed find that the more mobile the state, the more "big box" stores it hosts (even after controlling for income and population). They also see that the more college students moved in their childhoods, the more they preferred national chains to local alternatives.[21]

Although they may revel in their newfound independence, many neophyte Westerners are nostalgic for the quirkiness of their native lands. "I niss the homes that had some style to them, that were built to be missed," ays Goldhor of New England. "I really hate ranch houses, and that's what)0 percent of the homes out here in Colorado are."

VCs and VFWs

Jp a level in the culture cycle, institutions reinforce and result from he independent interactions and individuals of the West. Perhaps the est-documented ecosystem of Western institutions is that of Silicon Val-ey, which produced the greatest uptick in wealth in human history.[22] Named for the silicon microchip, the brain of the modern computer, the rea of Northern California that later became Silicon Valley had a leg p on innovation even before computers came on the scene. The U.S. nilitary was already investing heavily in the area's aerospace and elec-ronics companies, which meant that plenty of talent, money, and infra-tructure were on the ground. A network of law firms then expanded to elp new companies take advantage of business-friendly laws. Venture apital firms stepped in to supply the many-figured funds that fueled the egendary growth of the region's companies. To match expertise with nterprise, headhunters and consultants leapt into the fray. Local universi-ies also got in on the act, forging unprecedented alliances with local in-ustries.[23]

Altogether, these institutions made it remarkably easy to start up a echnology company in Silicon Valley in the latter part of the twentieth entury. These startups, and the multinational behemoths many grew up) be, continue to advance the cause of the independent self through their aily interactions. "Creative people don't wear uniforms," writes Richard lorida in *The Rise of the Creative Class*, so Silicon Valley companies have eplaced the corporate suit with the casual dress code. Creativity is also otoriously difficult to schedule, so many of the area's companies allow exible hours. And to free workers from the everyday business of living) that they can chase their next great idea, many companies offer free ieals, on-site day care, medical services, and other perks.[24]

Rounding out Silicon Valley's innovation-inspiring offerings are prac-ces that encourage demographic diversity, including benefits for same-sex artners. By signaling their openness to diversity, the region's institutions attract open-minded people from an array of backgrounds. The wide variety of thoughts, feelings, and actions that these migrants bring with them then flow into the region's pool of ideas.[25]

The flip side of the hustle and diversity that Western institutions promote are the calm and solidarity that Midwestern institutions support. Compared to the rest of the nation, the Midwest has the most civic organizations of the sort that inspire lifelong memberships among like-minded people. For instance, Moose International, Kiwanis International, and Rotary International are all headquartered in the Midwest. And though the South gets the "Bible Belt" moniker, the Midwest has an equally high number of churches per capita. Midwesterners amply support their institutions, turning out for more club meetings, volunteer opportunities, and elections than do residents of any other region.[26]

Somewhere between the unfettered independence that Western institutions inspire and the cozy interdependence that Midwestern (and, as we will show, Southern) institutions sustain is the tempered independence that Northeastern institutions build. Home to most of the nation's first and oldest institutions, New England and the Mid-Atlantic states are steeped in tradition. Nevertheless, their functions and goals reflect the founding independence of the nation. As the columnist Brian McGrory wrote of Boston, "We are a city shaped by the past that always leads to a better future."[27]

Rebel Yells

More famous than the differences between the West and the rest are the historic divides between the North and the South. About this gulf, Alana knows a fair amount. A native of Memphis, Tennessee, she grew up with dozens of stories of how family members redressed perceived insults with violence. Some of these tales are funny. When Alana's raven-headed great-grandmother discovered a long blonde hair in the zipper of her husband's overalls, for example, the elderly woman said nothing. Instead, she grabbed an axe and hacked the garment to bits. When Alana's very pregnant, very hormonal mother broke down into sobs because she couldn't make the ironing board stay upright, Alana's father defended her honor by tearing apart the insolent device with his bare hands.

But some of Alana's family stories are tragic. For instance, at a University of Arkansas party in 1926, Alana's great-uncle publicly scolded a male classmate for harassing a woman. The insulted classmate drew a gun and shot Alana's great-uncle dead.

Until Alana moved to New England for college, she assumed that all families had lore like this. After all, most of her friends in Memphis did. But she soon discovered that her Southern stories amazed and alarmed her Yankee friends. She also learned that her own reactions to perceived incivilities were peculiar. In response to good-natured teasing, for instance, her roommates did not feel their blood pressure rise, their cheeks flush, and their fists clench. In debates about the finer points of Kant's *Critique of Pure Reason*, her classmates did not experience one another's mid-sentence interruptions as physical assaults. And upon encountering a surly salesperson, her friends did not mutter, "Well, aren't you just as useful as a trapdoor in a canoe?"

After years of comparing notes, Alana learned that many transplanted Southerners similarly concluded that their heads were too hot for the Northeast. They also felt bruised by the low-level rudeness that Yankees constantly dish out. The Southerners who leave the South are usually not the ones who take the most offense when, say, someone starts eating before everyone is served, or when men do not hold doors for women. Nevertheless, after heading North, many Southerners come to appreciate the less-heralded pleasures of their homeland's etiquette: salespeople who go out of their way to help, strangers who greet you on the street, drivers who never use their horns, bosses who observe weekends and holidays, and neighbors who bake cookies to welcome you into your new home.

"There's a sharpness to things here in the Northeast that wasn't there," says Jason Long, also a native Memphian who is now an architect in New York, "a brusqueness in people's demeanor, from the corner-store clerk, to the waiters, to the people I work with. It's easier to feel lonely here."

Southern Swells

Migrating in the other direction, many Northerners discover that they rather like the interdependence of Southern culture cycles. "The people really are friendlier here," notes a Bay Area native now practicing law in Atlanta. He doesn't want to be identified, he says, "because I'd hate for my old colleagues to think that I'm slacking. But come Friday night, work is over and the weekend begins. People make time for family, and sports, and church. And they invite the new guy to come along."

This is the better part of Southern chivalry: the desire to make other people feel good by entertaining them and helping them feel at home. This interdependence is why many Southerners don't just say, "He's fast," or "I'm surprised." Instead, they exclaim, "He's like a scalded dog with ears laid back!" or "Well, knock me down and steal my teeth!" It's also why Southern storytelling, preaching, politicking, and music-making have so powerfully shaped the nation as a whole.[28]

But Southern politeness has its dark side. For centuries, the mythology of well-mannered Southern belles and the protections they required provided many of the excuses for keeping Blacks separate from Whites, lest the former sully the alleged purity of the latter. Even today, the unwritten Southern code of behavior is used to maintain racial, class, and gender divides. Elaborate shibboleths reveal not only whether you know which fork to use or what shade of white to wear after Labor Day, but also who your people are and how much respect they get. Common courtesies sustain injustice in another way: when individuals are bending over backward to be civil to one another, they may be too busy to notice the larger incivilities built into their culture cycles' interactions, institutions, and ideas.

Most contemporary Southerners know that the rest of the country does not think too highly of them, and many feel great shame about their homeland's troubled past. Thus hospitality, writes Southern scholar Diane Roberts, "is also a function of the desire to present the South—where the populace is accustomed to being represented as stupid, backward, poor, prejudiced, and degenerate—as a place full of tremendously nice people who'd gladly give you their last piece of Jimmy Dean sausage."[29] But as transplanted Southerners serve up ever-healthier portions of politeness, many feel an even greater gulf between their kindnesses and others' insults.

The Culture of Honor

In graduate school, Alana learned that her sensitivity to affronts and appreciation for good manners were not crazy, or even unique. Instead, her ways were just part and parcel of the Southern *culture of honor*, a cocktail of violence and politeness that makes the U.S. South a charming place to visit but a slightly dangerous place to live.

For most of U.S. history, the South has been the nation's most violent region, logging the highest rates of homicide, domestic violence, corporal punishment, capital punishment, gun ownership, and support of wars. Yet individual Southerners do not unleash their wrath for just any old reason. Instead, psychologists Richard Nisbett and Dov Cohen find that Southerners disproportionately use violence to protect their reputations and restore their honor. For example, although Southerners comprise less than one-third of the White population of the United States, White Southern men commit 49 percent of lovers-triangle murders (where someone gets killed as the result of one partner cheating on the other) and 40 percent of argument-related homicides. Similarly, among White women, Southerners are responsible for 55 percent of lovers-triangle killings and 52 percent of argument-related murders.[30] These findings add steel of a different sort to the "steel magnolia" archetype, which portrays Southern women as hiding a flinty will beneath their delicate manners.[31]

Southerners also go out of their way to protect the honor of others, which is one reason they are so courteous. Southern politeness isn't just an empty stereotype. In a comparison of thirty-six American cities, psychologist Robert V. Levine and his colleagues discovered that Southerners are the most likely Americans to return a stranger's dropped pen, make change for a quarter, help a blind person cross the street, and retrieve magazines for a person with a hurt leg.[32] Southerners agree that they are kind. In a nationally representative survey of more than three thousand American adults, Southerners rated themselves as more soft-hearted and caring than did residents of any other region.[33]

At the center of this paradoxical mix of hostility and hospitality lies an interdependent self that rises and falls with public opinion. Because reputation is so important to selves in the Southern culture of honor, "Sticks and stones break Southerners' bones, *and* names deeply hurt them," says Cohen. Reputation is also important in the so-called *face cultures* of Asia, where people go to great lengths to save themselves and others from shame and "losing face." But unlike their counterparts in Asia, interdependent selves in the Southern culture of honor don't rely on other people to right a wrong. "It's up to you to respond to the affront," explains Cohen, "not a superior, or the group, or a court."

Without a posse backing them up, Southerners choose their battles wisely. But when they do exact revenge, they do so completely. Hence the adage "A Southerner is polite up until the point when he is mad enough to kill you."

The dynamics of insult, politeness, and violence are different for Northeasterners. Theirs is what Cohen calls a *culture of dignity*, which holds that all selves are born equally good.[34] With a solid self as their birthright, Yankees rely less on the opinions of outsiders in constructing their selves and more on the truths they discover within. (Although recall that Northeasterners are more concerned about social approbation than are Westerners.) More intent on expressing themselves than courting the opinions of others, Northeasterners tend to dispense with the niceties, express their anger early and often, and not take anyone else's guff too personally.

Duck

Cohen and his research team captured the violent politeness of Southern interdependence and the toothless ire of Northeastern independence in a highly entertaining laboratory experiment. Billing their study as a "simulated art therapy session," the researchers invited individual college students (half of them Southern men, half of them Northern men) to spend an hour drawing pictures inspired by their childhoods.

Sounds fun, right? The only problem with this scenario, each man soon learned, was their session's other participant—an obnoxious, six-foot-tall oaf. This fellow participant was actually in league with the researchers—an actor trained to deliver eleven escalating annoyances. Annoyance 1 was innocuous enough: the actor reached across to the participant's desk, took two crayons, and said, "Let me get a couple of your crayons, Slick. I'll give them back later."

But the annoyances quickly became more offensive. Here are examples from the experimenters' script:

> Annoyance 2: [actor crumples a drawing and shoots it at the garbage bin, but hits the participant instead] "Watch out there, Slick."
>
> Annoyance 7: [hitting the participant with another paper wad] "You're sitting there like a sitting duck. Maybe I'll call you Duck instead of Slick."

Annoyance 9: [aiming paper wad at participant] "Duck, you need to duck."

Annoyance 11: [hitting participant with paper wad] "I don't know about your drawings, Slick, but you make a pretty good target."

Throughout the experiment, a researcher watched the proceedings through a live video feed and made observations at regular intervals. Analyses of these observations revealed that Northerners did what Northerners do: they showed their pique early, but never flashed much hotter than their initial warning flare.

Southerners, in contrast, initially showed *less* anger than Northerners. During Annoyances 1 through 5, they seemed amused by the actor's antics. They went along to get along. But by Annoyance 6, their amiability had flipped into full-blown rage. Indeed, two of the Southern participants "physically confronted" the actor, to quote the research report.[35]

Death before Dishonor

Although North-South differences in reactions to insults, the desire for politeness, and notions of the self are large and clear, many people from these regions are not aware of them. "If you ask Southerners about the culture of honor," says psychologist Joseph Vandello, "they can't necessarily articulate the norm. They just know that if someone insults you, you punch him."

The same is true for people everywhere, he adds: "We don't know where we learned the rules, and we might not be able to say the rules at a conscious level, but when the occasion arises, we know how to act." The invisibility of these cultural rules is what makes them so powerful; when you can't explain why you are doing something, you infer that you're doing it because it's the only thing to do.

Yet a quick spin through the culture cycle of the South uncovers the many daily interactions that require and reproduce its unique form of interdependence. Starting in childhood, for example, young Southerners get more spankings from their parents, who in national surveys more strongly agree with statements such as "It is sometimes necessary to discipline a child with a good, hard spanking."[36] Southern children also get more licks from their teachers than do Northern children.[37] Southern adults expect children to be more aggressive—although, once again, not indiscriminately; in one study, for instance, Cohen and Nisbett found that more Southerners than Northerners would want a ten-year-old boy to fight his bullying tormentor.[38]

The years following school also seem to be more violent in the South than in the North. The South has always sent disproportionately more of its young people into the armed forces. In 2007, for instance, the South supplied 43 percent of new recruits to the U.S. military, although it harbored only 36 percent of males between the ages of eighteen and twenty-four.[39] By joining the armed forces, these soldiers put their M-16s where their mouths were: Southerners consistently elect politicians with hawkish platforms.[40]

Aiding and abetting the wide spread of violence is the wide spread of guns, an everyday artifact that makes murderous interactions easier to commit. Whereas 47 percent of Americans as a whole keep guns in their homes, 54 percent of Southerners keep a hearthside firearm.[41]

Southerners are not only more likely to kill one another, but are also more likely to be killed for doing so. Since the death penalty was reinstated in 1976, Southern states have carried out 82 percent of the nation's executions.[42] Yet Southern judges, juries, and media are more lenient toward the perpetrators of honor-related crimes than are their Northern counterparts. And once a murderer has done his time for an honor-related crime, Southern employers are more sympathetic to him than are Northern employers.[43]

Murder is more commonplace in the South than in the North, but it is still a rare event. And given the rules of the Southern culture of honor, trouble is rather preventable, notes the sociologist John Shelton Reed: "The Southerner who can avoid both arguments and adultery is as safe as any other American, and probably safer."[44]

Charm School

All those guns may have another desirable side effect. As author Robert Heinlein noted, "An armed society is a polite society."[45] Guns don't do all the work of keeping the South congenial. To help out, a panoply of daily interactions and artifacts reinforces the importance of good manners and, more broadly, interdependence in Southern culture cycles.

Most obvious to the Yankee ear is how Southerners speak English. Despite the influence of national media, the Southern dialect is still strong. And it's not just a matter of drawing out vowels or swallowing *r*s; Southern speech reveals a deep concern with not offending other people. For example, many Southerners of all ages and ranks still use the honorifics "ma'am" and "sir" to show deference.[46] Southerners also frequently communicate a desire to "avoid imposing their version of the world on others," notes linguist Barbara Johnstone. Whereas a Northerner might say, "Juneau is the capital of Alaska," for instance, a Southerner would soften his assertion by saying, "I reckon that Juneau is the capital of Alaska." And whereas a Northerner's polite request for aid is "Please help," a Southerner's is the less insistent "If you could help, I'd be much obliged."[47]

With their own children, Southern mothers are not so subtle, drilling their charges in the finer points of table manners, dress codes, holiday traditions, family obligations, formal comportment, and the many other domains of etiquette. Despite the centrality of these teachings, Southerners have produced few books on good manners. That's because "Southerners prefer to learn proper behavior from mothers rather than from books," historian Charles Reagan Wilson explains.[48] As Southern mothers enter the workforce, however, they are increasingly enlisting finishing schools, etiquette classes, and beauty pageants to help with the rearing of genteel offspring.

When it comes to entertaining guests, Southerners are less shy about consulting printed references, notes Diane Roberts: "The success of *Southern Living* magazine, which was selling 'lifestyle' years before Martha Stewart waxed her first camellia, testifies to the near obsession with 'proper' entertaining shared by the middle classes across the color line in the South."[49] This obsession endures throughout the lifespan and no matter the circumstances, as revealed in titles such as *Being Dead Is No Excuse: The Official Southern Ladies Guide to Hosting the Perfect Funeral.*[50]

Institutions, and the Lack Thereof

Southerners and Northerners do not have to wake up every morning and decide which practices and artifacts to interact with or, more generally, which kinds of selves to construct. Instead, institutions, especially laws, make some actions and selves much easier to realize than others. For example, Southern teachers are more likely to spank their students because laws protect their right to do so in all but two Southern states (Virginia and West Virginia).[51] In contrast, most Northern states have outlawed corporal punishment in schools. Southern state laws also protect the use of force to defend property more so than do Northern state laws, and erect fewer obstacles to buying firearms.[52] And underlying the higher number of executions in the South is the fact that all but one Southern state (West Virginia) allows capital punishment.

Although the South is noteworthy for institutions that endorse violence, it is even more noteworthy for its historical lack of institutions. Indeed, the lawlessness of the South is a major force in its culture cycles, driving the region's violence, politeness, and interdependence.

The lawlessness of the South goes back five hundred years, when Europeans began making incursions into what would later become the United States. The main settlers of New England and the Mid-Atlantic states were English, Irish-Catholic, and other European agriculturalists and artisans. Farmers in the habit of cooperating, these settlers worked together to establish the political and legal systems that would ultimately free them to pursue their independent interests.[53]

But the main settlers of the American South were Scotch Irish mostly from the borderlands between Scotland and England. Because the forbidding climate and terrain of their native lands did not allow for much farming, the Scotch Irish were pastoralists—pig herders, to be exact. Their skill at squeezing a living out of unforgiving environments served them well not only in the old country, but also on the Southern frontier.[54]

Even when the Scotch Irish settled in areas of the United States that could support agriculture, they tended to stick with herding and slash-and-burn horticulture. This was a fateful choice. Although advanced agriculture is a risky business, farmers enjoy the security and stability that come with tying their wealth to the land.

But for herders such as the Scotch Irish, wealth wandered freely and widely on four legs. Often poor, they were sometimes tempted to nab a neighbors' animals. But if someone nicked their pigs—the seminal event in the Hatfield-McCoy feud—most Southerners couldn't go crying to the law, because there *was* no law. The low population density of the region meant that lawmakers and law enforcers were few and far between. When done wrong, a Southerner had to take matters into his own hands.[55]

Vigilante justice is seldom as much fun as it seems in the movies, so Southerners devised a method to deter would-be pig thieves: cultivate a reputation for being badasses. This entailed reacting violently not just to major threats to property, but also to the slightest threats to reputation. Fear of instant and cruel retribution could protect a Southerner's property where the short arm of the law couldn't reach and his own eyesight fell short. His property, moreover, included his livestock, his womenfolk, and, as the South's "peculiar institution" of slavery spread, his slaves. To avoid the wrath of the Southerner, elaborate manners developed.

Meanwhile, back in the more densely populated agricultural Northeast, institutions to protect the individual flourished. In case of theft or other affronts, Yankees could turn to the police and the courts to set matters right. Not needing to flex their tough-guy reputations, they could tolerate other people letting off a little steam. And they could mouth off without worrying about getting shot down like a dog in the street.

The Scotch Irish did not invent the culture of honor. Herding economies the world over combine a sensitivity to insult and willingness to aggress with impeccable manners. Nisbett and Cohen list just a few of these groups: Sardinians, Corsicans, Druze, Bedouins, and many of the traditional societies of Africa and the steppes of Eurasia and North America.[56] Another inhospitable and lawless terrain, the poor inner city of many U.S. metropolises is also thought to encourage cultures of honor, where insults must be answered with violence, and residents follow strict politeness codes so as not to raise the hackles of their heavily armed neighbors.[57]

Modern Tribes

At first blush, Southerners' scrappiness may seem to smack of a more independent self, while Northerners' live-and-let-live attitude may seem to suggest a more interdependent I. But as the world grows smaller and cross-national studies get larger, scientists are seeing that punishing outsiders to protect insiders is more typical of interdependent selves, while adopting a middle-gray neutrality toward everyone is more typical of independent selves.

For instance, a research team headed by Simon Gächter, an economist, watched students in sixteen cities all over the world play a classic economics game in which groups of four students (all strangers) first had to use a complex set of rules to distribute tokens among themselves. In subsequent rounds, each player could punish the greedy by taking back tokens. Punished players could then either restore the peace by giving more tokens to fellow players or retaliate by taking away their loot.

In independent Boston, the students readily penalized the greedy and, when penalized themselves, responded with generosity. So did students in western European countries such as the United Kingdom, Germany, and Denmark. But half a world away, in the more interdependent cultures of Turkey, Saudi Arabia, and Russia, the play was a little rougher. Students were not only less generous initially but also more vindictive when punished.[58]

"In these societies," explains Gächter, "you cooperate with people inside your network, which is organized along family and friendship lines." But in the anonymity of the lab, "everyone is an outsider," he says, so the nastiness ensues.[59]

Make Your Self at Home

No matter which region they call home, Americans still have a lot in common with each other. Many of us watch the same television shows and movies, celebrate the same national holidays, obey the same federal laws, pledge allegiance to the same flag, speak the same language, even dine at the same food chains and shop at the same franchises. Because of these shared institutions and interactions, we often underestimate just how large the differences between the culture cycles of the West, Midwest, Northeast, and South really are. So when a new job or promising relationship crops up in another locale, we more readily leap upon it than do people in many other nations.

American corporations also worry less about transferring their workers than do employers in other countries. For instance, when Walmart attempted to expand to Germany, the company assumed that German executives would go where the jobs were. They wouldn't, which left Walmart scrambling for talent. This is one of many reasons Walmart failed to break into the German market.[60]

Perhaps Americans should adopt a similar wariness toward picking up and moving on. Though some migrants such as Lisa Radloff and Rob Goldhor wind up loving their adopted homes, many others find that their selves just won't align with their new culture cycles (at least at first). Transplanted to the more independent coasts, many interdependent selves from the Midwest and South find themselves craving the deeper relationships, clearer roles, and stronger traditions back home. Independent pegs likewise labor to fit into interdependent holes, as they struggle to pursue their individual interests, express their uniqueness, and exercise choice.

Just as culture cycles erect and echo these different selves, so, too, can selves use culture cycles to make cross-regional sojourns less traumatic. At the institutional level, employers, schools, and other organizations can take the edge off relocation stress by linking transplants hailing from the same region. For instance, Princeton University hosts both a West Coast students' club and a Southern Society.[61] "International students have all sorts of resources for adjusting to life at Princeton," a club founder told the *Daily Princetonian*, "but no one seems to realize that it might be just as hard for those of us from the other end of the country to feel comfortable." Organizations such as these give migrants a secure and familiar base from which to explore their new environments.

Region-hoppers can also do a lot at the interaction and individual levels of the culture cycle to make their selves at home. As is so often the case in psychology, admitting the problem is the first step. Migrants should acknowledge that regional cultures are real, and do matter. Armed with this insight, Southerners and Midwesterners transplanted to the coasts should take a walk on the independent side by opening their minds to the new ways around them. "People who are more open are going to experience much less difficulty acclimating to the new environment," says psychologist Peter Jason Rentfrow, who studies regional differences in personality. "Their curiosity makes it easier [for them] to overcome some of the obstacles." For Southerners in particular, opening your mind to the possibility that Northerners are often just venting their spleens rather than personally attacking you can go a long way toward taking the sting out of Yankee gruffness.

In return, the independent selves on the coasts should extend some interdependence to their friends from flyover country. Rather than honking at the car with Mississippi plates doing the speed limit in the fast lane, for instance, the Pennsylvania driver should first consider how insulting his actions might seem. Before canceling drinks with the new coworker from Indiana, the Oregonian should think about how hurt the Hoosier might feel. And before sharing that great new West Virginia joke, the New Yorker should pause and reflect that, for some interdependent Southerners, them's fighting words.

In contrast, the independent souls from the coasts will need to get in touch with their interdependent sides to make the most out of their spells in Dixie or the Heartland. These transplants will probably not need to make the first move; neighbors and coworkers will likely extend invitations to dinner or a weekend event. And when that weekend event is "church," accept it. Your interdependent friend isn't trying to convert you; she's just trying to plug you into one of the most important social networks in town.

The interdependent selves of our nation's interior, in turn, have to cut the coastals some slack when they show up late, empty-handed, and underdressed. They likely aren't putting on airs, defying tradition, or cutting a figure. Bless their hearts, they just don't know any better.

Dress the Part

Mark Zuckerberg does know better. A Northeasterner by birth, the cofounder and CEO of Facebook comes from a culture that knows how to wear a suit. But now a Californian, Zuckerberg is almost as famous for sporting a gray hooded sweatshirt as he is for making $17 billion before the age of thirty. In Silicon Valley, his attire isn't a problem; Steve Jobs broke the CEO dress code a generation before when he adopted a black turtleneck and jeans as his power suit.

But on buttoned-down Wall Street, Zuck's hoodie causes an uproar. The Northeast establishment sees the young entrepreneur's refusal to don at least a jacket when he is in New York as a sign of disrespect. Potential investors worry that Zuckerberg is unreliable and immature.[62]

Should Zuckerberg shed his casual threads to make nice with the Northeast crowd? Or is he right to stick to his Silicon Valley guns and flaunt his independence?

At the risk of betraying our own Silicon Valley allegiances, we think

Zuckerberg (and all culture-crossers) should strategically deploy both his elves. Zuckerberg may think his hoodie is critical to his independence, ust as Jobs regarded his own sartorial choices as necessary for his success. Yet as Jobs's biographers now note, the Apple founder's stubborn individuality may sometimes have hindered him more than it helped.[63]

By being interdependent in interdependent places, Zuckerberg could eceive even more support for his independence. The advice of Ambrose Bierce, another stridently individualistic region-trotter, still applies: "When n Rome, do as Rome does." This flexibility can win friends and reap prosperity not only in Rome, Italy, but also in Rome, Georgia; Rome, New York; Rome, Indiana; and Rome, Oregon.

CHAPTER 7

Getting Religion

Faith Cultures

The conservative Protestants vying for the 2012 Republican presidential nomination left many mainline Protestants wondering wha had happened to their religion, not to mention their country. Fo most of the United States' history, science had been the helpmate of Protestants, who viewed it as a gift from God to help them learn about thei world and make more pious choices. Those years of persecution back i Europe had also impressed upon them the benefits of building a high wal between religion and government.[1]

Yet here was Ron Paul, a Southern Baptist, rejecting evolution as jus "a theory."[2] Rick Perry, who attends a Southern Baptist church, similarl told a schoolboy that evolution is "a theory that is out there—and it's gc some gaps."[3] Michele Bachmann, an evangelical Lutheran, dismissed nc only evolution, but also climate change, calling it "voodoo, nonsense, ho kum, a hoax."[4] Rick Santorum, a conservative Catholic with a stalwar conservative Protestant following, also called climate change "a hoax." Mitt Romney, a Mormon, acknowledged that the weather is getting weirc but wondered whether humans were causing the change.[6] And though h sometimes seems to believe in both climate change and evolution, New Gingrich, an evangelical Lutheran turned Southern Baptist now Catholic nevertheless betrayed the scientific community by implying that researchers kill children for stem cell research.[7]

Meanwhile, conservative Protestants were wondering what had happened to *their* religion and *their* country. Unlike their mainline brethren, conservative Protestants consider the Bible the inerrant word of God, seek "born again" experiences that bring them closer to that God, aim to convert other people, and think that religious teachings should guide daily life, including education and politics.[8] Understanding the United States to be "one nation, under God," these Americans want their laws to reflect Christian values and beliefs, rather than scientific findings and theories. Yet here was their president saying that two men should be able to legally wed, even though the Bible often does not smile upon such configurations. Here was a Supreme Court upholding abortion, even though the Bible says, "Thou shalt not kill." And here were legions of lawmakers enforcing the separation of religion and government, following in the footsteps of America's only Catholic president, John F. Kennedy, who said, "I believe in an America where the separation of church and state is absolute."[9]

Santorum reported that when he first read these words, he "almost threw up."[10]

How is it that the two sides of the Protestant coin are now diametrically opposed? At the heart of their acrimony, we see yet another clash between independence and interdependence. Although both groups sail under the Protestant flag, their culture cycles make and mirror decidedly different selves. On the one hand, the group that came to be known as mainline Protestants were the original independent selves in the United States. Firing up the Protestant Reformation in sixteenth-century Germany, their ancestors ditched the popes and priests of the Catholic Church in favor of direct relationships with a personal god. (See chapter 2 for more about the Protestant Reformation.) The Puritans brought their zest for independence with them when they settled the United States, where they formed the first of the mainline Protestant branches, which now include the Methodist, Lutheran, Presbyterian, Baptist, and Anglican/Episcopal churches. For some four centuries, mainline Protestant groups were the most popular religions in the country, and now claim some 18.1 percent of the population.[11]

On the other hand, the sects that came to make up conservative Protestantism took a turn for interdependence. In the conservative Protestant tent you'll find evangelical and fundamentalist groups such as the Southern Baptist, Assembly of God, Church of God in Christ, and Pentecostal churches. Compared with their mainline counterparts, these interdependent selves have a greater yen for warm family relations,[12] tight community bonds,[13] clear social hierarchies,[14] and traditional moral codes.[15]

Conservative Protestants also want more God in their lives, more of the time, than do mainline Protestants. Their God is the kind of deity you want to have around. As anthropologist Tanya Luhrmann relates in her book *When God Talks Back*, He is "a deeply human, even vulnerable God who loves us unconditionally and wants nothing more than to be our friend, our best friend, as loving and personal and responsive as a best friend in America should be." The conservative Protestant relationship with this God is not like the distant, abstract ties that many mainline Protestants maintain with their God. Instead, it is "the free and easy companionship of two boys swinging their feet on a bridge over a stream."[16]

But just as conservative fathers both hug and spank their children more than mainline fathers,[17] the conservative God is at once warmer and more wrathful than the mainline God. In their book *America's Four Gods*, sociologists Paul Froese and Christopher Bader recount that many conservative Protestants think of their God as angrier and more punishing, while many mainline Protestants conceive of their deity as more benevolent and forgiving.[18] The conservative God uses his stormy side for interdependent ends, keeping His flock from wandering too far from traditional roles and rules.

Numbers testify to the appeal of this more intimate, personal, and present divine: conservative Protestants have supplanted their mainline counterparts as the leading denomination in America, claiming some 26.3 percent of the population.[19] That number jumps to 34.9 percent when scholars include both Mormon and historically Black churches, which share some of the same practices and beliefs as conservative Protestants.[20]

As conservative Protestants continue to challenge the mainline's four-hundred-year-old foothold on the souls of Americans, we predict many more clashes of the Protestants. The tighter binding of religion and politics has not helped matters. Over the past three decades, many conservative Protestants and their interdependent allies (e.g., conservative Catholics such as Rick Santorum) have aligned with Republicans, while many mainline Protestants and their independent fellow travelers (e.g., the nonreligious, who make up a full 16.1 percent of the country,[21] and secular Catholics and Jews) have sided with Democrats.[22] Consequently, politics is no longer about how to steer the nation forward; it's about who has the better soul. Because discussions about the relative goodness of souls rarely end well, the two sides of this cultural divide are now shouting past each other, rather than working together to lead the country.[23]

The United States can find some solace in its past. The nation has a long, relatively peaceful history of incredible religious diversity. Although Protestants have always been the majority religion, they have never been the only game in town. Catholics, who we shall show are a more interdependent set, carved out a niche from the start, and now make up 24 percent of the American population.[24] Another interdependent religious group, Jews, was also present at the founding of the United States, with a band of twenty-three arriving from Spain and Portugal in 1654.[25] At 1.7 percent of the population, Jews tie with Mormons as the third-largest religious community in the United States.[26]

When we look at the culture cycles of these groups, we see ways that mainline and conservative Protestants can mend their fences. Mainline Protestants and their independent allies must access their interdependence to detox their discourse with conservatives. Rather than scorning the more conservative set, mainline Protestant institutions, interactions, and individuals must extend empathy and respect so that the two sides can find common ground. In many cases, independent religions can easily tune their messages for more interdependent ears.

At the same time, conservative Protestants and their confreres must step up their independence to meet their adversaries halfway. Allowing dissent within their institutions, including debate in their interactions, and encouraging critical thinking among their individual members would all hasten the healing of religious rifts.

As mainline and conservative Protestants align their culture cycles, they can hone better ways to work with growing religious minorities, including Muslims (0.6 percent of the population), Buddhists (0.7 percent), and Hindus (0.4 percent)—all whose culture cycles sustain and stem from more interdependent selves.[27] (See chapter 9 for more about Islam, Buddhism, and Hinduism.) Likewise, observers in other countries that are contending with conflicts between independent and interdependent religious groups can apply our approach to their own culture clashes.

Before delving into the details of America's two sorts of Protestants, we drop back in time to examine how the culture cycles of different religions feed and flow from different notions of the self. This story begins long before the Abrahamic religions (i.e., Judaism, Christianity, and Islam) emerged, at a time when humans were dodging glaciers to become the species we know and love today.

More Interdependent Than Thou

Until the Late Pleistocene (about fifteen thousand years ago), people were still hunting and gathering. Because they lived pretty much hand to mouth, they did not amass wealth. And as everyone knew everyone else (indeed, most people were related), Pleistocene neighbors were "probably pretty nice to each other," says psychologist Ara Norenzayan.[28]

Although these hunter-gatherers had deities, their gods were largely uninterested in what the humans were up to. They weren't *moral* gods, says Norenzayan. Instead, "these gods seemed indifferent to human affairs. Many were like your crazy grandfather. You know he exists, but you don't pay much attention to him. Sometimes he acts up and does crazy things. You try to calm him down. You give him food. But you don't really take him that seriously."[29]

But then *Homo sapiens* started settling in towns and growing food. With better nutrition and technology, populations boomed. Small bands of relatives became big towns of strangers who, like many people today, were loath to meddle in the affairs of people they did not know. With extra food, people now had stuff to accumulate and, thus, to covet. Lying, cheating, fighting, and stealing entered the scene.

To keep from self-destructing, these larger, anonymous communities needed an institution that would induce people to cooperate. A fatherly eye in the sky fit the bill. All of a sudden, "Watchful gods were everywhere," says Norenzayan, "and they became much more serious. They started punishing wrongdoing. They became supernatural monitors who were intimately involved in human affairs."

As cultures with these moral gods became larger and more successful, they crowded out the older, smaller communities with crazy-grandfather gods. Modern religion was born. And as it linked people in relationships, required them to adjust to a shared moral code, and rooted them in communities and traditions, religion became a major force for interdependence.

Fast-forwarding to the twenty-first century, Norenzayan and his colleagues show that contemporary humans still react to even subtle evocations of divinity by straightening up and flying right. In one study, for example, he and psychologist Azim F. Shariff first asked college students (and, later, older adults) to unscramble sentences that had either religious words (such as *spirit*, *divine*, and *God*) or neutral words embedded in them. All the participants then took part in a classic economics game where they divided ten dollars between themselves and another participant (who was actually a confederate in cahoots with the researchers). The researchers found that just reading a few random religious words led participants to divide the money more fairly than did reading the neutral words.[30]

Studies that measure personality also suggest that religious people are more interdependent than nonreligious folks. For instance, completing a meta-analysis of more than seventy-one studies from nineteen countries, psychologist Vassilis Saroglou and his colleagues discovered that the more religious people are, the more their personalities are agreeable and conscientious—that is, the more they wish to get along with others and do what is right. Perhaps this is not surprising, given that even the most stridently independent forms of Protestantism entail getting together with a community to worship the same deity, perform the same rituals, share the same beliefs, and preserve the same traditions.[31]

Although scientific studies cannot determine whether these exertions please a deity, they do show that religion confers health and well-being upon its practitioners. No matter their denomination, religious people have more friends, suffer fewer illnesses, feel more happiness, and live longer lives than their godless counterparts.[32] Religion is good medicine for those who take it. And even for those who don't, having religious neighbors can be a boon. Compared to people who are not part of a religious community, those who are give more money to charity, donate more of their time, and are more active in community life.[33]

Think Right or Act Right?

Now let's jump ahead some fifteen thousand years to another great parting of religious ways, this time between Christians and Jews. For many Americans, the closest association with the word *Jewish* is the word *guilt*. Yet if President Jimmy Carter is any indication, Christians also haul around their fair share of remorse. In a 1976 interview with *Playboy* magazine, Carter (then the governor of Georgia) confessed, "I've looked on a lot of women with lust." So far, nothing unusual there. But then the Baptist leader concluded, "I've committed adultery in my heart many times."

This way of thinking strikes psychologist Adam Cohen as strange. "For Jews," he says, "if you're just thinking about doing something bad, it doesn't have moral significance so long as you don't act on it." In other words, as long as you do the right thing, contemplating doing the wrong thing is harmless.

But to Carter, just thinking about sinning was a sin. Our former president isn't alone, and he wasn't just sharing his personal philosophy. Instead, he was quoting the New Testament: "But I say unto you," Jesus commanded in his Sermon on the Mount, "That whosoever looketh on a woman to lust after her hath committed adultery with her already in his heart."[34] Perhaps reflecting the depth of his faith, Carter was quoting scripture to America's favorite nudie mag.

Cohen wondered how deep these differences in religious dogma drill into individual psyches. So, with psychologist Paul Rozin, he set out to discover whether Christians (in particular, Protestants) and Jews indeed think about morality differently. In a series of studies, the researchers asked participants to read about characters who were *thinking* about doing something naughty (having an affair, poisoning a professor's dog) and about a character who did nice things but had naughty thoughts (taking care of parents, but thinking ill of them). Next, participants gave their impressions of these characters.

Cohen and Rozin found that the Jewish participants evaluated characters with bad thoughts but good deeds much more positively than did the Protestants. This was not because the Jewish participants let sinners off lightly; indeed, Jews disdained an actual adulterer just as much as did Protestants. Instead, what drove the differences between Protestants and Jews were their beliefs: Jews really don't care what's happening under the hood as long as people's deeds are good. Protestants, in contrast, pay just as much attention to the action between a person's ears as to their actions in the world.[35]

In addition, Cohen and his team find that Protestants more firmly believe that people can control their thoughts, and that thoughts compel actions, but Jews see thoughts as less controllable and less consequential. "Judaism says that people have good and bad impulses," says Cohen, "and you just try to do the best you can."

Another set of Cohen's studies highlights that, in matters of religion, Jews pay more attention to the traditions and people surrounding them (an interdependent tendency), while Protestants pay more attention to what's going on inside themselves, and between themselves and God (a more independent way of being). In one study, Jewish and Protestant adults talked about a moment that changed their lives forever. Cohen's research team then coded whether these narratives mentioned God, community, both God and community, or neither.

In this narrative, for example, a Protestant participant offers a God-centered story:

> The most important experience in my life was the moment that I first accepted that Jesus Christ really was God Himself. . . . I was angry because I knew that I wouldn't be able to go on living however I wanted. . . . In spite of all my anger and frustration, I put my trust in Him for the first time.

And in this narrative, a Jewish participant focuses on his community:

> When my brother died my father started attending *minyan* [Jewish services] every day. He said it comforted him greatly. I was aware that it was the rituals and other men there that made him feel better—not any idea that God

> had intended this. . . . I understood then that my human relationships were all that gave meaning to my life.

Across 126 participants, Cohen found that Jews shared more stories about community, while Protestants shared more narratives about God.[36]

Argue Together or Pray Alone?

Jews and Christians come by their different selves honestly. The daily interactions of both religions scaffold their distinct ways of being. This is all the more remarkable considering how many daily interactions Jews and Christians originally had in common. Both Abrahamic religions, Christianity and Judaism share a foundational text—what Christians call the Old Testament and Jews call the *Tanakh*. How they use this text, however, diverges. Christians feel free to interpret the Bible themselves—no fancy scholars are necessary. This results in a more literal, concrete interpretation of scripture.

In contrast, for Jews, "there are multiple levels of interpretation of religious texts," says Cohen. For instance, in one interpretative method, called *gematria*, scholars substitute letters with numbers, and then look for patterns. Another method entails looking for connections between the same word across different texts. "These methods are helpful because there are parts in the Bible that seem to conflict," Cohen notes, such as the two creation stories in the book of Genesis.

Was Eve made from clay or Adam's rib? Was the world created in six days or one? Was God pleased or displeased with his handiwork? Jewish scholarship is more about grappling with such questions and inconsistencies than about resolving them, argues psychologist Edward Sampson. In contrast, much of Christian scholarship, especially Protestant scholarship, is about finding *the single correct* answer among the inconsistencies.[37]

Jews' greater emphasis on questioning, relative to Christians' greater emphasis on answering, is apparent not only in religious practices, but also in earthlier pursuits. The studies of psychologists Kaiping Peng and Richard Nisbett suggest that Jews more readily employ "dialectical thinking"—accepting contradictions—than do Christians.

Peng and Nisbett stumbled upon this finding by accident. In one of their early studies, they discovered that an encyclopedia of Chinese proverbs contained far more dialectical sayings—"too humble is half proud," "beware of your friends, not your enemies"—than did a comparable American proverb book, which almost exclusively contained more straightforward adages such as "for example is no proof" and "one against all is certain to fail."[38]

The researchers wanted to test whether Chinese participants preferred the dialectical proverbs while European-American participants preferred the consistent ones. Being good scientists, though, they needed a control group of proverbs that were neither Chinese nor American, to rule out the possibility that participants simply preferred whichever proverbs were more familiar to them. To their delight, the researchers discovered that a book of Yiddish proverbs also featured many dialectical sayings. As was the case with Chinese proverbs, Chinese participants liked the Yiddish dialectical proverbs more than the Yiddish nondialectical proverbs.

"Jewish folk beliefs seem to be very much like Chinese folk beliefs: there are two sides to everything, and the world is full of change and uncertainty," says Peng. He sees a connection between this more dialectical way of thinking and a more interdependent view of the self: "When your self is defined by relationships, contexts, and histories, you don't think of yourself as fixed. Instead, you have different aspects of your self, and some aspects may be contradictory."[39]

Given or Chosen?

The finding that Jews and Christians hold different worldviews and self-views is not surprising, writes Sampson. Like a younger sibling fighting his way out of an older sibling's shadow, Christianity had to find its own niche in the Jewish world. It did so partly by promoting a more independent notion of self, one that could arrive at truth by itself, rather than by relating with others, the past, or the environment.[40]

So Christians ditched Jewish dietary laws and many Sabbath customs. Though they did not discard the Old Testament, their New Testament revised many of the Old's teachings. For instance, Jesus' Sermon on the Mount is a rejoinder to the Ten Commandments. Whereas the old text stressed behavior, the new text stressed feelings and thoughts. For Jesus, it was no longer enough not to kill; you must not even *feel* hatred toward people. It was no longer enough not to sleep with your neighbor's wife; you must not even *think* about sleeping with your neighbor's wife.

In response to Christianity, Judaism dug in its heels, holding fast to its own, more interdependent doctrines and practices. As Tevye says in *Fiddler on the Roof*, "Because of our tradition, every one of us knows who he is and what God expects him to do."[41] And though Tevye is no Jewish scholar, the Yiddish playwright who created him, Sholem Aleichem, channeled Jewish culture's regard for history and ritual.

That regard starts before birth; Christians are made, but Jews are usually born. As a religion mainly of descent rather than assent, Orthodox and Conservative Judaism holds that a person is a Jew only if his or her mother is a Jew. Although Judaism does offer a conversion option, so-called "Jews by choice" are the exception, not the rule. When an adolescent boy becomes a Bar Mitzvah (and, more recently, an adolescent girl becomes a Bat Mitzvah), he does so mostly to learn about the roles, responsibilities, and traditions of Judaism so that he may completely participate in the Jewish community.

Being a Christian, on the other hand, requires individual choice. Just because your parents are Christian does not mean that you are. Instead, your parents must choose to baptize you. And sometimes even that isn't enough; conservative Protestant denominations require adherents to "accept Jesus Christ as [their] personal savior" through confirmations, adult baptisms, and public testimonials.

"In Judaism, doing something because it's tradition is enough and even valued," Cohen concludes. "But in many Protestant denominations, you have to find a personal reason to do what you're doing."

Cohen, Peng, Sampson, and other scholars who compare Jews to other groups do so gingerly, and with good reason. Centuries of anti-Semitism, culminating in the Holocaust, show how such comparisons can turn invidious. As a result, many well-intentioned people have worked overtime to argue that Jews are no different from anyone else.

Yet a careful examination of the culture cycles at work among Jews and Christians reveals that the ideas, institutions, interactions, and I's of these two groups are decidedly different. Shining a light on Christian ways further reveals why these differences may have been interpreted as essential, racial, and therefore grounds for violent action: the independent ways of thinking to which Protestants hew can lead to essentialist thinking. Many Christians, especially Protestants, think behavior comes from stable internal traits, see group behavior as the sum of individual behaviors, and thus view group differences as internal and stable.

Perhaps by applying a more interdependent style of thinking to the question of why people are different, Christians and Jews alike can better appreciate how contexts, histories, environments, and one another shape and reflect individual psyches. This more interdependent approach may then lead to more peace-promoting culture cycles.

Catholics in the Middle

Some 1,500 years after Jews and Christians went their separate ways, Protestants and Catholics set off on different paths. As we shall see, Protestant culture cycles produced and proceeded from a more independent self, while Catholic culture cycles reinforced and resulted from a more interdependent self.

For much of U.S. history, Protestant Americans considered Catholics to be the foreigners in their fold. This perception wasn't completely wrong. The American Catholic Church is largely made up of successive waves of immigrant groups: first Germans, then Irish people, then Italians, then Latinos and Filipinos.[42] Partly because of their large immigrant contingent, Catholics have also been the poorest religious group in the United States.[43] Yet since the election of Kennedy in 1962, Catholics have secured their place in the American mainstream. Non-Hispanic Catholics are now among the most upwardly mobile people in America.[44]

Nevertheless, Catholics still feel slightly out of step with the United States' predominantly Protestant ways. In the 1990s, cultural psychologists began bottling exactly what is different about Catholics. They are finding that, for all their assimilation and mainstream success, Catholics harbor a more interdependent sense of self than do mainline Protestants.

Among the first to examine Catholics' more interdependent selves under the bright lights of the laboratory was psychologist Jeffrey Sanchez-Burks. He invited Protestant and Catholic men to complete a task while dressed either in dress shirts and ties (the business condition) or in Hawaiian shirts (the casual condition). Thus bedecked, the participants listened to recordings of positive-emotion words (for instance, *lively*, *hope*, and *laugh*) and negative-emotion words (for example, *rude*, *evil*, and *horrid*). After each word, participants had to judge whether the word's meaning was pleasant or unpleasant.

The catch was this: sometimes, the word's intonation did not match its meaning. For example, *evil* lilted with brightness and cheer, while *laugh* sank with dread and despair. In these cases of mismatched sound and meaning, Sanchez-Burks wanted to know how much the word's social and emotional connotations interfered with participants' ability to judge its meaning.

In the casual condition, Protestants and Catholics struggled equally with the mismatched tones and meanings. But in the business condition, Protestants showed a unique ability to tune out the socioemotional input and home in on the information. Catholics, in contrast, could not as easily ignore the human, feeling side of the recording, and had much slower reaction times when words and intonations did not match no matter what they were wearing.

Sanchez-Burks concludes that, while on the job, Protestants check their hearts at the door. As we will discuss in the next section, they aren't doing this to be unkind. Instead, they are simply following what Sanchez-Burks terms the Protestant relational ideology: that is, "beliefs dictating that attentiveness to relational concerns ought to be restricted in work-centered contexts." With limited exposure to this ideology, Catholics more readily wear their hearts on their sleeves in the workplace.[45]

Relative to Catholics, Protestants' greater independence is also apparent in how they describe everyday behavior. As we discussed in the introduction and chapter 2, making so-called situational attributions for everyday behavior is a more interdependent style that assumes people are driven largely by relational concerns and environmental influences. It's okay to say that your mother or the devil made you do it. Making so-called dispositional attributions, in contrast, is a more independent style that assumes people are driven largely by their internal traits and preferences. For this sort of self, it's best to say that your behavior sprang from inside.

To study the attribution styles of Catholics and Protestants, Cohen and colleagues asked participants to read about two characters who did something good (a pharmaceutical executive who donated malaria medicine and a professional baseball player who volunteered at a camp for poor kids) and two characters who did something bad (a doctor who hid a mistake that led to a patient's death and a public official who took bribes). Participants then rated how much they agreed with internal explanations for each character's actions (e.g., character, attitude, temperament) and external explanations (e.g., social atmosphere, social norms).[46]

The researchers found that Protestants made more internal attributions than did Catholics, as predicted. They also dug a little deeper to figure out why Protestants have this attributional style, and discovered that Protestants believe more strongly in souls, and worry more about their condition, than do Catholics. "Protestants had been handed a fearsome mandate by Luther," the researchers write. "They as individuals, and not the church, were now responsible for the condition of their own souls." So Protestants tend to pay more attention to the inner working of themselves and other people than do Catholics.

Of course, Catholics also believe that people have souls, and they also worry about them. But Catholic teachings hold that participating in the sacraments is a fine way to attain salvation. Indeed, the researchers report, the Catechism of the Catholic Church includes fifty-four entries for the words *sacraments* and *sacramentals* but only six entries for the word *soul*.[47]

Although more interdependent than Protestants, Catholics seem not to be quite as interdependent as Jews. The most direct evidence for Catholics' more interdependent notion of self comes from Cohen's studies on self and religion. As was the case with Jews, Catholics felt that religion was more about participating in rituals, traditions, and community and less about having a personal relationship with God. On a few measures, Catholics even tied with Jews on the more interdependent measures. But on most indices, Catholics were between Protestants and Jews.[48]

By the Book or per the Pope?

Examining the different practices, artifacts, and institutions of Catholics and Protestants has been the pastime of many social scientists. Plotting these findings reveals several forces that have maintained and reflected an independent self among Protestants and an interdependent self among Catholics.

Perhaps the most famous work on the ways of Protestants was Max Weber's *The Protestant Work Ethic and the Spirit of Capitalism.* Weber's jumping-off point was a slightly indelicate question: Why are Protestants so much richer than Catholics? His answer was that Protestants harbor a special set of beliefs called the Protestant work ethic. One of these beliefs is the notion that people have a "calling," a heaven-chosen line of work. Because the idea of the calling elevated work from a necessary evil to a moral imperative, everyone was suddenly willing to work a lot harder.

A second wealth-accruing belief peculiar to the early Protestants—also known by their less fun name, the Puritans—is that people's spiritual fate was predestined, that God had already chosen who would go to heaven or hell. On its surface, this idea would seem to be bit of a buzz kill for the laboring Protestant. Instead, though, its effect was to make people not only work harder, but also consume less, and less conspicuously. This was because Protestants came to view worldly success (that is, wealth) as a sign of spiritual fitness and, conversely, to view worldly failure (that is, poverty) as a sign of spiritual bankruptcy.

A third belief that contributed not only to Protestants' success, but also to their slightly frosty work style, was that concerning oneself with the feelings of coworkers would detract from one's calling. So Protestants adopted the Protestant Relational Ideology, which is, in short: Don't mix business with pleasure. All work and no frivolity makes for a lot of productivity. This is why Protestants quickly became the most successful capitalists and the richest Europeans, Weber argues.[49]

More recently, economists Sascha O. Becker and Ludger Woessmann identified a different route from Martin Luther to Protestant prosperity. During the Holy Roman Empire, clerics did most of the reading in Europe. And they did it in Latin. The early Protestants realized that if they were to have an unmediated relationship with God, they needed to get literate. As a classical education was a luxury that most could not afford, the early Protestant Church undertook to translate the Bible into local languages. It then set about teaching converts to read by building schools and haranguing parents. Consequently, Becker and Woessmann show, the emerging Protestant world had much higher rates of literacy than the surrounding Catholic world—a trend that persisted until the twentieth century.[50]

Reading does not have to be a solitary activity. And books do not have to be individuating artifacts. Likewise, prosperity does not necessarily lead to a more independent way of being. Yet in the hands of the early Protestants, the practices and products of literacy and prosperity fed and were fed by the ethos of self-reliance. Consequently, Protestants were able to turn more and more inward in their pursuit of spiritual fitness, and more and more away from religious leaders and communities.

Meanwhile, back in the Catholic realms of Europe, the Catholic Church continued to mediate adherents' relationship with the divine. Then as now, the Church held that the pope is Christ's ambassador on earth, and that the pope realizes Christ's will through the hierarchy of cardinals, bishops, and priests. To know and act upon the will of Christ, parishioners must participate in the institutions of the Church. Yet historically, the Church offered masses and the Bible only in Latin, which left parishioners highly dependent on clerics and one another for guidance on how to be good Catholics. To this day, being a good Catholic entails performing rituals, observing sacraments, and tithing (that is, contributing 10 percent of one's income to the Church). With hundreds of feast days, saint days, celebrations, and masses, Catholics have a reason to interact with their church almost daily.

Once at church, Catholics can enjoy opulent paintings and sculptures, lush music, and fragrant incense. Rich decorations tell the life of Christ, the Stations of the Cross, and other Bible stories. Mother Mary uplifts parishioners with her patient beauty. Jesus himself is present, most notably in depictions of his suffering on the cross. In contrast, Protestant churches offer a starker aesthetic. The cross in Protestant churches is always empty—a sign that worshippers should invest their energies in the future, when Jesus returns, rather than in mourning the past or seeking solace in the present.[51]

American Catholicism and Protestantism have diverged considerably from their European roots. Indeed, some sociologists argue that the American branches of the two churches have more in common with one another than they do with their modern European counterparts.[52] Nevertheless, the culture cycles at play in the fields of modern American Catholicism and Protestantism still encourage the use of different selves.

The New Protestants

The latest arrivals to the American religious landscape are modern-day conservative Christians. The United States has undergone several "religious awakenings," during which speaking in tongues, hallucinating, and going through other unusual and immediate experiences of the divine were more commonplace. The first of these periods dates back to 1730, recounts Luhrmann. But the current interest in the direct, personal experience of God "exploded in the 1960s," she writes.[53]

One reason behind this newfound enthusiasm for the ecclesiastical is that the nation as a whole was opening itself to more emotional and intuitive experiences. Another impetus was the social upheaval of the time, including loosening sexual mores and widespread rebellion against mainstream institutions.[54] The turmoil that these changes wrought left many people feeling adrift. Some turned to the Church for a sense of community and order.[55] With its warm God and clear rules, the conservative Protestant Church was just the institution that many were seeking.

Psychologist Ian McGregor and colleagues captured these dynamics in a set of experiments. In one, for example, the researchers frightened undergraduates by making them read a graduate-level statistics lesson that had been edited to be incomprehensible. Compared with students who had read a nonthreatening passage, these aggravated undergrads reported greater religious zeal, more fervently endorsing statements such as "I would support a war that defended my religious beliefs" and "My religious beliefs are grounded in objective truth."[56]

No one has directly measured the selves of conservative Protestants, but many scholars have examined the personalities of political conservatives, whose circles overlap with those of religious conservatives. Psychologist John Jost and his colleagues conducted a sweeping meta-analysis of eighty-eight of these studies from twelve countries. They discovered that, compared with political liberals, political conservatives are less open to new experiences, need more closure and order, and have lower self-esteem.[57] As we discussed in previous chapters, these personality features are more typical of interdependent selves.

Coffee with Jesus

The emotional lives of conservative and mainline Protestants likewise seem to divide over the independence-interdependence line. Psychologists Ingrid Storm and David Sloan Wilson followed eleven conservative Protestant teens and thirty-nine mainline teens over the course of one week. Roughly every two hours, a preprogrammed personal digital assistant (PDA) cued these participants to answer questions about what they were doing and how they felt about it.

Storm and Wilson found that, consistent with a more interdependent self, conservative Protestant teens spent less time alone and were happier when they were with other people. They were by themselves only 17.5 percent of the time, as compared to 26 percent for mainline Protestants. All by their lonesome, conservative teens reported feeling lonelier, weaker, and more bored and self-conscious than when they were in the presence of others, including friends and family.

For the mainline Protestant teens, being with other people had little effect on their feelings, except that being with family made them feel slightly *lonelier.*[58]

Storm and Wilson also analyzed data from a survey of more than three hundred respondents. True to the interdependent practice of observing hierarchy and tradition, conservative Protestant teens reported that their parents had more control over which friends they spent time with and which people they dated than did mainline Protestant teens. And true to the independent practice of cultivating uniqueness and self-expression, mainline Protestants more readily agreed that their families made them feel special on birthdays and holidays, and let everyone express opinions—even when they differed.[59]

Conservative Protestants spend more time not only with friends and family, but also with Jesus. As a member of the Vineyard Christian Fellowship Church, Luhrmann explored how conservative Protestants develop their friendly, loving relationships with their savior. She discovered that conservative Protestants invite the divine into their lives many times a day. Interactions such as pouring coffee for Jesus, setting aside a weekly date night with the Lord, and learning how to differentiate His voice in your mind from your own voice are just a few of the regular practices that conservatives undertake.[60]

Save or Be Saved?

Conservative Protestants reveal and reinstate their interdependence not only in how they raise their teens and talk to God, but also in what they do with their money. An extreme act of interdependence is to forgo personal gain for the sake of your community. Conservative Protestants do just this: of all religious groups in the United States, they donate the greatest portion of their wealth to their churches.

By giving away so much of their wealth, conservative Protestants are hewing closely to the reported words of Jesus Christ, finds sociologist Lisa Keister. About 10 percent of New Testament verses are about finances, she notes,[61] including verses such as "Honor the Lord with your wealth, with the first fruits of all your crops; then your barns will be filled to overflowing, and your vats will brim over with new wine" (Proverbs 3:9–10). Likewise, the conservative Protestant writer Randy Alcorn noted in his 2003 book, *The Law of Rewards*, "[Jesus] spoke about money and possessions more than heaven and hell combined."[62]

With a literal interpretation of the Bible as their distinguishing feature, conservative Protestants more strongly endorse statements such as "The purpose of church is to give money back to God," "Money is the root of all evil," and "I think a great deal about the connection between religion and personal finances." This holds true for both White and Black conservative Christians. "If you remember Hurricane Katrina," Keister says, "there were a lot of people who didn't have $40 to rent a car and drive away." Among this stricken lot were many conservative Protestants.[63]

One side effect of giving away so much wealth is that conservative Protestants are among the poorest Americans. Using data from more than six thousand respondents to the National Longitudinal Survey of Youth, Keister shows that conservative Protestants had a median net worth of $26,000 in 2000, whereas the sample as a whole had a median net worth of $66,200. She also demonstrates that these differences in net worth were due more to conservative Protestants' failure to accumulate assets than to their starting out with less wealth. And though other cultural practices in conservative Protestant circles—getting less education, having more children at younger ages, and sending fewer women into the workforce—certainly add up to less in conservative Protestants' coffers, religious beliefs and the financial practices they promote also exert a strong influence.[64]

The humbler circumstances of conservative Protestant culture cycles push I's in a more interdependent direction. As we examined in chapter 5, poorer Americans tend to use their interdependent selves more than do wealthier Americans. The reasons for this are many: the less money a person has, the more she must rely on friends and family to meet daily needs, the fewer resources she has to act on personal preferences and realize personal goals, the less control she has over her environment, and the more she must accept things as they are. When combined with the institutions and interactions of conservative Protestantism, lower socieconomic status supports and reflects a particularly robust form of interdependence.

Calm the Elephants

"When two elephants fight, it is the grass that suffers." So warns a Ugandan proverb. Likewise, as conservative Protestantism has grown to be the largest religion in America, its clashes with mainline Protestantism (and the latter's independent allies) are eroding public discourse and the ties that bind Americans to one another.

Culture cycles twisted us into this stalemate, and culture cycles can wind us out. Although mainline Protestants are now the numerical minority, their deeper roots in American institutions put them in the better position to offer the olive branch to their conservative counterparts. To elevate the national conversation on religion, mainline Protestants and their allies should welcome conservative Protestants into their institutions. The U.S. National Institutes of Health blazed this trail by appointing geneticist Francis S. Collins, a self-described "evangelical Christian," to be its director in 2009. The former head of the Human Genome Project, Collins weds faith with evolution in a viewpoint he calls BioLogos, which holds that God created the universe fourteen billion years ago, put in place the processes that would lead to human life, and then sat back and watched.[65]

Mainline Protestants, in contrast, should take a more active role in helping conservatives feel more welcome in their midst. A first step in building warmer interactions is to stop trying to convince conservative Christians that their values and beliefs are wrong. Most people think and speak poorly when they feel that the core of their self is under attack. So creating a safe space for cross-faith conversations means checking the collected works of Christopher Hitchens at the door. Although the daedal argumentation and searing rhetoric of Hitchens (and of Richard Dawkins, Sam Harris, and other verbally adroit atheists) score points with the Oxbridge set, they only alienate conservative Protestants.

Instead, the better tactic is to discover what goals you already share, and then go from there. Or, as the psychologist Morton Deutsch put it, "Learn the difference between 'positions' and 'interests.' The positions of the conflicting parties may be irreconcilable, but their interests may be concordant."[66] What you will miss in the way of converting a few people to your way of thinking, you will enjoy in the way of mobilizing a lot of people toward a better way of acting. As the old adage says, "An insincere peace is better than a sincere war."

For Reverend Richard Cizik, this means appealing to broadly shared Christian ethics when stumping for the planet. "My message really isn't to persuade anybody of the science of climate change," explains Cizik, the president of the New Evangelical Partnership for the Common Good. "It's rather to persuade them of their own biblical responsibility. . . . There's no way you can love God and your neighbor if you're polluting his or her air."[67]

Political candidates who are less popular with conservative Christian voters should likewise change their messages to emphasize interdependent concerns over independent ones. Mainline Protestants and their allies often talk about their policies in terms of serving self-interest, maximizing economic returns, protecting individual rights, and expanding choices. Instead, Luhrmann recommends, "They could talk about the way their policy interventions will allow . . . those of us who support them [to] better ourselves as we reach out in love. They could describe health care reform as a response to suffering, not as a solution to an economic problem."[68]

Individuals can also work on their own psyches to make way for better interfaith conversations. One quick cognitive intervention is to consider that valuing fairness, equality, and freedom above all else is *itself* a moral code. Psychologist Jonathan Haidt gives this code a name, the *morality of autonomy*, and points out that it is unusually prevalent in wealthy, educated, industrialized, and rich democracies. In the rest of the world, and among conservative Christians, two other ways of being good (the moralities of *community* and *divinity*) command larger audiences.[69] It's easy to keep ourselves blind to these other moral codes. But if you wish to build bridges between religion and, increasingly, politics, you must at least dip your mind into the possibility that all three moralities are, as Haidt writes, "manifestations of deeply conflicting but equally heartfelt visions of the good society."[70] This sort of good faith can go a long way.

What Would Jesus Drive?

While mainliners are harnessing their interdependence to reach out across the religious divide, conservatives must access their independence to think for themselves and speak up for their beliefs. Conservative Christians have already created several institutions and interactions that support the free flow of ideas within their faiths. For instance, the Evangelical Environmental Network hosts an active debate about climate change research. One of the organization's most successful projects is its "What Would Jesus Drive?" bumper sticker campaign. The nonprofit also publishes *Creation Care* magazine and operates an institute "to equip, inspire, disciple, and mobilize God's people in their effort to care for God's creation," according to the organization's website.[71] The evolution debate likewise has a flagship evangelical-led organization, the BioLogos Foundation, which hosts an online forum where dissenters and supporters of theistic evolution can air their views.

At the individual level, conservative Protestants should take the trouble to read the Bible, rather than relying on church leadership to tell them what to believe. Through this act of independence, many have discovered that the scripture's list of dos and don'ts is not so clear-cut. For example, the Bible does indeed mention sex between men in a few passages, going so far as to call it an abomination (an unclean act) in Leviticus. Yet as biologist Joan Roughgarden documents, Jesus never mentions homosexuality, and no scripture mentions sex between women. Moreover, Roughgarden contends, the Bible's many inclusive statements about eunuchs and intense same-sex friendships (Naomi and Ruth, Jonathan and David), and the church's embrace of "transvestite saints" such as Thecla and Joan of Arc, suggest that sex and gender are rather bendy in Christianity. Grappling with these and other complexities, rather than hiding them under half the story, may strengthen both individual faith and the institution of the Church.[72]

The Devil Inside

The founding documents of the United States are likewise inconsistent about exactly how religion should fit in to the fabric of our nation. On the one hand, the Declaration of Independence puts a deity front and center: "We hold these truths to be self-evident, that all men are created equal, that they are endowed by their Creator with certain unalienable Rights." On the other hand, the U.S. Constitution doesn't mention God at all. Instead, its first amendment cleaves church from state: "Congress shall make no law respecting an establishment of religion, or prohibiting the free exercise thereof."

In a pluralistic society with a growing population and diminishing resources, deciding how to interpret these unclear messages, how to balance church and state, is a crucial project. Understanding how the clash of independence and interdependence can sidetrack that project can put it on a more productive course. The devil isn't in the other side's values and beliefs; it's in the details of how to harness independence and interdependence for a more productive peace.

CHAPTER 8

Love's Labour's Lost

Workplace Cultures

The XO is as cute as a laptop can be, with its bright green buttons, chunky handle, and bubbly logo. In 2005, MIT professor Nicholas Negroponte unveiled the idea of selling the XO for a mere $100 so that children in poor countries could use it for school. Intel, Google, and several other technology giants were eager to get in on the feel-good moment. So they became official partners of Negroponte's nonprofit, One Laptop Per Child (OLPC), pledging cash, materials, and expertise.

Soon, however, one partnership began to fray. Beholding the huge market at the bottom of the world's wealth pyramid, Intel began to manufacture its own low-cost laptop, the Classmate PC. Because Intel's Classmate would directly compete with OLPC's XO, Negroponte asked Intel to stop selling its machine in regions where his nonprofit was active. But Intel was unwilling to let OLPC put the kibosh on a profitable venture. In 2008, Intel backed out of the partnership. An offended Negroponte summarized the organizations' conflicting visions by saying, "[OLPC] views the children as a mission; Intel views them as a market."[1]

Intel and OLPC are not alone in their mutual exasperation. As social and environmental problems take on global proportions, many nonprofits and corporations are attempting to join forces to fight for the common good. Their alliances are catalyzing a bevy of workplace innovations. Taking a cue from their charitable comrades, for example, the business world is spawning social entrepreneurs, triple-bottom-line companies (supporting people, planet, and profit), blended-value propositions (which include economic, social, and environmental components), corporate social responsibility initiatives, and other activities that are both magnanimous and money-making. And at the urging of their for-profit partners, nonprofits are launching revenue-generating ventures, posting quarterly performance dashboards, and lowering their operating costs. Governments are also getting in on the action, undertaking more public-private partnerships and borrowing ideas from both the business and nonprofit worlds.

Despite their best intentions, many sector-hoppers soon lock horns. Jim Fruchterman has a particularly bitter tale of a nonprofit-government clash. Fruchterman is the founder and CEO of Benetech, a Palo Alto–based nonprofit that develops new technologies to help people and protect the environment. In 2000 he learned that a company called Quantum Magnetics had invented a new device for detecting land mines. He wanted to work with the company to refine the invention for humanitarian organizations in war-torn regions. Quantum Magnetics agreed that "using the technology for humanitarian purposes [rather than just military ones] was incredibly cool," says Fruchterman. So the two organizations began collaborating in earnest.

There was a hitch, however. Because Quantum Magnetics received funding from the U.S. government, and because the land mine detectors could be used offensively, Benetech would have to get permission to adapt the new technology from the Department of Commerce, the Department of Defense, and maybe even the State Department. "Actually, we weren't quite sure whose permission we needed," recalls Fruchterman.

Undeterred, Fruchterman sought the required clearances. "Everyone in government agreed that humanitarian land mine detectors were a great idea," he learned. "But nobody actually got around to signing on the dotted line to give us access to the technology." After two years of daily promises that the signatures were on their way, "we finally put the project on ice," he says. "We realized that we just didn't understand the culture of government."

What exactly is that culture? Why does it so often rub nonprofits and corporations the wrong way? And why do so many nonprofits and corporations likewise chafe in each other's company?

By now you can probably guess our answer: the business world is home to more independent selves and to the ideas, institutions, and interactions that support and reflect this way of being. But the nonprofit and government sectors hone more interdependent culture cycles, each one distinct from the other.

In short: you are where you work, to a surprising degree.

When these distinct workplace cultures collide, progress on fixing the world hits the skids, and sometimes even grinds to a halt. To avoid these clashes—and maybe even make the world a better place along the way—businesses, nonprofits, and government agencies must meet one another halfway. For their part, businesses need to brush up on the basics of interdependence and focus more on their relationships, both with their partners and within their organizational walls.

Nonprofits must take a different medicine. Because they are so focused on maintaining their relationships, charities too seldom speak truth to power, which hinders their ability to get what they need from their partners and serve their missions. A strong dose of independence could help them speak up for themselves and their beneficiaries.

Governments also suffer from too much interdependence, but of a different sort. They are in a quagmire of absurd hierarchies and obsolete traditions. To break through their own red tape, they need more independence to take risks, tolerate failure, and reward innovation.

Having amped up their independence, both nonprofits and governments should wield it for an additional end: to fight the businessification of everyday life. Over the past decade, both nonprofits and governments have increasingly adopted the practices and metaphors of the business world. Nonprofits are now honing their "competitive advantages," for instance, and their donors are "seeking social returns" on their investments. Governments are outsourcing their work to for-profit firms whose goals are all too often at odds with those of the public.[2] And people in all sectors are hailing profitable solutions over charitable or policy ones.

Although many organizations can benefit from the efficiencies that business practices lend, a knee-jerk preference for the culture of business—and, by extension, for independence—is not the wisest reflex. As the philosopher Michael J. Sandel argues in his book *What Money Can't Buy: The Moral Limits of Markets*, not all problems have market solutions, and not everything should be for sale.[3]

If you have worked for more than one organization in your life, you will doubtless know that we are rolling over much of the variability within each kind of workplace. The unique business cultures of Apple and Microsoft, Southwest and American Airlines, and Toyota and General Motors are the stuff of bestsellers.[4] Likewise, some nonprofits have so little in common with each other that critics routinely debate whether the category makes any sense. After all, the same nonprofit umbrella shelters Yale University and the Yazoo County Fair, the Southern Baptist Convention and the North American Man/Boy Love Association, and the Bill and Melinda Gates Foundation and the Last Chance Ferret Rescue. Likewise, few government agencies are created equally. A trip to the Department of Motor Vehicles is a decidedly different experience from a trip to the Smithsonian Institution.

In all this noise, however, we see signals. Business workers striving to make the biggest profit build, and are built by, a different culture cycle than nonprofit workers aspiring to serve the social good, or government workers intending to maintain the social order. Even when these diverse selves sincerely want to work together, the gears of their different cycles don't always align. So before you boldly spearhead that cross-sector partnership, or even try out that best practice touted in the *Harvard Business Review*, take a spin through the culture cycles of business, nonprofits, and government agencies to learn what clashes you might encounter.

For Love or Money

Like many Silicon Valley entrepreneurs, Peter Thiel, a cofounder of PayPal, would like to make the world a better place. But he avoids investing in "people with a nonprofit attitude," he recently told *The New Yorker*, because they allegedly think, "We're doing something good, so we don't have to work as hard."[5]

Thiel is half right. Compared to employees in the business sector, nonprofit workers indeed march to the beat of a more interdependent drummer, as do employees in the government sector. No research has directly examined workplace differences in models of the self. Yet many studies uncover that nonprofit and government workers are more cooperative and altruistic than for-profit workers, which suggests that they take more interdependent selves to work. In contrast, businesspeople are more competitive and self-interested, which suggests that their workaday selves are more independent.

In one early study, for instance, James R. Rawls and his colleagues found that business-school students who later pursued careers in nonprofits and government agencies valued being cheerful, forgiving, and helpful more than did students who headed for the corporate world. The more socially minded MBAs also scored higher on measures of cooperativeness. The business-bound students, in contrast, valued being ambitious and prosperous more than did their social-sector classmates. Notably, the groups did not differ in intelligence, creativity, or problem-solving ability.[6]

More recently, psychologists and sociologists have created a measure called *public service motivation*, which reflects people's commitment to the public interest, compassion for the less fortunate, and willingness to sacrifice themselves for others.[7] Researchers find that both nonprofit and government workers register higher levels of public service motivation than do business workers, even in countries with less aggressive business sectors such as Canada, the Netherlands, and Australia.[8] After the workday ends, nonprofit and government workers continue to walk the walk of interdependence, logging more volunteer hours than do their corporate colleagues.[9]

To be sure, the business world is interdependent in many ways. To serve their stakeholders, businesses must rally their workers around a common set of values and closely coordinate their activities. And quite a few for-profit workers chase hefty paychecks and comfy corner offices as independent means to interdependent ends, such as funding charitable causes.

Yet in business settings (especially in the Global North), the collective pursuit of profit and the individual quest for wealth and status take on a decidedly independent tone. Businesses and businesspeople must identify their unique talents and achievements, express them clearly and broadly, and then, ultimately vanquish the competition. According to some models of human nature (see, for example, Richard Dawkins's *The Selfish Gene*[10]), this pursuit of self-interest is people's primary, basic, natural motivation. Partly because these theories enthrone independence as the natural and good way to be, observers such as Peter Thiel conclude that businesspeople will work harder than those with more interdependent imperatives.

Yet no studies show that for-profit employees work harder, longer, or better than nonprofit or government ones. To the contrary: the evidence suggests that nonprofit workers in many industries work just as many hours, for less money, to produce the same or higher-quality goods and services as do for-profit workers.[11] For instance, a recent study of some 14,400 nursing homes showed that the quality of nonprofit and public facilities outstripped that of for-profit homes.[12]

One explanation for the greater productivity of nonprofit workers is that when people operate out of social motivations, rather than extrinsic motivations such as money, they like their work more and therefore work harder. Nonprofit workers indeed chart higher levels of job satisfaction than do for-profit workers.[13]

Dan Portillo has witnessed the gusto of the nonprofit worker firsthand. For five years he led hiring for Mozilla, a nonprofit whose best-known product is the open-source Firefox Internet browser. Because Mozilla employs a "drastically smaller" workforce than its main competitors, says Portillo, one Mozilla employee does the work that several hundred people do at larger, for-profit companies. "There are no small jobs at Mozilla," he observes, "and so the organization attracts people who want to handle big, hairy projects."

Mozilla's employees may come for the challenge, but they stay for the mission. "People work at Mozilla because of what it stands for: open choice in innovation and pushing the boundaries of the Web," says Portillo. He notes that during his years at the nonprofit, the average employee tenure was longer than that in corporate settings, where employees were "counting their minutes until their vesting was up."

Like their nonprofit brethren, government workers also report working more hours than for-profit workers.[14] But they aren't as happy doing it. Despite their altruistic motivations, government workers routinely report the lowest levels of work satisfaction and commitment.[15] The culprit lies not in the selves of government workers, but in the institutions and interactions with which they must contend. As we shall see, their culture cycles are clogged with so much bureaucratic nonsense that even the most dedicated workers lose sight of government's lofty goals.

Business Ends

For many culture cycles we discuss in this book, seeing differences at the institutional level requires considerable scholarship. But the institutional differences between workplace culture cycles are quite obvious. When it comes to public corporations, for example, the law of the land is clear: their primary legal obligation is to maximize financial returns to shareholders. Full stop. So although corporations are legally "persons," as the U.S. Supreme Court affirmed in 2010, they have few responsibilities to other persons other than to make them money.[16]

"That's why it's called the 'bottom line,'" says Steve Beitler, manager of community and government affairs at Agilent Technologies, which is based in Santa Clara, California. "What started out as an accounting term has become a widespread cultural phrase." In business, that phrase narrows the aperture onto one outcome: profit.

Ben Cohen and Jerry Greenfield learned the hard way that in public corporations, profit trumps all. The two entrepreneurs founded their ice-cream company, Ben and Jerry's Homemade, on a bedrock of social responsibility, sourcing local and organic ingredients, dedicating 7.5 percent of their profits to community programs, and blazing the trail with many other people- and planet-friendly practices. But when their board accepted Unilever's $326 million offer to buy the company, the founders had little choice but to comply; they were legally required to sell the company to the bidder that would increase the company's share price the most. Since this sale, the founders have lamented that their company has shifted away from its original social mission.[17]

The Interdependent Sectors

Compared with businesses, charitable nonprofits have a decidedly different legal mandate, as spelled out in section 501(c)3 of the U.S. tax code.[18] According to this riveting read, 501(c)3 nonprofits are entities "organized and operated exclusively for religious, charitable, scientific, testing for public safety, literary, or educational purposes, or to foster national or international amateur sports competition, or for the prevention of cruelty to children or animals." To put it in plain English: nonprofits are up to good—or, at least, their notion of what is good. Because our government is presumably not in the business of dictating what is good, it grants nonprofit status to a wide range of organizations.

For their pursuit of the good, nonprofits are exempt from paying many taxes, and their donors get a tax deduction for their contributions. Despite these breaks, nonprofits' operational burdens can be considerably more onerous than those of for-profit firms. Businesses must track only one performance measure (profit), for a single audience (shareholders), in the short term (usually on a quarterly basis). By contrast, nonprofits must keep their eye on several, often ill-defined outcomes because measuring progress in, say, poverty alleviation or world peace, is not straightforward. They must also serve many audiences, including clients, communities, board members, donors, funding agencies, and partners. And they must track their outcomes for however long it takes to achieve their mission, which is seldom a short-term proposition.

Governments have a clearer legal goal than nonprofits, but they must fuss with a still gnarlier tangle of expectations and constraints. Although political philosophers and parties may disagree about the fine print, many agree that a major goal of government is to maintain social order.[19] In capitalist democracies such as the United States, this job description also entails being accountable to voters. To dispense with these duties, government agencies must track an even larger dashboard of more complicated outcomes, for pretty much everyone all the time. And they must do so by following very strict rules while everyone scrutinizes them.

Of the three sectors, business is by far the largest, generating 77 percent of the nation's gross domestic product and employing about 75 percent of its workforce. Government comes in second, contributing some 12 percent of the nation's GDP while employing about 16 percent of its workers. Nonprofits, in turn, make 5 percent of the nation's output using 10 percent of its workers.[20]

For Profit, But Zero Sum

Farther downstream in the culture cycle, institutional differences breed different ways of working. In businesses, everyday interactions have a decidedly independent flavor. Managers are encouraged to make quick decisions and take risks in order to seize opportunities that will add dollars to the bottom line. When their speed, daring, and judgment generate more profit, they receive financial and status rewards, which are in greater supply in the business sector. For most job descriptions, financial incentives are higher in commercial enterprises than in nonprofits and government agencies.[21]

These material incentives need not ignite interpersonal attacks and winner-take-all smackdowns. But all too often, tensions rear their ugly heads in business settings, says Kerry Patterson, coauthor of the *New York Times* bestseller *Crucial Conversations* and cofounder of VitalSmarts, a corporate training consultancy.[22] "I've spent the last thirty years making my living trying to undo the cutthroat tactics that people learn in business school," says Patterson. He sees the seeds of the agonistic culture of business in business schools, where students are pitted against one another "like gladiators" to crack real-life case studies. "The professor cold-calls students, watches them struggle to answer the question, and, when they fail, invites their peers to tear them apart." The message is clear: to be a good businessperson, you must be right, be right first, and be right at the expense of others.

Nonprofit Cat Herding

Nonprofits, in contrast, rely on more interdependent practices to meet their missions and make their hay. Because nonprofits have so many stakeholders, managers must confer with many more people before making decisions. These stakeholders often have different understandings of the organization's mission, and so managers must build consensus around their plan of action. They must then rally workers around the plan, as the latter are more motivated by values than money. And because nonprofits tend to be understaffed, underfunded, and underresourced, they must often reach out to partners for help. In many cases, the addition of new partners starts the consensus-building process all over again.

With these constraints, nonprofit managers do not decide and direct so much as rally and respond. "It reminds me of what someone said life as an ambassador is like," says Philip Lader, former U.S. ambassador to the

United Kingdom, of his stint as the president of Winthrop University, nonprofit. "There you are at the helm of the great ship, with everyon scurrying about. Only after about four months of steering the wheel d you realize that it is not connected to the rudder. Everyone is saluting yo and saying 'aye aye,' [and then] they go below to steer the ship themselves In many nonprofits, that genuinely is the case."[23]

Government Red Tape

As Lader's musings on ambassadorships hint, daily life in governmen agencies is likewise rife with interdependence, albeit of a different sort. I addition to having many stakeholders and broad, hard-to-measure objec tives, government agencies operate in fishbowls. Everyone's got his eyes o the government. To avoid incurring the wrath of this very large public government agencies have generated reams of rules that employees mus follow, "even if those rules lead to stupid outcomes," says Richard Boly the director of the Office of eDiplomacy at the U.S. State Department.

The technical term for these "good rules gone bad" is *red tape*, an their plentitude in government agencies is what puts them in a league a their own.[24] Of course, we want public servants to account for their tim and spending, and to make their processes transparent. But often, all tha accounting and revealing suck up an alarming portion of governmen workers' jobs, which is one reason government employees love their job least.[25]

In his classic report on red tape, Vice President Al Gore recounts sev eral examples of the rules that make government employees miserable For instance, a new Energy Department petroleum engineer requested high-end calculator to do her job, completing all the necessary paperwor and receiving all the necessary permissions. "Three months later," Gor writes, "she received an adding machine. Six months after that, the pro curement office got her a calculator—a tiny, hand-held model that coul not perform the complex calculations her work required. Disgusted, sh bought her own."[26]

Rigidly adhering to rules not only bums employees out, but also quell risk-taking and innovation.[27] Witness the Benetech–Quantum Magnetic partnership, whose land mine project sank in an abyss of regulations tha government employees themselves did not understand. They were likely not motivated to understand the innovation, as government workers have few incentives to take risks. "If you take a tremendous risk in Silicon Valley," explains Boly, "you get a job with stock options, and a ton of money, and invitations to all the cool parties, and a speaking slot at South by Southwest and TED. But if you take a risk in government? If you're a whistleblower, you might get on *60 Minutes*. Otherwise, the only thing you've likely risked is your job."

Business, Try a Little Tenderness

The clashes between the culture cycles of different workplaces need not only provoke conflict. They can also inspire innovation and promote the greater good. Many businesses are finding that when they add interdependence to their tactics, they make cooler products, higher profits, and healthier communities. Meanwhile, many nonprofits are discovering that when they polish their independence, they can kick bigger dents in the problems they are trying to solve. Government agencies are likewise learning that taking a walk on the independent side can enhance their ability to serve their constituents.

In the business world, social innovators are hard at work infusing a little interdependence at every level of the culture cycle. The big news at the institutional level is the advent of the B Corporation. The *B* in *B Corporation* stands for "beneficial." Unlike other corporate forms, B Corporations change their bylaws so that their boards must consider the interests of their employees, their communities, and the environment. The Pennsylvania-based nonprofit B Lab administers the B-Corp certification process, screening applicants, offering legal counsel, and lobbying state legislatures to recognize B Corporations. For their part, B Corporations comply with the B Lab's certification standards, pay an annual licensing fee, and sign the organization's so-called declaration of interdependence.

Businesses that receive the B Corp seal of approval not only attract socially and environmentally concerned consumers, but also protect their companies from assaults on their missions. Had Ben and Jerry's received B-Corp certification, for example, it might have staved off Unilever's buyout. (The buyout took place in 2000; B Lab was formed in 2006.) As of 2011, more than five hundred companies have registered as B Corporations, and seven states have passed benefit corporation legislation.[28]

At the level of daily interactions, adopting a few relationship-focused practices not only makes business employees happier and healthier, but may also thicken the companies' bottom lines. First among these practices is what consultant Dev Patnaik calls the "no-zinger policy." The rule? Fire employees who regularly insult their coworkers.[29]

"Insults stop people from being collaborative, which in turn makes them less creative," explains Patnaik. As CEO of Jump Associates, he helps Fortune 500 companies innovate by developing highly collaborative cultures. (Among his firm's successes: "We spent the last ten years helping Target morph into *Tarzheh*," he says, referring to a campaign to give the big-box store a more upscale image.) He also advocates other empathic practices, such as making sure that you are listening more than you're talking, and not assuming that the behaviors you see in others mean the same thing as when you perform them. For example, when your coworker smiles at your off-color joke, she might very well find it as hilarious as you do. But she might also just be trying to act polite.

Kerry Patterson agrees that a little workplace civility can go a long way. "If you shut down one person, then everyone else starts shutting down." As the silence spreads, brilliance dies on the vine. To make it safe for people to express their opinions, leaders have to model how to disagree without being disagreeable. Rather than "stripping people naked to show how wrong they are," he says, leaders should approach differences of opinion by asking, "What do people like about this argument?" or "What do you think I can learn from this argument?"

The raging success of online shoe retailer Zappos proves that nice corporations can finish first. Above all else, Zappos values its culture, whose big idea is captured in the title of CEO Tony Hsieh's book, *Delivering Happiness: A Path to Profits, Passion, and Purpose.*[30] Happy employees, reasons Hsieh, make for happy customers, and underlying all that happiness are warm personal relationships. To foster those relationships, Zappos requires managers to spend 10 to 20 percent of their work time "goofing off" with employees, encourages sales representatives to spend more (not less) time on the phone with customers, and hosts spontaneous Conga lines and other events to encourage cross-departmental friendships. Zappos also communicates that it cares for its employees by paying for their health care, lunches, and snacks.

Hsieh has repeatedly gone to the mat to protect Zappos's highly interdependent culture, staving off buyouts and mollifying board members who disliked his emphasis on relationships over profits. Zappos's commitment to its interdependent culture has paid off: in 2009, Amazon bought the company for $1.2 billion in a deal that preserved Hsieh's role and dismissed several profit-fixated board members. Since that time, the company has placed in the top twenty-five of *Fortune*'s "Best Companies to Work For" every year.

The success of interdependence-breeding companies such as Zappos is probably not anomalous. In several studies, psychologist Jennifer Chatman shows that organizations that emphasize collectivism and interdependence better harness the creative power of diverse work groups than do organizations that emphasize individualism and independence.[31] A large meta-analysis likewise reveals that the more that team members value collectivism (including interpersonal harmony, solidarity, and cooperation), the better they perform.[32]

Talking about a Revolution

At the individual level of the culture cycle, for-profit workers and managers can make smaller declarations of interdependence by watching their language. Psychologist Lee Ross and his colleagues randomly assigned Israeli pilots and American college students to play a game that was named either the Wall Street Game or the Community Game. In fact, all participants played a version of the Prisoner's Dilemma, an economics game in which participants take turns either allotting rewards or extracting penalties according to rules that pit cooperation against self-interest. The researchers discovered that when the task was called the Community Game, participants cooperated more than when it was called the Wall Street Game.[33]

In another set of studies, Lee Ross and Aaron Kay similarly found that planting even subtler seeds of cooperation in people's minds—say, by having them unscramble sentences that included words related to cooperation, such as *fair* or *alliance*—induced them to prefer cooperation over self-interest. In contrast, participants who unscrambled words related to competition, such as *tournament* or *cutthroat*, took the self-interested route in the game.[34]

Although laboratory experiments are a long way from your average Fortune 500 workday, these findings suggest that a few quick linguistic fixes could spawn a more collaborative, and therefore more creative, workplace. Why argue when you can discuss? Why throw down a competition when you can raise a challenge? Why go for the jugular when you can go for the gold? By taking a moment to choose more interdependent words, you could transform a snake pit into a brain trust.

Be a Good Partner

As businesspeople put their own houses in more interdependent order, they should extend their sensitivity to the nonprofits and government agencies with which they work as program partners, donors, volunteers, and board members. To do so, they must overcome a common yet troublesome obstacle: misapplying their cultural assumptions and practices to the nonprofit sector.

For instance, because businesspeople track profits on a quarterly basis, they want to see nonprofits and government agencies "move the needle" on performance outcomes with similar alacrity. Yet moving the social-change needle often takes more time and effort than does turning a profit. In the late 1950s, for example, researchers in Ypsilanti, Michigan, randomly assigned 123 poor Black children to either the HighScope Perry Preschool program or to a comparison group that did not attend the preschool. Several years later, the preschool graduates were not faring much better than their counterparts in the control group. Based on this low initial "return on investment," many contemporary funders would have pulled the plug on the preschool.

But some forty years later, researchers revisited the study participants. They discovered that the HighScope Perry graduates were more likely to have a college degree, job, spouse, and savings account; to own a home and car; and to have raised their own kids than the control group. They were also less likely to have been on welfare, to have been arrested, or to have been sentenced to prison. Those short-term-return-focused funders would have killed a program that has yielded over twelve dollars on every dollar invested.[35]

For-profit folks who want to get in on the business of social change must practice patience. "The problems that nonprofits are tackling aren't going to get solved by next week," says Beitler of Agilent. "Corporations need to stick around for the long haul."

Businesspeople must also learn to appreciate how difficult it is to measure social change. At base, calculating profit is just a matter of math. But the social sector does not have an analog to profit. Success indicators for an arts organization in New York City are entirely different from those of a homeless shelter in Pine Bluff, Arkansas, a microlender in Bangalore, India, or an environmental advocacy group in the Amazon River Basin. And because many innovative programs are just one step ahead of the issues they have been formed to address, they often do not yet know which indicators they should be tracking.

"The next time corporate board members or donors get on an evaluation kick," recommends business professor Chip Heath, "ask them about the return on their investment in their R&D unit, or their advertising expenses. They won't be able to tell you. And yet outcomes in the corporate world are much easier to [track] than those that nonprofits are routinely asked to measure."[36]

The Nonprofit Starvation Cycle

Measuring those outcomes, moreover, is a luxury that many nonprofits cannot afford. Even the most successful nonprofits wrestle with resource shortfalls that would be unheard of in the corporate world, including nonfunctioning computers, outdated software, and chronic understaffing.[37] The for-profit mind-set is complicit in creating these shortfalls, argue Ann Goggins Gregory and Don Howard, both of the Bridgespan Group, a consultancy for nonprofits. In the absence of a nonprofit analog to profit, many for-profit folks rely on overhead ratios—the proportion of indirect expenses (operations, finances, human resources, and fund-raising) to program-related expense—to decide which nonprofits to support. Funders say they use this metric because they want to fund the action on the ground, rather than the infrastructure that makes the action happen. To win these donors' dollars, many nonprofits report artificially low overhead ratios. These misrepresentations of how much it actually costs to run a nonprofit then feed funders' already unrealistic beliefs.

The result is what Gregory and Howard call "the nonprofit starvation cycle": funders underestimate the cost of running a nonprofit, and assume that nonprofits with higher overhead ratios are simply inefficient; nonprofits misrepresent their costs, and therefore receive less funding; infrastructure suffers, and nonprofits become more inefficient. In the worst cases, high-quality programs fold for lack of adequate support.

Because funders are the more powerful parties in this dynamic, ending the nonprofit starvation cycle begins with them. Gregory and Howard suggest that funders work with nonprofits to define their shared goals, and then invest in the infrastructure needed to make those goals a reality, rather than imposing their own language, metrics, and priorities. In other words, funders need to have more respect for what nonprofits do, and more empathy for what nonprofits need.[38]

Market Failure

Jan Masaoka suggests one technique that businesspeople can apply to make empathy flow more readily. As the former executive director of CompassPoint, a San Francisco–based consultancy for nonprofits, Masaoka has brokered her fair share of cross-sector partnerships. She learned that corporations make better partners when they treat nonprofits as they would a small business. "For some reason, people in corporations understand that if you partner with the local pizza parlor, you cannot expect it to have its own lawyer," she says. Corporations are also more understanding of small businesses' slower decision-making and turnaround times.

A final step that businesspeople can take to help out their nonprofit brethren is to acknowledge the limits of markets. With the rise of social entrepreneurship, social enterprise, and other business solutions to social and environmental problems, many people have lost sight of the fact that not all problems have business solutions. Indeed, two of the most important roles that nonprofits and governments play are to intervene where markets fail and to fix the problems that markets created in the first place. Nonprofit and government-owned medical clinics, for example, accept patients so sick or impoverished that businesses could not profit from treating them. Likewise, many environmental nonprofits and government agencies act on behalf of people whose health has been harmed by unscrupulous businesses. Rather than trying to crowd out this good work by starving organizations or governments, the more business-minded among us should support our partners in all sectors.

Nonprofits, Pipe Up for Progress

On the more interdependent side of the labor pool, nonprofits should not just wait for the business sector to grant them their proper place at the economic table. Instead, workers in the charitable sector need to amplify their independence by speaking up for what they need. Yet because the selves of this sector are so steeped in interdependence, they sometimes fail to get out their biggest guns: their voices.

At the institutional level of culture cycles, speaking up means lobbying local, state, and federal governments. Lobbying lets citizens shape the new laws of the land, and so it is nonprofits' biggest lever. Yet many organizations avoid lobbying because they mistakenly believe it is illegal (or at least completely sleazy). The truth of the matter, however, is that nonprofits can spend up to $1 million on advocacy annually (the actual amount depends on the size of overall budgets). They can also speak their truths to power in less formal ways, including educating government officials about pending legislation, or alerting them to the consequences of policies already in place.[39]

"You have to show up," says Jim Fruchterman of Benetech, which devotes considerable time and money to lobbying. "The people who are defending the status quo are working full time to bend the ears of policy makers. When you don't show up, policy makers don't know that there's an alternative, and reform doesn't happen."

Fruchterman gives the example of an early Benetech project: the Bookshare online library for people with visual or learning disabilities. Although the technology was ten times more cost-effective than an older program's approach, the latter received government earmarks to the tune of $14 million. When Benetech, then an unknown player, lucked out and competed successfully for record-breaking funding from the Department of Education, "I started getting calls from congressional staff saying that we were crooks because they didn't know who we were."

To stay on the radar of policymakers, Benetech now employs the

Sheridan Group, a government-relations firm that primarily serves nonprofits. Fruchterman also spends ten days a year on Capitol Hill. Consequently, the work of Washington now reflects some of the ideas he espouses. Benetech can also feel a more tangible benefit of its advocacy: the nonprofit's annual budget has grown from $3 million to $12 million, "a big chunk of which is government contracts," Fruchterman says.

Many corporations would like to hear from nonprofits as well. "I want you to pester me," says Beitler of Agilent. "If I had to initiate all the learning I need [in order] to do my job well, my job would be a lot tougher, and I wouldn't be able to learn as much about what different groups are doing." A big part of his job is to partner with nonprofits working on STEM education. Because these nonprofits are much closer to the people who are grappling with the daily details of teaching STEM, they often have the best insights into how to improve it. In addition to briefings from these organizations, says Beitler, "I need them to be very frank about their needs and how we can be helpful."

Nonprofits must also speak up to break the nonprofit starvation cycle. Left to their own devices, many donors invest in pet programs or eponymous real estate. But with calm reasoning at strategic times, nonprofits can convince donors that an organization's programs and facilities are only as good as their management and maintenance.[40]

In their everyday communications with the outside world, nonprofits should also flaunt both their competence and their kindness. Word on the street has it that nonprofits are warm but not too smart, while businesses are clever but cold. Because of these different stereotypes, people would rather buy products or services from the allegedly sharper for-profit sector than from the allegedly less capable nonprofit sector. In one experiment, for instance, psychologist Jennifer Aaker and her colleagues found that participants wanted to buy a laptop bag from WorldofGood.com, presumably a for-profit company, more than they wanted to buy a laptop bag from WorldofGood.org, presumably a nonprofit. Yet when participants learned that the staunchly competent and independent *Wall Street Journal* had endorsed the dot-org bag, participants wanted to purchase it more than the dot-com one. The *Journal*'s endorsement made the nonprofit seem *both* warm and competent (both interdependent and independent), which is a combination that consumers find quite enticing. Nonprofits that speak to both heads and hearts may ultimately win more donor dollars than ones that advertise only their warmth.[41]

Governments, Fail Fast to Win Big

Government agencies should get hip to independence of a different sort: the willingness to take risks. For this shift, Richard Boly of the State Department recommends that institutions adopt the "fail-fast mantra of Silicon Valley." This is the mentality that made Apple, Google, and design firm IDEO famous. Rather than tiptoeing into a project by knocking out its easiest features, the fail-fast method makes organizations dive headlong into the hardest part of a project, see if it's doable, and if not, recalibrate.

Built into this approach is the message that "it's okay to fail," says Boly. This reassurance frees people up to dream bigger, try harder, and build better than do more conservative mind-sets. It makes people embrace risk rather than avoiding it.

It can also help break the stalemate of red tape. In government, the highest hurdle is often getting the approval of the relevant hegemons, as Fruchterman woefully learned. Applying the fail-fast mantra means that the first action items on an ambitious project's to-do list are to get the most persnickety stakeholders in the room, present the idea, encourage them to poke holes in it, and then iterate solutions that respond to stakeholders' concerns. By enlisting the toughest audiences early, workers in the government sector wind up not only better serving their stakeholders, but also getting their buy-in.

"Don't complete 80 percent of a project in stealth mode only to find out that you can't finish it," advises Boly. "That's been the fate of too many government projects."

Government agencies are also discovering that ripping off the red tape and flattening the hierarchy so that all stakeholders can let their unique ideas fly win efficiency and effectiveness. At the State Department, for example, Richard Boly's eDiplomacy was born from a $16 million failure: the Foreign Affairs System Integration. FASI was an old-school, top-down, command-and-control system for sharing information within the agency. The system was a flop. "People just won't go fishing through a gigantic 'databasement' to find what they need or to share their knowledge," he says. They will, however, happily ask questions and post their greatest ideas on Wikis, blogs, Twitter-like feeds, ideation platforms, and other social media.

To harness the creativity of the State Department staff, Boly and his team established half a dozen open-source platforms behind the department's firewall. These sites have shaped not only what the agency does, but also how it gets things done. For example, a perennial problem in Washington, D.C., is that government buildings are too far apart for people to walk to meetings, but taxis are too scarce to ride to them. Fare reimbursement is also a tedious process.

To fix these problems, employees used an ideation platform, the Secretary's Sounding Board, to suggest, and then to implement, a greenly efficient plan: purchase a stable of twenty bicycles that employees can check out. Since the program's beginning, employees have put more than three thousand miles on the bikes.

Saving Starfish

A change-the-world story that is making the conference rounds goes like this: "A man walking along a shore covered with washed-up, dying starfish notices a boy throwing them back into the ocean, one by one. The man says to the boy that there are miles and miles of beach and hundreds of starfish, and that he'll never make a difference. As the boy throws a starfish back into the ocean, he says, 'I just made a difference to that one.'"

Although the starfish story has warmed the cockles of many an independent heart, Rich Tafel's is not among them. As founder of the nonprofit Public Squared, he trains nonprofit leaders and social entrepreneurs in public policy. He objects to the starfish story because it exalts a lone hero who is reacting to the problem right in front of him, rather than reaching out to others to understand what is beaching the starfish in the first place, and then stopping it at the source.

"Real world problems usually result from a broken ecosystem," Tafel notes, "and solutions most often require some kind of change to the rules." For instance, when thousands of starfish really did wash up on the shores of Kent, England, the Marine Conservation Society (a charity) and the Environment Agency (a government office) discovered that it was because local businesses were too aggressive in their fishing of mussels—a problem whose solution will likely require the government to create new laws, as well as companies to cooperate with the laws and nonprofits to monitor the progress.

In other words, identifying and addressing the root cause of the mass stranding will require the cooperation of all three sectors. Kids will always throw starfish back in the sea, and well they should; independent approaches have an important place. But to make the kinds of change that twenty-first-century problems require, all three workplaces will need to work together interdependently.

CHAPTER 9

The Economic Equator

Cultures of the Global North and South

In early 1998 a famine descended upon southern Sudan,[1] despite a United Nations–led effort to monitor and alleviate food shortages in the region. Aid workers suspected that military and tribal chiefs had been hoarding the food, so they began delivering rations directly to the most vulnerable people: nursing mothers, children, the ill, and the elderly. To the workers' dismay, however, these beneficiaries rerouted the rations right back to their leaders. The aid workers concluded that corruption and inequality were so ingrained in the local culture that the least powerful people were colluding in their own destruction.

Anthropologist Simon Harrigan was sent in to investigate. One day he followed an elderly woman after she had received her ration. She indeed secreted the food away to her chief, rather than eating it all by herself. But instead of digging in to his newly supersized supper, the chief added the woman's contribution to a collective pot. He then split the pot equitably among his people, including the elderly woman. Harrigan discovered that these redistribution practices were the norm, while so-called resource capture by leaders and other elites was relatively rare.[2]

Indeed, the Sudanese chiefs did such a good job apportioning food that no individual suddenly starved. Instead, the entire group slowly starved together. This proved disastrous; because aid workers were trained to look for early and isolated cases of severe malnutrition, they missed the subtler signs of a gradual mass starvation. As a result, when the effects of malnutrition finally became apparent, they were widespread and catastrophic. In 1998 alone, the famine claimed more than seventy thousand lives.

Aid organizations eventually realized that the immediate cause of the food crisis was not inefficient resource distribution. Instead, the problem was not enough resources to begin with. The crisis halted when the agencies simply sent more food.[3]

Yet more food is only a temporary fix for a bigger problem. Every year, the wealthy nations of the Global North spend billions of dollars to save the poor nations of the Global South from starvation, infectious diseases, ethnic tensions, and inefficient markets. If headlines are to be believed, however, this aid decays into second helpings for corrupt leaders, fake drugs for sick customers, stolen arms for civil wars, and special privileges for sketchy companies.

The culprit? "Culture," many experts say, although they seldom explain what culture is, how it works, or how it transforms aid into evil. We agree that culture is partly responsible for charity gone wrong. Unlike many of these experts, though, we lay the blame not on any one culture, but on the collision between the cultures of donors in the Global North and recipients in the Global South.

The Global North-South divide is mostly one of wealth, and is admittedly fuzzy. Nations with the highest gross domestic products (GDP), per capita incomes, levels of industrialization, standards of living, and development of infrastructure are called the Global North. Most, but not all, of these nations are in the Northern Hemisphere (notable exceptions include Australia and New Zealand). The remaining nations comprise the Global South, and include Mexico, Central America, and South America; the Middle East and North Africa (MENA); the rest of Africa; Southeast Asia;[4] and India.[5]

Despite their amazing diversity, the people of the Global North have in common a sense of their selves as independent. For them, including the aid workers in Sudan, people are unique individuals, separate from their groups, in control of their fates, equal in rank, and free to act in their own self-interest. Indeed, for many economists in the Global North, the definition of being rational is acting in one's own self-interest.

In contrast, the amazingly diverse people of the Global South have in common a sense of their selves as interdependent. For them, including the Sudanese famine victims, people live their lives through relationships, and see themselves as strands in a web, nodes in a network, or fingers on a hand. As a result, ties to kith and kin drive individual actions. For instance, in their analysis of the Sudanese aid fiasco, economists Vijayendra Rao and Michael Walton conclude, "Survival of the kinship system was considered almost as important as physical survival." In other words, people would forgo food for themselves to preserve the ways of their group. "Even a cursory reading of the anthropological literature on southern Sudan [would have revealed this and] could have resulted in a more effective response," the authors write.[6]

When the Global North attempts to help the Global South, the clash of independence and interdependence undermines many of its efforts. On the wealthier, northern side of the equation, scientists, policymakers, and aid workers assume that people everywhere operate according to the ground rules of the independent self. In the Sudanese famine, for instance, aid workers assumed that a person given food would keep it for herself, with no regard for the needs and practices of everyone else in her kinship group. Largely trained in the Global North, these workers strove to deliver their aid with efficiency, accountability, and transparency.

On the poorer, southern side of the equation, what donors call "irrationality," "corruption," and "inefficiency" are what many aid recipients call "sound operating principles." The mistrust that pervades West Africa the cronyism that besets India, the conflicts that pepper the Middle East and the slow pace that hobbles Mexico are the flip sides of interdependen qualities, including a profound sense of history in West Africa, of duty in India, of honor in the MENA region, and of *simpatía* (Spanish for "pleasan and harmonious social relations") in Mexico. The culture cycles supporting these different aspects of interdependence have brought meaning and order to the Global South for the past few millennia. And though the shape that interdependence takes in each of these regions is distinct, al versions promote and proceed from a notion of the self that is relational similar, adjusting, rooted, and ranked.

The polite term for the poor countries of the Global South is *developing nations*. Many assume that once these interdependent cultures are al grown up, they will adopt independent culture cycles. Although GD and independence are correlated,[7] some of the most successful nations of the world (for example, Japan, Korea, and India) do not seem to be trading in their interdependence for independence. Indeed, to many Global Southerners, the efficiency and detachment of Global Northerners seem cold and soulless. Our best guess is that most of the Global South will embrace the parts of independence that are useful to them, and leave the others behind.

In this chapter, we predict which independent elements will migrate into the culture cycles of the Global South. We also suggest how the Global North can boost the interdependence in its culture cycles to quell and even avoid conflicts with its neighbors down south. By wisely wielding both independence and interdependence, selves on both sides of the economic equator can help bridge the differences between them and better leverage each other's strengths.

Irrationality in West Africa

In 1997 the Ghanaian newspaper *People and Places* ran an article with the headline "Fear Grips Accra." The article read:

> These so-called jujumen [i.e., witchcraft practitioners] who are operating under cover "infect" innocent people with mysterious "disease" through bodily contact, especially by shaking hands with their victims. Soon after this, the victims allegedly experience a burning and realize that their manhood has disappeared. According to the reports, whilst these innocent victims are going through this nightmarish experience, a member of the syndicate quickly approaches them claiming to know someone who could restore their manhood for an exorbitant fee.[8]

This was not the only article that summer about penis shrinking. Psychologist Glenn Adams, who was doing a Peace Corps stint in Sierra Leone at the time, was intrigued by the number and variety of these sensational stories, and by constant rumors of the evil eye, the invisible hand, and other unseen malevolent forces. He also knew that he was not living among primitive or paranoid people. So he wanted to find out, what is the local logic behind these beliefs that, to a Northern observer, seem so irrational?

Several years later, Adams returned to West Africa,[9] this time to Ghana. He and his colleagues studied newspaper reports of penis shrinkings. They interviewed witnesses, victims, and skeptics. Some of their sources thought witchcraft, or juju, was the culprit, sent in by enemies to settle old scores. Others asserted that the accusers didn't believe in witchcraft themselves, but were cynically exploiting other people's beliefs to bring down enemies.

Noting the common theme of enemies, Adams settled in to study the social science literature on enemyship. His discovery? There was no literature. He found plenty of studies on friendship, and on romantic love and familial love. He also found plenty of studies on stereotyping, prejudice, and intergroup hostility. But an idea that was very real and prevalent in West Africa, the idea that enemies are everywhere, was nowhere to be found in Northern social sciences.[10]

So Adams established a new area of study. At first, he simply surveyed people from various walks of life (students, urban professionals, rural dwellers) in Ghana and the United States about their enemies. The results were dramatic: In Ghana, from 60 to 90 percent of people reported that they believed the world harbored "people who hate you, personally, to the extent of wishing for your downfall or trying to sabotage your progress." Their belief in these enemies was emphatic: "Even Jesus Christ had enemies," said one respondent. "Who are you? If you want to live in a fool's paradise, fine. But as for me . . . I know I have enemies."[11]

Yet in the San Francisco Bay Area, a hotbed of cut-throat entrepreneurialism and corporate intrigue, only 10 percent of respondents thought they had enemies. In the Midwest, that figure rose to 20 percent. (See chapter 6 for more about the interdependence of the Midwest.) Adams also found that who makes up the enemy pool differs. Ghanaian respondents thought that enemies came from close to home: family, friends, neighbors, and schoolmates. "Even your best friend, somebody who might be close, might be your enemy," said one Ghanaian man. The few Americans who did perceive enemies, in contrast, saw them outside their own circles: business competitors and members of different social, ethnic, or political groups.[12]

Why would the supposedly interdependent selves of West Africa drive wedges of animosity between themselves and the people closest to them? The answer, ironically, lies in interdependence itself. West Africans see interdependence everywhere—between the self and others, mind and body, spirit and matter, past and future, long-gone ancestors and newborn children.[13] Instead of "I think, therefore I am," in West Africa they say, "I am because we are, and because we are, therefore I am."[14]

With so many social ties, even the most conscientious interdependent self is bound to cause a tangle. So when bad things happen to themselves or others, many West Africans look first to the people close to them, seen and unseen, and try to understand what the bungle was. They then attempt to appease their tormentors or otherwise undo their influence.

In contrast, Americans with independent selves construct their worlds in terms of choice. If a partner doesn't play nice, the offended can simply choose to end the relationship. Easy come, easy go. As one of Adams's American respondents put it "I think [having enemies] is up to the individual. If someone dislikes me then they can, but that does not make them my enemy. That is up to me to decide, and I choose not." An American woman likewise cited individual choice as the linchpin of enemyship: "I cannot quite understand how someone would make an enemy, or why one would continue to interact with somebody one did not like."[15]

Yet in West Africa, as across the Global South, relationships are seldom voluntary. They cannot be unmade when they become troublesome. People do not choose relations based on their preferences. Instead, people work overtime to maintain balance in their networks. Interdependence is a full-time interpersonal housekeeping project, and failing to keep the lines of relationship clear can result in accusations, threats, and even bodily harm.

The Bug inside Your Own Cloth

Why are West Africans so preoccupied with enemyship? A close look at the culture cycles in this region uncovers interactions and institutions that simultaneously nurture deep roots and distrust.

Songs, poems, painted slogans, and stickers everywhere warn, "No Man Is without Enemy," "I Am Afraid of My Friends, Even YOU," and "Let My Enemy Live Long and See What I Will Be in the Future." Many people display amulets to ward off envy, sabotage, and juju. In a practice also common in the Mediterranean, families seclude newborns and their mothers to avoid the "evil eye" of envious observers. And lest anyone forget where the enemies live, a popular proverb advises, "If an insect bites you, it comes from inside your clothes."[16]

Reflecting and reinforcing these interactions, in turn, are powerful institutions—and the powerful lack thereof—that sow mistrust throughout West Africa. The most powerful of these was the slave trade that plagued the region for more than four hundred years. From 1500 to 1900, slave traders forced between seven and twelve million Africans to undertake the infamous Middle Passage across the Atlantic. At least one million people died during this harrowing voyage, and unknown numbers more died during their capture.[17]

Interviews of slaves in the 1850s reveal the violence, deceit, and betrayal inherent in the practice of enslaving Africans. Many of the respondents told linguist Sigismund Koelle that they were kidnapped and forced into slavery. Others were taken during war. Some recounted being tricked onto a slave ship by a friend or relative. Still others were enslaved through a rigged judicial process that found them guilty of witchcraft and then bundled them and their families off to a slave ship.[18]

Although the slave trade in West Africa has been largely dormant for more than one hundred years, the institution fuels West African culture cycles to this day. Economists Nathan Nunn and Leonard Wantchekon used archival data to map the intensity of the slave trade in sub-Saharan Africa over five hundred years. They then compiled several contemporary studies on current attitudes in seventeen West African, East African, and South African countries, including measures of how much people trust their neighbors, relatives, and local government. They discovered that the more their ancestors encountered the slave trade in the past, the more modern-day residents mistrust each other in the present. An ugly history has left an ugly scar.[19]

The horrors of slavery are still palpable in contemporary interactions. In a local language of Benin, for instance, the definition of the word *untrustworthy* is "capable of tricking one's friend or neighbor into slavery." Similarly, many West African countries have proverbs such as "He will sell you and enjoy it."[20]

European colonialism from the early nineteenth century to the mid-twentieth century also did much to sow mistrust in the region. Pursuing a divide-and-conquer strategy, imperial powers manipulated existing tribal rivalries and created new conflicts. When the colonizers departed, the animosities remained. As a result, West African countries have had great difficulty establishing stable economic and legal institutions. Although Ghana and Nigeria score fairly well on the World Justice Project Rule of Law Index, other West African countries rank among the lowest in the world.[21] Without strong institutions to keep them in check, civil wars and crime are widespread. And because police and courts are often corrupt, vigilante justice is rampant.[22]

When we examine West African culture cycles, we see that the mistrust and instability in the region are not irrational, and rumors of penis shrinking are not the result of paranoid delusions. Instead, they are the understandable responses of interdependent people to horrifying histories. "You're not paranoid if they're really following you," the old saying goes. Moreover, if you have an interdependent self that is exquisitely sensitive to relationships, you more gravely bear the marks of a violent and treacherous past.

Cronyism in India

Interdependent in a different way, India inspires a different complaint from the Global North: you can't get anything done for all the corruption. The form of corruption that gets the Global North's goat is cronyism, the practice of appointing friends and family to positions of authority, regardless of their qualifications. Because of cronyism, families control businesses, and political parties control almost everything else. The results can be large and bad. An emerging view holds that the Asian economic crisis of 1997 came about because bank officers made too many loans to friends and family who could not repay them.[23]

At a more local level, cronyism makes life harder for the little guy, reports journalist Edward Luce in his book *In Spite of the Gods: The Rise of Modern India.* The political culture, he writes, includes "preferential access to a whole range of public goods, from free first-class plane and rail tickets, the opportunity to jump queues, the ability to pull strings, and the availability of free services for which the poor have to pay. . . . If you are rich and important, you rarely pay. If you are poor, you usually pay through the nose, and there is no guarantee you will get what you pay for."[24]

India pleads guilty to these charges of cronyism, and has spawned its own dissenters and instituted its own reforms. At the same time, however, many Indians ask, how *else* could you run a business or government? Don't organizations work best when people know and trust one another? And if you had the ability to lift an entire village out of poverty, why would you choose a village of strangers over a village of your own relatives?

A quick survey of the interdependent culture cycle of India reveals that cronyism is not always the result of greedy villains grabbing the fat of the land for their own people. Instead, it follows from a millennia-old moral code that stresses interpersonal duties over abstract notions of justice, law, and individual rights. In such a cycle, the Global North's cry for impartiality rushes headlong into India's understanding of morality.

Psychologist Joan Miller and her research teams have spent the past few decades documenting how European Americans and Hindu Indians solve dilemmas between relational duty, justice, and choice. To experience one of her studies, imagine this scenario: A man named Ben is on his way to his best friend's wedding, bearing the bride and groom's wedding rings. But then his wallet is stolen, leaving him without enough money for a train ticket. To arrive at the wedding on time, he must catch the very next train. While he is trying to figure out what to do, he notices that a well-dressed man sitting next to him in the train station has left his cashmere coat. Ben sees a train ticket sticking out of the pocket.[25]

Ben must think fast: should he break the law and steal the ticket so that he can get to the wedding in time and deliver the rings to his best friend, or should he leave the ticket alone, even though it means letting his best friend down? What would you decide?

If you are European American, you likely think that Ben should obey the law, as did the majority of European-American participants in this study. But if you are a Hindu Indian, you likely think that Ben should put his buddy's needs first and nick the ticket. In the Hindu moral universe, obligations to people you know rank higher than obligations to such abstract principles as "justice," "individual rights," and "rule of law."

With dozens of findings like this under her belt, Miller concludes that European Americans hew to a justice- or rights-based moral code, while Hindu Indians follow a duty- or caring-based moral code.[26]

Obligations to other people shape more mundane decisions in India, as well. Along with Hazel and Alana, psychologist Krishna Savani asked middle-class Indians and Americans how much they liked many types of shirts, shoes, watches, and other consumer goods shown to be equally desirable and familiar to both groups. We then asked these same participants to choose which of these items they would most like to have for themselves. Like good independent I's, the Americans chose the items they liked the most. In other words, their preferences and their choices were tightly correlated. But for the Indians, personal liking was less closely linked to their choices.[27] Savani explains: "Indians habitually consider what other people in their lives would choose for them before making their own selections. And so you often wind up choosing what you think your mom thinks you should have, or your sister or other people you know; not what you personally want."

A Basket Case

Hindu Indians also put more weight on the welfare of others than on their personal druthers. Consider this classic parable:

> A man and his wife lived with the husband's elderly father. The daughter-in-law was always thinking of how they could get rid of the old man. One day she had an idea. She told her husband, let us carry Father to Puri [a Hindu pilgrimage site] in a basket. There we will leave him on the Great Road in front of the Temple of Jaganath. . . . The husband agreed to this plan. But their son had overheard everything. He first warned his grandfather of the plot. Then he went to his father and said, "Father, you leave Grandfather at Puri just as you have said. But please do not leave the basket. Bring the basket back. Otherwise, what shall I use to carry you to Puri when you

become old?" The husband understood. He confessed everything to his father and begged his father's forgiveness.

Anthropologist Richard Shweder first heard this story in rural Bhubaneswar, Orissa, India, and reported it in his book *Why Do Men Barbecue?*[28] Shweder finds that India is awash in stories like this one—stories about putting duty above your own personal preferences.

Americans also tell stories about their duties to friends and family, and feel closely connected to the important people in their lives. But when the needs of family or friends conflict with their own personal needs and preferences, European Americans tend to opt for the latter.

For instance, imagine that you have a brother, and he has asked you to help him move to a new apartment. You share many interests with your brother and have a warm and affectionate relationship with him. How willing are you to help him?

Now imagine that you are not similar to your brother and do not feel close to him. How willing are you to help this brother?

If you are a European American, you are likely to feel more responsibility to help a brother you like than a brother you do not like, as did the European-American participants in a study from Joan Miller's lab. Whether you help depends on your personal preferences. It is a matter of choice. But if you are a Hindu Indian, you are equally willing to help both brothers. A moral obligation is a moral obligation. Whether you like your brother or not, helping him is a matter of right and wrong.[29]

Beds, Betrothals, and Bollywood

Examining the culture cycles in Hindu India, we see that daily interactions and institutions reinforce the idea that relationships with family and friends come first. Take a peek into the windows of many Hindu Indian homes at bedtime and you will see just how complete the weaving of individuals into families is. Most Hindu Indians live with three generations under the same roof. Parents wouldn't think of letting their children sleep alone—even older children, and even in families wealthy enough for every member to have his or her own room. In contrast, recent American bestsellers include *Solve Your Child's Sleep Problems*, in which Robert Ferber details his famous method for training children to sleep by themselves; and *Go the F★★k to Sleep*, a bedtime story for grown-ups whose children's lack of sleep is impinging on the parents' independence.[30]

To show how important it is to Indians to sleep next to their children, Shweder and his colleagues gave U.S. and Indian participants the task of arranging the following family members into two rooms for sleeping: father, mother, son (age fifteen), son (eleven), son (eight), daughter (fourteen), and daughter (three).

Among the Indians, 75 percent selected an arrangement in which the father slept with the three sons and the mother slept with the two daughters. Meanwhile, 44 percent of the Americans picked a sleeping solution that no Indians chose—the father and the mother sleeping with two daughters in one room, and the three sons sleeping together with no parent in another room. Many other Americans said the problem could not be solved; more rooms were needed.[31]

Because families, not individuals, are where the action is for Hindu Indians, whom to marry is a decision the whole family helps make. Even today, more than 80 percent of all marriages in India are arranged.[32] Brides- and grooms-to-be usually guide the search, and the woman usually (although not always) has the power to veto candidates. Once Indian families arrange a match, the couple schedules multiple meetings in person or over the phone to see if they fulfill each other's qualifications.

To find their son- or daughter-in-law, some pragmatic Hindu Indian parents advertise online and in publications, stressing their family's origins, heritage, and social standing. One recent ad reads, "Patel parents invite professional for their U.S.-raised daughter, 26, (computer science); family owns construction firm." Contrast this with the ad of a European-American woman searching for her own match: "Where shall I kiss thee? Across Sierra shoulder, skiing? Between acts of *Aida*, sharing? Forthright, funny, fiery, fit, seeking perceptive, profound, permanent partner." Instead of the Indian goal of matching families, the American ad aims to match personal preferences and traits.[33]

Many Westerners are certain that arranged marriages are oppressive, especially for women. Yet studies of arranged marriages suggest that these couples are no less satisfied than couples in so-called love marriages.[34] Many Indian women also disagree with the Western insistence that people choose their own partners. In her 2009 book, *First Comes Marriage:*

Modern Relationship Advice from the Wisdom of Arranged Marriages, British journalist Reva Seth interviewed three hundred women whose parents chose their spouses. "Over the long term that takes a lot of pressure off a relationship," she writes. When families get involved in a marriage from the beginning, they also bring with them a huge support network to help the couple work it out, she finds. And arranged marriages are not without love. "In India, they say first we marry, then we fall in love."[35]

Bollywood, India's film industry and one of the largest centers of film production in the world, does its part to support and reflect the importance of duty and obligation in relationships, just as America's Hollywood does its part to support and reflect the importance of choice and self-actualization in relationships. In one Bollywood hit, *Hum Dil De Chuke Sanam* (released in the English-speaking world as *Straight from the Heart*), a handsome man and beautiful woman fall in love, but the woman's parents don't approve of the marriage. The man leaves India for Italy, and the woman marries the man who received the parental okay.

The new husband feels so responsible for his wife's needs and happiness that he takes her to Italy to find her lost "true" love. Not knowing of her marriage, the first love proposes again. At this instant, the woman recognizes that she has already found true love, as "true" love comes from fulfilling obligations to the family.[36] She happily returns to India with her husband.

When European-American college students watch this film, many are perplexed. The husband's denial of his own desires makes little sense to them. But in an Indian culture cycle that turns on duty and obligation, sacrificing for others is not tantamount to depriving the self. Instead, it is a way of strengthening the interdependent self and being a good, moral person.

Long before Bollywood blockbusters, Hindu stories institutionalized the core ideas of interdependence on the Indian subcontinent. Hinduism is the most widespread of India's religions, and its themes, plots, and characters infuse everyone's daily life—from children's cartoons, to political campaigns, to the air fresheners swinging from rearview mirrors throughout the country.

One Hindu tale that drives home the centrality of familial duty is that of Ganesh and Karthik's race around the world. Ganesh is the Hindu god of beginnings and the remover of obstacles. With a human body and an elephant's head, he would seem less fleet than his younger brother, Karthik, who appears as a beautiful human boy.

Ganesh and Karthik set up a competition to find out who can complete a lap around the world the fastest. Karthik is confident that he will win, not only because of his grace and strength, but also because of his pet peacock. With a mouse as his sidekick, Ganesh's victory seems highly improbable. What Ganesh lacks in aerodynamics and feathered friends, however, he makes up for in wisdom. Reasoning that his parents represent the entire universe, he folds his hands and, with great devotion, walks around them.

"What are you doing?" Ganesh's father asks.

"I am your son," explains Ganesh. "To me, you two make up my whole world." When Karthik returns from his globetrotting, he accepts that Ganesh has won the competition. With a celebration that foreshadows Bollywood musical extravaganzas to come, everyone praises Ganesh.[37]

Violence in the Middle East and North Africa

In the mind's eye of the Global North, the Middle East and North Africa (MENA) region conjure images of rock throwing, grenade launching, and suicide bombing. Even before the attacks of 9/11 and the U.S. wars in Iraq and Afghanistan, the Global North's view of MENA was extremely negative. Recall, for instance, the opening song of the Disney film *Aladdin*, which portrays the Middle East as a barbaric, camel-ridden place where lopping off other people's ears is a common pastime.[38]

MENA is not the world's most violent region—that distinction belongs to Central America.[39] Yet MENA violence has a distinctive quality that lands it on the front pages of newspapers and the ten o'clock news. Recall, for example, the autumn of 2005, when the Danish newspaper *Jyllands-Posten* published several cartoons depicting the prophet Muhammad in less-than-adulatory fashion. One frame showed Muhammad wearing a turban shaped as a bomb with a burning fuse. Another featured him in heaven, greeting a line of sooty suicide bombers with "Stop! Stop! We ran out of virgins!"[40]

To Western audiences, the cartoonists were just exercising their freedoms of speech and religion. But among some MENA audiences, the perception was decidedly different. Protestors took to the streets, calling the cartoons Islamophobic and racist. They burned European flags. They attacked Danish embassies, setting fire to several and bombing the compound in Pakistan. By the time the dust had settled, more than a hundred people were dead.[41]

Most people do not like caricatures of their religion's leaders, but they seldom respond with murder and mayhem. Why did the cartoons provoke such a violent spasm in the Middle East and North Africa?

Part of the reason is that the cartoons were a direct assault on Islamic beliefs, which hold that depicting Muhammad is a sin. This affront to the traditions and values of Islam then ignited the form of interdependence unique to the region. Like the U.S. South, the Middle East harbors a culture of honor.[42] You rely on other people to grant you status by showing you respect. But other people can also take away your status by insulting you. To restore your status, you must answer the insult, often with force. (See chapter 6 for more on the U.S. South's culture of honor.)

More than selves in the U.S. South, MENA selves travel together. If you insult my honor, you also insult the honor of my parents, siblings, children, and cousins (and maybe also the honor of my grandparents, neighbors, and business partners). I must answer your insult on behalf of everyone in my network. The prime minister of Turkey, Recep Tayyip Erdoğan, displayed the MENA brand of interdependence at the 2009 World Economic Forum in Davos, Switzerland. Erdoğan was in the middle of an angry rebuttal to a fellow panelist, Israeli president Shimon Peres, when the panel moderator cut him off. (The moderator was enforcing a time limit.) Erdoğan abruptly left the stage. He later explained that his swift exit was necessary "to protect the honour of Turkey and Turkish people." Upon his return to Turkey, he was given a hero's welcome.[43]

When a Middle Easterner or North African does not adequately retaliate, the many people in his or her network may join in to help. Erdoğan sufficiently countered the moderator's seeming disrespect. But the public humiliation of the prophet Muhammad and, by extension, all Muslims could not be rectified by one or two people. So large swaths of MENA stepped up to settle the score against the Danish newspaper. For many of them, declaring neutrality in the matter would have been tantamount to harming the people in their networks and, thus, themselves.

Shared Selves

Managing the honor of one's entire social network is not just the business of prime ministers. In the Middle East, according to anthropologist Lawrence Rosen, "the defining feature of a man is that he has formed a web of indebtedness, a network of obligations that prove his capacity to maneuver in a world of relentless uncertainty."[44] Middle Easterners and North Africans of many stations and ranks keep close tabs on the relative standing of their friends, family members, and associates. From this interpersonal bookkeeping, they also derive their sense of their own social standing.

Batja Mesquita is one of the first psychologists to study interdependent selves in MENA. Comparing Turkish and Dutch college students she finds that many college students in MENA have stories like this one: "I was admitted to Turkey's most competitive university. . . . My parents had invited all their relatives and neighbors over to their house to celebrate this success. . . . Without me knowing it, my mother had taken [my student ID] to show to them." Other Turkish participants shared similar tales of family members basking in one another's triumphs and agonizing over one another's defeats.[45] They describe events in terms of their impact on one's relationships. Dutch respondents, in contrast, describe events in terms of their consequences for individual goals: "I felt relieved when I gave my final presentation at the university."

Middle Eastern and North African selves do not just feel the joys and pains of the people in their social networks; they sometimes feel them *more deeply* than they experience their own emotions. Sociologist James Greenberg asked respondents in Yemen and in the United States to list instances when they felt an emotion. Not only did the Yemeni respondents list more events that involved others (a friend did well on an exam, many people died in an earthquake), they also reported that events that happened to *other people* hit them harder than events that happened to them personally. This helps explain why, say, college students in Syria would get so upset about a few cartoon panels in a Danish newspaper. They feel the offense of other Muslims at least as intensely as they feel their own.[46]

The solidarity that the interdependent selves of MENA feel is apparent even on subtler measures. In one study, researchers asked Omani and European-American participants to view several large shapes made up of smaller shapes. For every large shape, one of the smaller shapes was unique and the rest were the same—for example, a square made up of eight circles and one triangle. Omani participants disliked the unique shape and preferred the common shapes, while the European Americans showed the opposite pattern.

The Ties That Bind

The culture cycles that reflect and reinforce MENA's unique variety of interdependence include daily interactions and societal institutions that knit people into far-flung yet tightly knotted networks. One everyday practice, for example, is calling people not only by their proper names, but also by their ties to family and place. The president of the Palestinian Authority, Mahmoud Abbas, is addressed in both formal and informal settings as Abu Mazen ("Mazen's father"), and Saddam Hussein's full name included "al-Tikriti" ("from [the village of] Tikrit").[47]

Another practice that keeps the networks connected is *wasta*, which roughly translates from the Arabic as "whom you know" or, more bluntly, "nepotism" or "cronyism." Similar to Indians, Middle Easterners and North Africans tender *wasta* to accomplish everything from putting in a phone line to getting out of legal trouble. Despite considerable influence from the Global North, *wasta* is still the main currency in MENA. A recent Gallup poll finds that the majority of youth in the League of Arab States believe that *wasta* is critical to their future success.[48] Their parents not only agree, but also lay the foundation for a *wasta*-enriched adulthood. Unlike their counterparts in the Global North, most Middle Eastern and North African parents do not endeavor to help their children leave home, choose a profession, and make their own independent lives. Instead they view their children as members of the family organization. These family organizations form the backbones of businesses, neighborhoods, religious orders, and political parties, many of which call their leaders "father."

As was the case in India, Middle Easterners and North Africans do not view *wasta* only as a cause of mismanagement and corruption. Instead they also see it as a source of ethical behavior. When you secure a phone line or a driver's license, you must let your relatives use your phone and give your friends rides. If you have a good job, you should help your sister get a good job.

Imagine the following situation: Your sibling is getting bad grades in college and is having difficulty finding a summer internship. As it happens, you have a friend who is well placed in a consulting firm. Would you ask your friend to arrange an internship for your sibling without an interview?"

In a recent study, 42 percent of European-American college students answered "yes" to this question. But a full 70 percent of Turkish students agreed that they would try to arrange the internship for their sibling. Most of the European Americans who declined did so because they were worried about their own reputations. But many Turks who agreed to ask a friend to pull strings did so for interdependent reasons. As one Turkish participant said, "I would do it because I am not selfish."[49]

For MENA interdependent selves, it is the failure to share the fruits of their labors or their good luck that is corrupt. "For most Arabs," writes Lawrence Rosen, "it is only realistic to believe that society is better served by webs of obligation than impersonal roles, and that institutions are always defined by their occupants and not by depersonalized powers."

"To grasp that," he concludes, "is to enter a world of enormous decency, even if it is not our world."[50]

To maintain that decency, the interdependent selves that erect and echo MENA's culture cycles work hard to keep their networks balanced. When one person gives a little more than she receives, she can count on the recipient later to have her back. And the more people she has in her debt, the more insurance she has when times are lean. Yet she wants to avoid being too indebted to any one person, as this would disturb her relationships with the many other people in her social web.

The economist Simon Gächter and his colleagues recently captured the intricate machinations of reciprocity among Middle Easterners. In their study, participants in Oman, Saudi Arabia, the United States, Great Britain, and Australia played an economics game in groups of four people. In a first round, players could give too much, not enough, or just the right amount of rewards to the group. In subsequent rounds, participants could either punish or reward their fellow players. The researchers observed something strange they had not seen in other places: As expected, participants everywhere punished so-called freeloaders who did not contribute enough to the group. But the Middle Eastern participants from Oman and Saudi Arabia also punished the "pushovers" who created an imbalance by giving too much to the group.[51]

MENA is a tremendously diverse region. Yet many culture cycles there reflect and reinforce an honor-bound, networked style of interdependence. The Israeli film *Footnote*,[52] for example, tells the story of a great rivalry between a father and son who are both professors of the Talmud. When the father is accidentally awarded a coveted national prize intended for the son, a heated debate ensues:

"There are a few things more important than truth," says the son.

"Like what?" asks an incredulous colleague.

"Family," he answers.

Inefficiency in Mexico

"Mañana, yes. Today, maybe no."[53]

The sense that tomorrow is as good as today, and maybe even better, routinely frustrates relations between the Global North and Mexico. Why is Mexico so comfortable in the slow lane? And why does Mexico's inefficiency and lateness so irritate Northerners? The answer: Mexicans have the time, but Northerners have the clock.

Mexicans need the time. Their particular form of interdependence revolves around the notion of *simpatía*, or pleasant relationships. Cultivating *simpatía* takes a lot of time, and putting relationships first means that many of the Global North's highest priorities (profits, individual achievement, and punctuality) take a backseat. Some impatient observers in *El Norte* suspect that the Mexicans are just slacking off, lazing around, or refusing to understand how business works. Yet they could not be further from the truth. Mexicans are very busy putting the "human" back in *human resources*. Global Northerners who want to break into business in Mexico must learn how to work on Mexican time and with interdependent Mexican selves.

Feel Better with *Simpatía*

As is true for all regions of the Global South, research on how culture and the self make each other up in Mexico is just beginning. A combination of studies with Mexican, Mexican-American, and other Latino participants begins to shed light on the workings of interdependence, Mexican-style.

In the 1980s, for example, pioneering cultural psychologist Harry Triandis gave vignettes to Latino participants and asked them to predict the behavior of a set of characters. When the characters were Latinos, participants guessed that they would be more sociable, more agreeable, and less negative than when the characters were European Americans.[54]

Just because people with Latin heritage think they are brimming with *simpatía* doesn't mean that they actually are. They could just be holding positive stereotypes of their own group. To test this possibility in a carefully controlled experiment, psychologist Renee Holloway and her colleagues joined European-American, African-American, and Latino students in either same-ethnicity or different-ethnicity pairs and asked them to have a conversation. Participants of all ethnicities rated their conversations with Latino partners as more involving and of higher quality than they rated conversations with non-Latinos. People with Latino partners wanted to have more future conversations than did people with African-American or European-American partners. So Latinos are not the only people who think they inspire harmonious and pleasant relations. European Americans and African Americans agree with them.

How do Latinos make their conversation partners feel so good? It doesn't happen automatically. Holloway finds that Latinos put more effort into promoting smooth relations than do African Americans or European Americans. Latinos actively focus on their partners' positive qualities; they try to feel good about their partners so that they can make them feel good. Latinos also smile and make more eye contact with their conversation partners than do European Americans and African Americans.[55]

Simpatía doesn't just make for scintillating conversation; it also motivates better cognitive performance. Psychologist Krishna Savani and his colleagues asked Mexican and European-American college students to write about times when they experienced good feelings either toward another person or toward themselves. Next they asked the participants to solve word puzzles. While the European Americans solved an equal number of puzzles in both conditions, the Mexican students solved the most puzzles after recalling a time when they felt good about another person.[56]

In worlds where cooperation is in higher demand than competition, *simpatía* pays off. Psychologist Millard Madsen and his team invited children between the ages of seven and ten to learn to play a marble game that, unbeknownst to them, rewarded them for cooperating and punished them for competing. The Mexican children readily figured out how to cooperate and win more marbles. The European-American children seemed to have trouble keeping their competitive tendencies in check, and thus won fewer marbles.[57]

Simpatía can have its downsides. European Americans commonly complain that in Mexico many people will give directions for, say, a church or a road, even if they have no idea where it is. What the gringos don't understand is that for these interdependent selves, the primary goal of the interaction is often to produce warm feelings, not to exchange information about objective reality.[58]

La Familia

Mexican families give their children plenty of opportunities to practice *simpatía* in their daily interactions. Studies show that people with Latino backgrounds spend much more of their time socializing with family than do European Americans.[59] And "family," by the way, "means your mom and dad and brothers and sisters and cousins and second cousins and cousins of your aunt's husband's sister and aunts of your mom's second cousin Dionisia from Veracruz," says Juan Faura, a marketing expert who targets the growing Latino population in the United States.[60]

A basic law of the Hispanic universe, he says, is that "family is always first."

Statements such as this elicit cries of "Stereotyping!" from many Latinos, who despair that their "pro-family attitudes" are the only thing that European Americans have ever noted about them. Yet central to understanding Mexican selves is that their devotion to family goes far beyond attitudes. People everywhere have pro-family attitudes. European Americans, for all their independent ways, cite "family" as the main reason their lives go well.[61] But in Mexico, the individual requires the family not just to thrive, but also to be a complete self.

Consequently, many Mexican adolescents do not aim, once they grow up, to individuate and leave home. In fact, just the opposite is the case. A one highly qualified Latina admitted to a prestigious U.S. college asked, "Why would I want to leave my home and fly across the country to live in a small room with a person I have never met?" In surveys of American college students, those of Mexican heritage report the most frequent contact with their parents.[62] Following college, many Latino graduates evaluate employment opportunities based on how they will affect the family. Families stick together even when they have the differences in activities, interests, and lifestyles that often drive European-American families apart. Both Mexicans and Mexican Americans rate their families as more cohesive than do European Americans.[63]

The quest for *simpatía* and family connection extends to other social relationships. When people become close in Mexico, they call each other by familial titles of "sister," "brother," or "cousin," instead of "friend" or "partner." When children are born, the family invites a man and woman to serve as godparents. These compadres (cofathers) and comadres (comothers) can be called upon for loans, jobs, and other types of support.[64]

As is the case in India and MENA, nepotism is widespread in Mexico. In an environment where many formal institutions are relatively new and impersonal, working in the family's business is the preferred occupation. "You trust your blood, and that's it," says Gregorio Chedraui, a member of one of Mexico's most successful business families, with interests ranging from retail to roads. Many of his countrymen feel the same way; 80 percent of Mexican respondents agree that "one should be cautious in relations outside the family."[65]

Doing business in Mexico, in turn, requires plugging into existing family networks. Julio Garcia, an American-trained social psychologist, now runs his family's avocado business in Mexico. "When you have a problem in the United States," says Garcia, "you think, 'How can *I* do this?' In Mexico you say, 'Who in my family can help me do this?'

"I needed to have [Mexican] government approval for a business project," Garcia recalls. "When I discussed this with a friend, he was surprised that I had not talked to an uncle who has experience doing this kind of thing. So off I went to talk to my uncle. After hearing me out, he gave me the name and number of a person to call. Most importantly, he gave me his business card, and said, 'When you talk to him, give him my card.' On the back of the card, he had written, 'Compadre, this is my nephew. Greetings.' "

Not long after meeting with the official, Garcia received the approval he needed."[66]

Strengthen Institutions

We do not presume to have specific solutions to all the problems of West Africa, India, the Middle East and North Africa, and Mexico. Each of these topics commands the expertise of thousands of academic departments, government agencies, nongovernmental organizations (NGOs), and corporations. Yet we do have a few general recommendations for how the Global North, by infusing more interdependence into its culture cycles, can alleviate suffering in the Global South. We also suggest a few independent tendencies that the Global South could adopt to partner more effectively with the Global North.

At the level of institutions, Global Northerners should make a greater effort to work with the laws, norms, policies, and social structures that are already in place in the Global South, rather than imposing their own. Two of the Global North's hottest exports are free-market capitalism and democracy. Many economists in the Global North believe that free-market capitalism is the fastest path to economic growth, and that economic growth is the foundation of stable democracies. Yet the relationships between free markets, wealth, and democracy are much more complicated. Plenty of rich countries are not democracies (think Singapore, China, and Saudi Arabia).[67] Plenty of rich democracies did not get that way because of their free markets (think Norway, Finland, and Japan). And plenty of democracies (including the United States) are finding that capitalism is eroding democracy, as weakened governments can no longer keep powerful corporations from trampling individual liberties.[68]

What stable, prosperous countries do have in common, contend economists Daron Acemoglu and James Robinson, are strong institutions. By protecting the long-term well-being of their citizens, these institutions encourage individuals to invest in their communities. Many society-stabilizing institutions are obvious to the Northern eye: judiciaries that check executives, police departments that don't accept bribes, food-protection agencies whose arbiters are not on the payroll of food companies. But many stabilizing institutions of the Global South are not immediately apparent to

Northern observers: for example, village kinship structures in Sudan that equitably distribute food, or family networks in India that lift entire regions out of poverty.[69]

Many of the most successful NGOs work to strengthen these home-grown institutions, rather than sidestepping or undermining them. Seattle-based Rural Development Institute (RDI) is one of them. In much of the Global South, the difference between poverty and prosperity is land. But most poor tenant farmers cannot amass the wealth they need to purchase a plot.

Historically, the most popular solution to the problem of widespread poverty and landlessness was a revolution. But RDI takes a more interdependent approach. Since 1967, the nonprofit has helped more than 400 million rural farmers in 40 countries take ownership of some 270 million acres (about 7 percent of the world's arable land). It has done so by working directly with governments to reform laws, and to develop programs that give old landowners a fair price for their property, and new landowners what they need to succeed. Although the organization's mission ("to secure land rights for the world's poorest people") is rock-solid, its tactics are highly flexible so that it can meet the unique needs and strengths of each region.[70]

The Positive Deviance Initiative is another nonprofit that works with local networks to make change. Monique and Jerry Sternin, a husband-and-wife team, developed the positive deviance approach to solving problems in the late 1990s as they worked to reduce child malnutrition in Vietnamese villages. (Although we do not delve into the culture cycles of Southeast Asia here, this region is considered part of the Global South.) The Sternins first asked, which children in these villages are *not* malnourished? And what are their families doing that is different? The couple discovered that the parents of the better-nourished children fed them tiny shrimp and crabs they collected from the rice paddies, and sweet potato greens. Local wisdom held that these foods were not good for children, but the health of the children eating them suggested otherwise. The Sternins then asked these "deviant" parents to teach their cooking techniques to fellow villagers.

In other words, the Sternins assumed that the villagers already knew how to solve their own problems and were the best people to teach their solutions to one another. Through their organization, the Sternins have bottled their approach to helping people define and solve their own problems, and have successfully applied it all over the world, to issues ranging from female genital cutting in Egypt, to MRSA infections in Colombian hospitals, to child prostitution in Indonesia.[71]

Represent Fairly

To improve the interactions in its culture cycle, the Global North must also improve its media representations of the Global South. In his survey of more than nine hundred Hollywood films with Arab characters, film scholar Jack Shaheen found that only a dozen included positive portrayals. For interdependent MENA dwellers who are already sensitive to insults, these unflattering representations hurt.[72] Hollywood also does a brisk trade in negative portrayals of Latinos as banditos, harlots, buffoons, and lovers, rather than as equal actors on the global stage.[73]

And though representations of African Americans in the U.S. media are numerous and negative (see chapter 4 for examples), representations of Africans are most notable for their absence. Stories about Africa comprised less than 5 percent of "Top News" or "Latest News" on the *New York Times* home page, and less than 2 percent on CNN's home page.[74]

Even *National Geographic* magazine, the Global North's beloved window on the rest of world, sullies the image of its subjects in the Global South. In their classic work, *Reading National Geographic*, anthropologists Catherine Lutz and Jane Collins analyzed more than six hundred photographs from across thirty-seven years of the magazine's history, and the methods behind snapping and editing the shots. They learned that editors and photographers adopted many practices to make their subjects in the Global South seem more exotic, primitive, and sexual, including asking subjects to put on more traditional clothing, changing skin tones to make them appear darker, and featuring the naked bodies of women of color (never White women).[75]

Get Out More

Unflattering media portrayals of the Global South are reflected in the individual minds of Global Northerners. In 2011, for example, a cartoon map titled "The World according to Americans" went viral on the

Internet. MENA was flagged with "Evil-doers!!" and "Bombs go here." South America's label read, "Coffee comes from here, I think," and Mexico's inglorious signage was "They do our laundry." India was mostly absent, although some malformed portion of it was lumped in with China under "They make our stuff."

And Africa? Africa was missing altogether. It wasn't even on the map.[76]

Because media representations of the Global South are so flawed, Global Northerners who have the time and money should make the effort to travel to the Global South. Travel helps not only broaden their knowledge, but may also expand their creative powers. Psychologists Will Maddux and Adam Galinsky tested the creativity of two groups of MBA students at a large business school in the United States, some who had lived abroad and some who had not. They gave participants a picture of several objects on a table: a candle, a pack of matches, and a box of tacks, all of which were next to a cardboard wall. Their task was to figure out how to attach the candle to the wall so that, when lit, its wax would not fall on to the floor.

Can you figure out the solution? It's difficult to conjure, but obvious when you see it: pin the tack box to the wall and use it to hold the candle. Sixty percent of the students who had lived abroad solved the problem, but only 42 percent of those who had never lived abroad were able to do so. And the longer students had been overseas, the more likely they were to come up with the right answer. The researchers explain that the creative problem-solving skills people develop when bridging cultural differences spill over to other domains. As Mark Twain observed, "Travel is fatal to prejudice, bigotry and narrow-mindedness."[77]

Upon alighting in the Global South, take the time to make and maintain relationships. This is especially true if you want to do business. In many parts of West Africa, MENA, India, and Mexico, the first order of business is sharing a meal, meeting family or friends, and discussing personal interests. Ignoring all that "soft stuff" and getting right down to business, as is the instinct of many Global Northerners, can seem rude.

Sidestepping relationships can also be counterproductive. Psychologist Jeffrey Sanchez-Burks and his colleagues trained one group of American MBA students to pay more attention to their own and other people's relational styles and social needs. They gave a second control group a standard training in cultural differences. The students then spent six weeks consulting to firms in Santiago, Chile. The researchers found that students who had received the standard training were less successful at getting the information they needed to do their jobs than were the students who had received the relational training.[78]

Leverage the North

Global Southerners can likewise take steps to work more effectively with their neighbors up north. By polishing their independent streak, for instance, they can leverage Northern institutions for Southern goals. Chief Almir Surui, leader of the Surui people of the Brazilian Amazon, did just this. Loggers, miners, and other developers were increasingly encroaching upon his people's ancestral lands, arguing that the areas had no proven value and were therefore up for grabs. The Surui needed to inventory the many natural and cultural resources in their neck of the woods. They needed a map.

Chief Almir heard of a U.S.-based company that uses GPS and the Internet to make detailed maps. Breaking with thousands of years of history—his tribe had no contact with Europeans until the 1960s—he got in touch with his independent side and reached out to this company, Google, and to other organizations in the Global North, including the Virginia-based Amazon Conservation Team and the California-based Skoll Foundation. Within three years, the partners had not only mapped the many treasures of the Surui homelands, but had also set up a surveillance system to detect illegal activities on the land. Google also anointed Chief Surui a "Google Earth Hero," which helped the tribe and its NGO partners secure more than $2 million to protect biodiversity and cultural diversity in the Amazon.[79]

The Global South can harness not only Northern institutions, but also Northern practices and products. With them, they can inspire people to speak up, act out, and change their local culture cycles for the better. A surprisingly potent cultural product that organizations throughout Africa, Asia, and Latin America are using to instill a little independence is that warhorse of daytime television, the soap opera. In 2002 in Ethiopia, for example, thousands of listeners religiously tuned into *Yeken Kignit*, a radio soap opera that followed the travails of a young woman whose husband contracts HIV from a neighbor. The heroine bucks tradition and bravely travels to a clinic to get tested for the dreaded disease. After discovering that she is negative, she forgives her husband, cares for him until his death, remarries, and lives happily ever after. The series inspired more than fifteen thousand letters from its listeners, many of them from women testifying that the program had prompted them and their husbands to get tested for HIV.[80]

Yeken Kignit is one of many soap operas that the Vermont-based Population Media Center has produced to endorse smaller families, elevate the status of women and girls, and reduce the transmission of HIV in Africa and Asia. The soaps draw heavily on the research of psychologist Albert Bandura, who has spent decades demonstrating how media role models can change the behaviors of their audiences.[81] Combining the science of the North with indigenous genius, the radio plays employ local writers, actors, and producers to create riveting characters and plots that encourage listeners to reconsider their traditions and beliefs.[82]

The play's also the thing for reducing ethnic tensions in Rwanda, Burundi, and the Democratic Republic of the Congo. Every week, millions of radio listeners tune in to *Musekeweya* (*New Dawn*), a Romeo-and-Juliet soap opera that teaches Hutus and Tutsis how to heal the wounds of the past and prevent future violence.[83] Like *Yeken Kignit*, *Musekeweya* mixes Northern science with Southern soap. Sociologist Ervin Staub has documented that most genocides follow a common course: social instability leads to the scapegoating of a less powerful group, and then to an ideology that justifies aggression against that group. But if enough people speak out against this us-and-them thinking and the leaders who would manipulate it, communities can avoid the spiral into violence.[84]

Musekeweya models this intervention. Characters who intercede in unjust activities, criticize divisive leaders, and mend rifts between neighbors become the show's heroes. These characters are now so beloved that parents are naming their children after them, reports Radio Benevolencija, a Dutch nonprofit that partners with local actors and writers to produce the show.[85] The soap is not just popular; it works, psychologist Betsy Paluck finds. Her carefully controlled evaluation showed that listeners were more likely than non-listeners to stand up to authority and voice their own opinions in their communities.[86] Anecdotes of *Musekeweya*'s effectiveness abound. For instance, surrendering rebels at the Rwanda-Congo border cite the show as their main reason for giving up the fight.[87]

Try a Little Meritocracy

Another independent practice that would not only elicit the North's trust, but also increase the South's effectiveness, is to hire and promote people because of their qualifications, not just their connections. Note that this suggestion does not preclude hiring friends and relatives. But cronyism and nepotism become major problems when incompetent people crowd out competent ones.

A strict meritocracy would solve this problem. But even the Global North, for all its independence, fails miserably on the meritocracy front (as we saw in the 42 percent of European-American students who would seek internships for their sisters). In the United States, for example, nine out of ten businesses are family-owned. This includes 40 percent of Fortune 500 companies.[88] "Family tradition and continuity exist in our society, even though we pride ourselves on valuing merit above all," says Adam Bellow (son of author Saul Bellow), author of the book *In Praise of Nepotism*. "We are more like Swiss cheese, where you have pockets of nepotism in a framework of meritocracy."[89]

Rather than insisting on a system that few can follow, both the Global North and the Global South might do better to follow a middle way: make sure the friends and family you are hiring are competent for the job, and then invest in making them even better. To our knowledge, no organization in the Global North is explicitly implementing this idea. But it does seem to be the common practice of many organizations the world over.

The Platinum Rule

Many traditions teach the Golden Rule: "Do unto others as you would have done unto you." But the Global North and South so often clash because what you want done unto you is *not* what others want done unto them. Interdependent selves do not want to be treated independently, and vice versa.

To sow greater peace and prosperity, we suggest that that Golden Rule get a makeover. We propose what sociologist Milton Bennett calls the Platinum Rule: "Do unto others as they themselves would have done unto them."[90] To this end, Global Northerners attempting to meet their Southern neighbors in the middle can try these tactics:

- Ask people what they need.
- Partner with local institutions instead of imposing your own.
- Place relationships first, business second.
- Accurately portray the Global South in the media.
- Travel southward.

Meanwhile, Global Southerners who want to partner with their colleagues to the north can consider implementing these techniques:

- Ask for help.
- Leverage the institutions of the Global North.
- Reward competence.
- Use media to spark action and debate.
- Look for options.

By polishing its interdependence, Global Northerners might more readily understand that Global Southerners are not inherently more irrational, corrupt, senselessly violent, or inefficient than they. Meanwhile, by honing its independence, the Global South might better partner with Global Northerners, rather than writing them off as frosty and exploitative.

CHAPTER 10

Self-Made

The Culture of You

Two women sit on a bench holding hands. They are mirror images of each other except for their clothing and accessories. The woman on the left wears a white Victorian dress with a stiff collar. Her bodice is open to reveal that her heart is sliced in half. The darker woman on the right wears a colorful Mexican dress. Her heart is also visible, but it is whole. A thin red vein connects the two women's hearts. The woman in white is clamping another vein, but blood still drips onto her skirt. The colorfully clothed woman is also holding a vein, but hers terminates in a locket with her husband's portrait, and does not bleed.

The Two Fridas is one of artist Frida Kahlo's most famous paintings. Her surrealist self-portrait captures the many culture clashes that made up her self. Born in Mexico in 1907 to a German-Jewish father and a Mexican-Catholic mother, Kahlo defied gender roles and artistic conventions to paint in her own distinctive style. Yet she struggled to win the approval of her husband, the much older artist Diego Rivera. In 1939, as the couple was divorcing, Kahlo painted *The Two Fridas* to express the battles inside and outside her self, not only between male and female, but also between European and Mexican, rich and poor, and modern and traditional.[1]

This attempt to reconcile her selves on canvas was not Kahlo's last. Of her 143 paintings, 55 were self-portraits, all of which blended the many identities with which she was contending.[2] She was ahead of her time not just in style, but also in subject. Today, more people are labeling themselves as "biracial" or "multicultural" than ever before.[3] On the 2010 U.S. Census, for example, some nine million people checked more than one box to indicate their race.[4] And the ranks of the multicultural are poised to explode; one in seven new marriages is interracial or interethnic.[5] Hybrid national, gender, and class identities are also on the rise.[6]

As Kahlo's art depicts, grappling with the many cultures you inhabit and that inhabit you results in a unique work: your self. In previous chapters, we have shown how culture cycles forge similarities among people. In this chapter, we examine how they feed individuality.

The culture cycles of hemispheres, genders, races, classes, regions, religions, workplaces, and global economic divides give people the raw materials for crafting selves. But because each person interacts with a unique set of culture cycles, no two selves are exactly alike. Also, no two people reconcile the tensions between their cultural identities in exactly the same way.

Consequently, what it means to be Polish, or a man, or middle class, or a firefighter depends on all the other culture cycles rolling through a particular life. Consider two Peruvians. A nineteen-year-old woman attending university in Lima will have a decidedly different self than a fifty-year-old man farming potatoes outside of Cuzco. Likewise, if you are a high-school-educated, Jewish, White, female nonprofit-food-bank employee in New Jersey, your self will differ in many ways from that of a college-educated, Baptist, Black, male oil company executive in Houston. The fact that you are both Americans, however, will mean that you share a similar strand of independence that comes with being citizens of the United States in the twenty-first century.

So what makes you unique is not just your quirky set of chromosomes. Your individuality also comes from all your cultures and how you combine them in your daily life. Like Kahlo, whose personal title was "the one who gave birth to herself,"[7] you, too, are an artist of your I, creatively mixing all your different cultural currents to make you *you*.

Unlike Frida Kahlo, however, you live in a world that not only welcomes many-sided selves, but requires them. Knowing when and how to be independent or interdependent is a twenty-first-century skill—one that will allow individuals to thrive in increasingly diverse societies, and to face the outsize environmental and social problems plaguing our planet. In this final chapter, we leave you with several tools that will help you understand, refine, and deploy both sides of your self.

Add It Up

You don't have to be an avant-garde *artiste* with family from all over to be multicultural. All of us interact with many cultures in a single day and across our lives. You are born into some of them, including your nationality, gender, race, ethnicity, region, religion, and class. You pick up others by, say, moving, getting a college education, choosing a particular career, or living in an ethnically diverse neighborhood. Some of these identities come with culture cycles that inspire more independence; others yield more interdependence.

What cultures make up *your* self? Given your cultural exposures,[8] do you tend to be more independent or interdependent? Or are you equally both? In this book, we've explored only eight of the dozens of cultural contexts that foster and flow from your self. Yet keeping up with even this small number of cultures can be difficult. To help you sort your self out, we suggest you use this scorecard:

NAME:

	Independent		Interdependent	
Hemisphere	*West*		*East*	
Gender	*Male*		*Female*	
Race/Ethnicity	*White*		*Of Color*	
Class	*Middle*		*Working*	
Religion	*Mainline Protestant, Not religious*		*Conservative Protestant, Catholic, Jewish, Other*	
U.S. Region	*Northeast, West*		*South, Midwest*	
Workplace	*Business*		*Government, Nonprofit*	
Global Region	*Global North*		*Global South*	
TOTAL				

To complete the scorecard, think about the culture cycles with which you have interacted for each of the rows. If you have mostly interfaced with independent cycles for a given culture, then give yourself a 1 in the "Independent" column and a 0 in the "Interdependent" column. But if you have rolled mostly with interdependent culture cycles, then mark a 1 in the "Interdependent" column and a 0 in the "Independent" column. And if you've interacted with both, then write a 1 in both columns.

In the case of "Hemisphere," if you have lived your whole life in the United States, for example, you should probably give yourself a 1 for "Independent" and a 0 for "Interdependent." But if you have spent all your days in Korea, you should mark 0 for "Independent" and 1 for "Interdependent." And if you've grown up mostly in the United States, but spent summers in Korea with family, then you get a 1 in both columns. After you score yourself for all eight cultures, add up the columns. The totals will suggest whether you tend to use your independent or interdependent self.

Exactly how your cultures come together to make your self is a big question. We do not mean to imply that you should be able to figure it out during your drive home from work or your summer vacation. But by contemplating all the culture cycles of which you are a part, and how they intersect within you, you may gain a greater understanding of your self.

More to You

You may think there are more sides to your self than the scorecard tracks. We agree. In addition to the eight cultural categories we cover in this book, many others impact the shape your self takes. When did your family immigrate to the United States, and did they come voluntarily? Are you straight, gay, bisexual, or some other sexual identity? Do you live in a city, suburb, or rural area? Do you have any psychological or physical challenges? Which sports do you follow? Which teams do you cheer for? How do you let off steam on a Saturday afternoon? These are just a few of the culture cycles that may nudge you toward a more independent or interdependent self.

One particularly powerful cultural force is the generation (or cohort) you were born into. The Greatest Generation (also known as the G.I. Generation, born between 1901 and 1924),[9] for example, came of age amid the Great Depression and World War II, and then went on to become the productive, civic-minded, team-playing heroes of the twentieth century. But their grandchildren, the Baby Boomers (born between 1943 and 1960) were a notoriously independent lot. Singing along with Bob Dylan's "The Times They Are A-Changin'," they protested the Vietnam War, rejected organized religion, experimented with drugs and free love, and demanded equal rights for African Americans, Native Americans, women, and other groups.

Now the Baby Boomers' children and grandchildren, Generation X (or the Gen Xers; born between 1961 and 1981) and the Millennials (born between 1982 and 2004) are giving their predecessors a run for their independent money. Psychologist Jean Twenge calls this cohort Generation Me because these Americans "take it for granted that the self comes first."[10] Twenge has been tracking generational changes in psychological features for more than a decade. With psychologist Stacy Campbell, she recently reviewed data from 1.4 million people who filled out personality, attitude, psychopathology, or behavior questionnaires between 1930 and today. The authors discovered that, over time, Americans have developed higher self-esteem, narcissism, confidence, and assertiveness, and lower need for social approval.[11] As Twenge explains in her book *Generation Me*, this cohort is even more individualistic than the Boomers, who did not slouch into their independence until young adulthood. Even then, when the Boomers turned on, tuned in, and dropped out, they did so *in groups*. In contrast, the Gen Xers and Millennials like to go it alone.[12]

Your Superpower

Beholding the complexity of your self, you may be thinking, wouldn't it be better to have a simpler, single-sided I?

Even if this were possible, it wouldn't be desirable. That's because self-complexity is your superpower. As Kahlo's oeuvre suggests, having all those selves at your behest is good for creativity. Recall from the last chapter that people who have traveled to other cultures generate more out-of-the-box solutions than people who stay put. Other studies show that globetrotters, compared to homebodies, come up with many more uses for a brick, generate more names of fruits (durian, anyone?), and spot more connections between seemingly far-flung concepts. (Quick: what word i related to *rough*, *resistance*, and *beer*?*)[13] Originality also comes more easily to people who speak more than one language, who work in diverse teams, and who live in societies that have opened themselves to the outside world.[14] Not only are these international I's more imaginative, psychologists Angela Leung and Chi-yue Chiu note, but they are also "less intimidated by the practices, artifacts, and concepts that are different from or even in conflict with those in their own culture."[15]

Complex selves are also good for coping with adversity. The more facets you have to your self, the more tools you have to deal with a variety of circumstances, finds psychologist Patricia Linville. For example, say you put all your psychological eggs into the basket of being the best engineer possible. Life might trundle along swimmingly until your company has to downsize, and you find yourself unemployed. Your I is no longer, and you are devastated. Yet if you've built a self that is not only an excellent engineer, but also a loving husband, a fun father, a skilled model-builder, and an enthusiastic soccer coach, you have more selves in reserve. These other selves may or may not pay the bills, but they can help stave off the anxiety and depression that often come with unemployment.[16]

For ethnic minorities, nurturing your psychological bazaar is especially important. Psychologists Veronica Benet-Martinez and Angela Nguyen reviewed multiple studies on how minorities should best mix with mainstream American culture. Rather than accepting the melting pot idea that immigrants should give up their first selves and assimilate to their new home, embracing all one's identities was the surest path to health and well-being.[17] This approach was also better than clinging only to an old-country identity.

Having a complex self is good not only for individuals, but also for society at large. When you appreciate your own complexity, your default assumption about people on the other side of a cultural divide is not that they're incompetent, uncaring, or evil. Instead, your first guess is that they are operating according to different culture cycles. So you ask questions, judge more slowly, and act more carefully. In so doing, you reduce the likelihood of conflict, and maybe even discover something new about the person, yourself, or the world.[18]

---

* The answer is *draft*.

Both Sides of Obama

A quick look at a few contemporary leaders reveals that their selves include both independent and interdependent elements. Consider Barack Obama, for example. Does Obama seem more independent, more interdependent, or equal parts of both?

To answer this question, let's fill in his scorecard, starting with the "Hemisphere" row. Although some diehard Birthers might argue otherwise, Obama was born and has lived most of his life in the United States. Yet from ages six to ten, he lived with his mother and stepfather in interdependent Indonesia, where he spent considerable time even after returning to the United States. So, on the "Hemisphere" dimension, we assign Obama two 1s.

As a male who identifies as such, Obama gets one point in the "Independent" column for "Gender." And although his mother was White and his father was Black, Obama refers to himself as Black. So in the "Race" row, he gets a 1 for interdependence and a 0 for independence. (If he considered himself biracial or multicultural, he would score 1s in both columns.) With a bachelor's degree from Columbia and a law degree from Harvard, Obama is highly educated, so in the "Class" row he scores a 1 for independence and a 0 for interdependence. And as a longtime member of a Black Protestant church, he gets a 1 in the "Interdependent" column for "Religion." (See chapter 7 for more on Protestant traditions.)

For the remaining rows, Obama gets 1s in both columns. The years he logged in the Northeast pursuing his degrees confer a 1 in the "Independent" column for region. But his roots in Hawaii[19] and Chicago also earn him a 1 in the "Interdependent" column. When it comes to "Workplace," Obama's years at a for-profit law firm put a 1 in the "Independent" column. Being a community organizer, professor, senator, and president, however, give him a 1 for interdependence. (Although "leader of the free world" may sound like an independent gig, at the end of the day, it's still a government job.) Obama also scores double 1s for "Global Region." He has spent most of his life in the Global North, which sends a 1 to the "Independent" column. At the same time, his early years in Indonesia and continued connections to family there earn him a tally for interdependence.[20]

If you guessed that Obama is equally independent and interdependent, you were correct. Here is his completed scorecard:

NAME: Barack Obama

	Independent	Interdependent
Hemisphere	1	1
Gender	1	0
Race/Ethnicity	0	1
Class	1	0
Religion	0	1
U.S. Region	1	1
Workplace	1	1
Global Region	1	1
TOTAL:	6	6

Bill Gates's Other I

Speaking of leaders of the free world, how about Bill Gates? Does he seem more independent, interdependent, or both independent and interdependent? Let's take a look at where he's been to learn a bit more about what kind of self he likely uses most.

The cofounder of the world's largest software company and the second-richest person alive was born in Seattle, Washington, and has lived most of his life near there, save for the two years he spent at Harvard University in Cambridge, Massachusetts (before dropping out). This lands him 1s in the "Independent" column for "Hemisphere" and "Region" (West), and 0s in the "Interdependent" column for these rows. A White male who avows no other gender or racial identities, Gates also gets 1s only for "Independence" in the "Gender" and "Race" rows.

Gates is also 1 and 0 for "Class" and "Religion." Although he technically does not have a bachelor's degree, his occupation and income have not suffered as a result. Moreover, both of his parents were college-educated executives who clearly conferred on their son no small number of advantages. They also raised him as a mainline Protestant (in the Congregationalist Church), though he now calls himself an agnostic. Both religious tendencies lean toward independence.

Proof that successful people who seem completely independent usually harbor interdependence as well, Gates gets double 1s for "Workplace" and "Global Region." He is an iconic entrepreneur, and showed a bent for business from a young age. Gates's sister reports, for instance, that when a teenage Bill borrowed her baseball mitt, he prepared a contract to limit his obligation. In recent years, Gates has also blazed the trail of philanthropy, pledging to give away 90 percent of his vast fortune. To this end, he cofounded the Bill and Melinda Gates Foundation, a nonprofit with extensive activity in the Global South. The work of the foundation has led Gates to spend considerable time traveling through and thinking about Africa, India, and South America. So although he has not taken up residence in the Global South, he is earning honorary citizenship there.[21]

As Gates's scorecard suggests, his independent self propelled him to the top of the business world. But his interdependent self is what may establish him as a global visionary.

NAME: Bill Gates

	Independent	Interdependent
Hemisphere	1	0
Gender	1	0
Race/Ethnicity	1	0
Class	1	0
Religion	1	0
U.S. Region	1	0
Workplace	1	1
Global Region	1	1
TOTAL:	**8**	**2**

The Mother of Interdependence?

Just as Bill Gates has a surprisingly interdependent side, Mother Teresa had an independent streak that moved her to practice her good works on a worldwide scale. Awarded the Nobel Peace Prize for her more than forty-five years of ministering to the poor and sick, Blessed Mother Teresa of Calcutta was born Agnes Gonxha Bojaxhiu in Skopje, Albania, where she lived until moving to India at the age of eighteen. With her life thus divided between East and West and the Global North and South, she gets a 1 in both columns of the "Hemisphere" and "Global Region" rows. Since she was a White woman, the "Race/Ethnicity" row of her scorecard reads 1-0, while the "Gender" row reads 0-1. Her "Class" is also 0-1, because neither she nor her parents received a formal college education.

As a Catholic nun, Mother Teresa posts a 0 for independence and a 1 for interdependence in the "Religion" category. And as an employee of the Catholic Church and founder of five hundred nonprofit missions throughout the world, she likewise nets a 1 for interdependence on the "Workplace" dimension.[22]

Summing the columns, we see that Mother Teresa is mostly interdependent, but with a healthy dose of independence:

NAME: Mother Teresa

	Independent	Interdependent
Hemisphere	1	1
Gender	0	1
Race/Ethnicity	1	0
Class	0	1
Religion	0	1
U.S. Region	N/A	N/A
Workplace	0	1
Global Region	1	1
TOTAL:	**3**	**6**

Settling Your Score

In accounting for how particular culture cycles have given rise to independent or interdependent selves, we have applied rather blunt rules. In the case of "Gender," for example, we gave the men a 1 for independence and the women a 1 for interdependence, regardless of how they might think or have thought of themselves. Yet people's gender identities are often more complex. Obama, for example, frequently notes how much women shape his actions—his top three foreign policy advisers are women[23]—so he might lobby to change his 0 for interdependence on the "Gender" row into a 1. Likewise, Mother Teresa was a woman, but many of her actions defied traditional female roles. At a young age, she walked away from her family and home, never to return.[24] Perhaps like many people called to the cloth, she might have felt that her self either transcended gender altogether or embodied both gender roles. Thus she might have given herself either two 0s or two 1s in the "Gender" row.

About these famous folks, we can only speculate. But you have the inside scoop on yourself. So, in calculating your own scorecard, feel free to apply more complex and subjective criteria.

Be the Right Who

Now that you know more about both sides of your self, what do you do with them? How do you know which self to use when? Although every situation is different, we've distilled the fine art of being the right person at the right time into a simple three-step process:

1. Lead with interdependence. In early interactions with people, try interdependence first. When you are in an interdependent frame of mind, you can better assess what selves others are bringing to the situation and adjust your self accordingly.

One way to summon your interdependent self is to think of how you are similar to other people. Psychologist David Trafimow and colleagues showed the power of this simple trick in an experiment with both American and Chinese participants. The research team first asked half the participants to consider how they were different from their friends and family, and the other half to consider how they were similar to their loved ones. They then asked the participants to describe themselves. When participants thought about their similarities to loved ones, their self-descriptions included more relationships and roles than when they considered differences.[25] Other studies show that reflecting on how you are similar to your conversation partners makes you pay more attention to them, which helps dispel stereotypes and pave the way to more peaceful and productive exchanges.[26]

2. Match or contrast. Next, if you want to go with the flow of the situation, match your self to that of other people. But if you want to change the state of affairs, then try a self that runs counter to the prevailing trend.

For instance, say you are a Philadelphian who has just taken a job in Duluth, Minnesota. Having surveyed the scene, you will likely conclude that your coworkers lean more toward interdependence than you do. If you like your job and your company is pleased with your team's progress, it's probably best to search your self for its more interdependent qualities, and learn how to bring them to the table more often. But if you've been hired because your company feels it is stagnating and wants to bring in a little "fresh blood," now is the time to let your independence shine.

Likewise, if you are a female nonprofit executive who is trying to rouse your mostly female employees to greater cohesion and productivity, you should probably use the matching strategy and let your interdependent self do the talking. Similarly, if you are pitching your $1.2 million idea to a roomful of business executives who might pony up for the project, matching your independent self to theirs will most likely bring in the bucks. But if that roomful of business executives is guilty of polluting your community's groundwater and you'd like them to stop, a plea from your contrasting interdependent heart might move them to better behavior.

In all these cases, your particular style of being independent or interdependent will not perfectly match that of the people you are trying to swim with or against. For instance, a middle-class Black female teacher's way of relating and adjusting will likely not be the same as her working-class White male students. Nevertheless, their mutual appreciation for connecting and enduring will help bridge this divide. Similarly, a Ugandan Protestant artist's manner of expressing her uniqueness and exerting control will not perfectly mirror her French-Catholic collaborator's. Yet their shared focus on individuation, mastery, and freedom will help them to make exciting art together.

3. Switch. If the first self you bring to a situation doesn't give you the results you desire, try the other one. For many people, the realization that you have two equally legitimate selves marks a 100 percent increase in psychological resources. Until you get the hang of which one works best where and when, experiment.

When you're in the thick of one way of being, though, it's sometimes hard to remember how to summon the other side. So here are a few fast tactics for calling forth each self:

How to Summon . . .

Independence

- Speak up.
- Think about how you are different from others.
- Remember that asserting yourself doesn't mean you're selfish.
- Consider each action a choice.
- Assume that you have as much authority as others.

Interdependence

- Listen.
- Think about how you are similar to others.
- Remember that adjusting to others doesn't mean you're weak.
- Consider how each action affects others.
- Assume that others have more authority than you.

Go Prime Time

Your individual thoughts, feelings, and actions are only one level of the culture cycle. You can also leverage the interaction and institution levels to bring out the self you want to use in a given situation.

As we have emphasized throughout this book, culture cycles operate largely at the unconscious level, nonchalantly steering the self without troubling the conscious mind.[27] Subtle cues in the environment (mostly practices and products at the interaction level of the culture cycle) do much of this heavy lifting. These cultural "primes" make it more likely that we will think, feel, and act in some ways rather than others. For instance, psychologist Wendi Gardner and her colleagues asked European-American students to circle all the pronouns in a story describing a trip to the city. Half the students were randomly assigned to read a story in which all the pronouns were independent (*I*, *me*, *my*, and *mine*); the other half were randomly assigned to read the exact same story, except all the pronouns were interdependent (*we*, *us*, *our*, and *ours*).

This simple activity jogged something that you wouldn't think could be so easily shaken: people's values. Participants who circled the "we" pronouns later rated interdependent values such as "belongingness," "friendship," and "respect for elders" higher than independent values such as "freedom," "choosing one's goals," and "living an exciting life." Most of these participants also thought they had a moral obligation to help a friend in need. In contrast, participants who circled the "I" pronouns rated the independent values more highly, and only half thought they were obligated to help their friend.[28]

Many cultural primes are like this: seemingly insignificant yet surprisingly powerful. Because cultural primes are so subtle, they can be difficult to change. This is why cultures themselves are so hard to alter; millions of tiny cues keep them rolling without much effort on any individual's part. But once you know what to look for, you can start shaping the primes in your environment and, by extension, the thoughts, feelings, and actions of your individual self.

Psychologist Ying-Yi Hong and her team demonstrated the power of cultural symbols to shift selves. They chose as their site Hong Kong, a former British colony on the south coast of China. Hong Kong hosts many of the independent elements of the United Kingdom's culture cycle, as well as many of the interdependent elements of China's. The researchers wondered how easily they could prime Hong Kong students to use their British or Chinese selves.

The outcome the researchers examined was how people explain one another's behavior. Recall from the introduction and chapter 2 that interdependent people more readily look *outside* at a person's situation and relationships for the causes of her behavior, while independent people more readily look *inside* at her dispositions and preferences. Psychologists Michael Morris and Kaiping Peng gave a fun demonstration of this difference. Showing participants an animation of one fish swimming in front of a cluster of four fish, they asked, "Why is the fish swimming alone?" True to their independent ways, American respondents offered internal explanations such as "He wants to lead the other fish" or "He doesn't want to be a part of the crowd." And true to their interdependent ways, Chinese respondents offered situational explanations such as "The other fish are chasing him" or "He is lost."[29]

Hong and colleagues guessed that, with a simple flip of primes, they could make Hong Kong students respond to the fish task as either situationists or dispositionists. They first showed half their participants classic Chinese icons: a Chinese dragon, the Great Wall, a rice farmer, and a Chinese dancer. To the other half they showed classic Western icons: Mount Rushmore, the Statue of Liberty, the U.S. Capitol, and a cowboy. These small prompts had big effects. After viewing the Chinese primes, Hong Kong students adopted a situationist style, explaining that the first fish was responding to pressures from the other fish. But after viewing the Western primes, students took a dispositionist stance, saying that the lead fish was acting on his own ideas and preferences.[30]

Watch Your Language

The languages we speak also prime which self we bring to a task. In Canada, Michael Ross and his coauthors randomly assigned English-Chinese bilingual students, all born and raised in China, to answer a questionnaire about themselves in either English or Chinese. Students who responded in English made significantly more positive statements than negative ones, reflecting the independent tendency to focus on one's uniqueness and positivity. In contrast, students who responded in Chinese made the same number of positive and negative statements, reflecting a more interdependent tendency to fit in and seek the middle way.[31] (For more about these tendencies, see chapters 1 and 2.) Indeed, organizational psychologist Donnel Briley has found that, when making decisions, Hong Kong bilinguals seek compromise and moderation more when they speak Mandarin than when they speak English.[32]

Even within a language, which words you choose can prime which self you use. In one study, for instance, psychologists Caitlin Fausey and Lera Boroditsky asked a large online sample of English speakers to read about Janet Jackson's "wardrobe malfunction" at the 2004 Super Bowl halftime show. Half the respondents read a more passive account of the incident: "a snap unfastened and part of the bodice tore!" The other half read a more active report: "[Justin Timberlake, Jackson's dance partner] unfastened a snap and tore part of the bodice!" Compared to respondents who read the passive language, respondents who read that Timberlake actively ripped the bodice blamed him more for the fashion gaffe and thought he should pay a higher fine. Although the authors did not directly measure the selves of respondents, their findings are consistent with the idea that highly agentic language primes an independent self, while less agentic language primes an interdependent self.[33]

Research on priming is a growth industry.[34] From these and other studies, we can make a few recommendations. Depending on which of your selves you want to prime, install the tchotchkes, enact the practices, and speak the language of a culture you associate with that self. In English, for example, use *I* and other individual pronouns when you want to elicit independence, and *we* and other collective pronouns when you want to evoke interdependence.

Build Two-Self Institutions

At the institutional level of the culture cycle, you can also create organizations that reflect and support different selves for different occasions. Stephanie Fryberg and her team are doing just that. A professor of psychology at the University of Arizona and a member of the Tulalip Tribes of Washington State, Fryberg now spends half her time as a school district administrator at the Quil Ceda and Tulalip Elementary School, which is located on the Washington State reservation where she grew up. The school's mission? To teach the children and their teachers to deploy both sides of their selves.

Some 71 percent of the school's 570 students are Native Americans, 10 percent are Latinos, and 19 percent are European Americans. Most of the teachers are European Americans.[35] And 95 percent of Washington's schools score higher than Quil Ceda and Tulalip on standardized tests.

Pained that the school was shortchanging its children, Fryberg decided "to bring together what I know from being my middle-class professor self with what I know from being my reservation Native self." From her own experiences, she knew that the roots of the problem at the underachieving elementary school were long and tangled: poverty (76 percent of students qualify for free lunches), discrimination, unemployment, substance abuse, and a long-standing lack of trust between Native and European-American communities. Yet as a cultural psychologist, Fryberg also knew that a few adjustments to the school's culture cycle could make a big difference. With the school's administrators on her side, she was ready to try a few ideas.

As in many large, underresourced schools, Quil Ceda and Tulalip Elementary has more than its fair share of discipline issues. One day, for example, Fryberg heard a young teacher struggling in vain to get Thomas,[36] a first-grade Native student with a difficult home life, to come out from under a table.

"Thomas," the teacher pleaded. "Think about what you're doing. Make the smart choice that you will be proud of. Come out from there."

Thomas did not budge.

Watching Thomas stand his ground, Fryberg intuited that he was probably using his independent self. Like African Americans and other groups that have actively confronted discrimination, Native Americans have high levels of both independence and interdependence. (See chapter 4 for more on the independence and interdependence of African Americans.)[37] Fryberg decided to try his interdependent side: "Look," she said, "you don't want your friends to see us pulling you out from there. That would be really embarrassing."

Within moments, Thomas was out from under the table and back at his desk as if nothing had happened.

Over time, Fryberg found that reminding young students of friends' and family members' expectations could be a very effective tactic. "Raina, what would your Grandma say if she saw you fooling around and not reading?"

But some of the teachers were worried about this approach, arguing that the children needed to do the right thing for themselves, not because of what others might think. Fryberg agreed that the school needed to hone student's independent selves alongside their interdependent ones.

So working together, the school's staff introduced a series of interventions. First, teachers adopted the jigsaw classroom technique we described in chapter 5, but with an independent twist. As per the usual intervention, teachers divided students into small groups to research Tulalip culture. Within each group, individual students were assigned a topic (food, religious traditions, economic systems, etc.). But unlike the usual jigsaw classroom, in which students next collaborate on a group presentation, the students wrote individual papers and made individual presentations that integrated their group's research. In this way, students cultivated both interdependent and independent skills.

Quil Ceda and Tulalip's staff also put in place a program called GROW, which features boosts to both independence and interdependence. Partly informed by psychologist Carol Dweck's research on growth mind-sets (see chapter 2), the program urges students to *G*row their brains at least six hours a day; *R*espect themselves, others, and all living things; *O*wn their attitudes and actions; and *W*elcome all people who come into the community. The school also developed a book in which a tribal elder explains to a young Native that if she works hard and grows her brain, she will always be able to help people.

Create Identity-Safe Spaces

To inspire its Native students and keep them in school, Quil Ceda and Tulalip Elementary also knew it had to do more to improve the image of Natives. Fryberg was well acquainted with the problem. Most people outside the Native community know very little about Native Americans. When they think of Natives at all, they usually conjure sports mascots—Atlanta Braves, Cleveland Indians, North Dakota Fighting Sioux—or Disney's Pocahontas. She also knew from experiments in her lab that these seemingly innocuous images undermine the self-esteem, efficacy, and academic motivation of Natives. Starved of images of themselves succeeding in school, many Native students surmise that they don't belong there.[38] To broaden the Hollywood vision of an American Indian, the school now highlights contemporary examples of Native lawyers, doctors, elected officials, scientists, and artists.

Through extensive interviews, Fryberg and her team also discovered that relations between teachers and student families were strained, which made Native students feel ambivalent about Quil Ceda and Tulalip. The teachers said that many Native parents were reticent to talk. The teachers also worried about appearing culturally insensitive or racist to the parents.

The parents, in turn, were not sure they should trust the school, as many of them had endured bad experiences there growing up. Because they respected the teachers' authority, they didn't feel comfortable sharing their ideas or criticisms. Observing the teachers' easier and more frequent interactions with European-American parents led the Native parents to feel like outsiders. The researchers also noted that although the teachers claimed to be color-blind, they sent Native students to the principal's office more often than European-American students.

With these observations, Fryberg worked with the school's staff to create a space where teachers, students, and their families would all feel that their multiple identities were valued and "safe." (For more on identity-safe spaces, see chapter 4.) Teachers were encouraged not only to push their students to achieve, but also to get to know students' families and to attend community celebrations. Instead of singling out individual students for recognition (the usual American practice), classrooms selected families to receive a bumper sticker that read, "Our Family Was Honored by Quil Ceda and Tulalip Elementary." And although district guidelines counsel against touching children, the teachers now routinely hug their students.

To get the entire community involved, the Quil Ceda and Tulalip team now actively recruits Natives to serve in various volunteer and paid roles. A newly developed teacher-training program will grant college credit to Natives working in the school. Over time, seeing more Natives as teachers and school leaders will signal that, contrary to what some Native students may have assumed, school *is* a place for them.

Taking their efforts up to more powerful institutions, parents and teachers are also lobbying governments at the state and local levels to ban Indian mascots in the public schools. Washington's neighbor, Oregon, has already passed similar legislation.

Welcome Both Selves

On the reservation and off, empowering people to use both their different selves requires making it okay to *have* two selves in the first place. On this count, independent cultures are more challenged than interdependent ones. Because independent selves are allegedly made up of stable, internal, unique traits, they are not supposed to vary too much across situations

When they do, disdainful observers have a few words for their more flexible brethren, including *hypocrite, phony, two-faced, inauthentic,* and *fraud.*

Now interdependent selves have a word for their more uniform counterparts: WEIRD. An acronym that stands for "Western, Educated, Industrialized, Rich, and Democratic," this is the term that economists and psychologists use to describe the historically, economically, and geographically odd people who, among other psychological anomalies, think that selves are and should be singular and consistent. Because most scientists are WEIRD, we know a great deal about WEIRDS but vanishingly little about the other 85 percent of people alive today.[39]

A second stumbling block that besets the two-self solution is many cultures' desire for national, racial, ethnic, tribal, or religious purity. In the United States, for instance, interracial marriage was not fully legal until 1967.[40] In addition, the so-called one-drop rule meant that if a child had one Black parent and one White parent, the child was considered Black in the eyes of the law.

In the past decade, however, movements to make way for multifaceted selves have heated up, with advocates acting at every level of the culture cycle. At the interaction level, parents of multiracial children have taken the lead by creating products and practices that reflect and support their children's selves. These products include children's books with multiracial characters and titles such as *Black, White, Just Right!*; guides for raising multiracial children; and toys and clothing targeted to the biracial market. T-shirts boast, "Mixed to Perfection!" and "Hybrid Vigor." Shampoos claim that they are specially formulated for "mixed chicks." The Real Kidz company produces mixed-ethnicity dolls, one of whose birth certificate reads, "Hi, my name is Willough. My mom is White and my dad is Hispanic. They created me out of love, and I am a perfect mixture of both!" News and social media target mixed-race audiences, and popular television shows such as *Modern Family* feature multicultural households.

At the level of institutions, many people hoping to legitimize their multiracial and multiethnic selves lobbied the U.S. Census Bureau to add a "multiracial" box to its forms. Their efforts were unsuccessful, however, partly because traditional civil rights organizations fought against them. These groups worry that the multiracial option will thin their ranks and thereby undermine their political power. (The federal government allocates money to community programs according to the size of the racial and ethnic groups they serve.) Multicultural activists did enjoy a partial victory: the current compromise, effective as of 2010, is to allow people to mark as many races and ethnicities as apply to them.

Meanwhile, multicultural people have formed their own grassroots organizations to help them face their unique issues. The Association of MultiEthnic Americans (AMEA), for example, founded in 1988, is a multiracial advocacy group that lobbies the U.S. Census on behalf of mixed, blended, or "hyphenated" groups.[41] Swirl, with chapters in locales ranging from New York City to Starkville, Mississippi, is another national multiethnic association that hopes to "challenge the idea that all should be able to fit in one neatly packaged identity," according to the organization's website.[42]

As we have stressed in previous chapters, people with more power (money, status, decision-making authority, etc.) can more easily alter culture cycles than can people with less power. Nevertheless, as the growing success of multicultural movers and shakers testifies, there is also strength in numbers and persistence. We expect that two-sided selves and the culture cycles that make and mirror them will become more common in years to come.

Harness the Energy

In 1954, Frida Kahlo passed away at the age of forty-seven. Whether she died of disease, an accidental overdose, or suicide is unclear.[43] But what is clear is that her dueling selves brought her both pain and inspiration until the end of her too-brief life.

Some fifty-seven years later, Amy Chua published *Battle Hymn of the Tiger Mother.* Although the world was beginning to recognize and even appreciate diversity, Chua also suffered from her inability to match her self to the selves of her daughters and to the culture cycles rolling around them all. Part of this was the world's doing; although some change has come, the calming of the clashes within and between our selves is still a long way off. Part was Chua's doing; she tried mightily to instill Chinese-style interdependence in the selves of her more multicultural daughters.

By the end of her book, it is Chua who gets the lesson. Her children teach her the importance of being more than one self, and of knowing which self to be when and where.

Embracing our many cultures and selves is an enormous challenge for all of us. But as the planet gets smaller, flatter, and hotter, we can no longer afford to fear or ignore diversity. Instead, we must harness the energy of our clashing cultures for a more creative, cooperative, and peaceful twenty-first century.

Acknowledgments

You can't be a self—independent, interdependent, or otherwise—by yourself, and you can't write a book alone, either. Many people gave all sides of their selves to help us produce *Clash!*, and to them we extend a thousand thank-yous and a lifetime supply of dinner parties. First in mind are our colleagues from the Stanford Culture Co-Lab and its affiliates, whose many hours in the lab and the field yielded the fascinating studies we showcase here. This crew includes Glenn Adams, Tiffany Brannon, Lisa Brown, Sapna Cheryan, Susan Cross, Katie Curhan, Geoff Fong, Stephanie Fryberg, Alyssa Fu, MarYam Hamedani, Keiko Ito, Heejung Kim, Batja Mesquita, Paula Nurius, Daphna Oyserman, Paula Pietromonaco, Victoria Plaut, Krishna Savani, Nicole Stephens, Sarah Townsend, Annie Tsai, Yukiko Uchida, Elissa Wurf, Shinobu Kitayama and his students, Jeanne Tsai and her students, and many, many other graduate students, undergraduate students, and research assistants. We are also grateful to the organizations that supported this research: the National Science Foundation, the National Institutes of Health, the John T. and Catherine A. MacArthur Foundation, the Social Science Research Council, and the Russell Sage Foundation, and to the institutions that nurtured the selves of the researchers, including the Psychology Department and the Institute for Social Research at the University of Michigan, and the Psychology Department, the Center for Comparative Studies in Race and Ethnicity, and the Center for Advanced Studies in the Behavioral Sciences at Stanford University.

Readers of earlier drafts contributed some of the better ideas you will find here. We are forever indebted to these smart, generous, and patient people, who include Mateo Aguilar, Adam Cohen, Marilyn Conner, Shinobu Kitayama, Cynthia Levine, Iris Mauss, Perla Ni, Victoria Plaut, Howard Rose, Jeanne Tsai, Krysia Zajonc, and Joe Zajonc. In the wee hours of the morning, their notes in the margins kept us sane and sanguine. In addition, we thank Taylor Phillips and Amrita Maitreyi for researching, referencing, checking, and checking again.

We also enlisted many friends and colleagues to serve as quoted sources. For their hours on the phone or over pad thai, we express our deep appreciation to Steve Beitler, Avi Ben-Zeev, Richard Boly, Adam Cohen, Dov Cohen, Susan Cross, Gail Davidson, Jim Fruchterman, Julio Garcia, Robert Goldhor, Deborah Gruenfeld, Stephen Hinshaw, Lila Kitayama, Jason Long, Jan Masaoka, Suzanne Miller, Ara Norenzayan, Shigehiro Oishi, Daphna Oyserman, Dev Patnaik, Kerry Patterson, Dan Portillo, Kaiping Peng, Victoria Plaut, Lisa Radloff, Jason Rentfrow, Steven Spencer, and Joseph Vandello.

When this book was just a chapter and an outline, Chip Heath and Ted Weinstein gave us invaluable feedback on the form it should take. Our agent, Gillian Mackenzie; our editor, Caroline Sutton of Hudson Street Press; and her assistant, Brittney Ross, then took up the project of shaping our sprawling ideas into a single volume. We thank these visionary souls for the encouragement and insights they have shared throughout this project.

Long before we proposed *Clash!*, our friends, families, and mentors championed our forays into the bright new field of cultural psychology. Hazel thanks Shinobu Kitayama for a collaboration that began with mutual astonishment over the details of each other's culture cycles and that continues to inspire and excite; Richard Shweder for his insistence that there is more than one answer to the question, What is good, true, and beautiful?; Pat Gurin for always modeling the value of diversity; and many other brilliant colleague-friends for a career's worth of sustaining interdependence, including Richard Nisbett, Bill Wilson, Eugene Borgida,

Richard and Nancy Moreland, Keith Sentis, Mayumi Karasawa, James Jackson, Toni Antonucci, Phoebe Ellsworth, Dale Miller, Paula Moya, Tanya Luhrmann, Carol Porter, Jennifer Boehler, Sarah Mangelsdorf, Carol Ryff, Lee Ross, Mark Lepper, Phil Zimbardo, Carol Dweck, Jennifer Eberhardt, Nalini Ambady, Greg Walton, and Geoff Cohen.

Hazel also offers her loving gratitude to Nancy Cantor, Steve Brechin, and Dorothy and Claude Steele for their steadfast friendship and decades-long conversation about diversity; to her family—Alice Rose, Krysia Rose Zajonc, Sharon Rose, Pat Shannon, Reid Shannon, Ben Shannon, Peter Zajonc, Renee Lemieux, Jonathan Zajonc, Joe Zajonc, Daisy Zajonc, Lucy Zajonc, Mike Zajonc, Batja Mesquita, Oliver Zajonc, and Zoe Zajonc—who commented on drafts, tolerated her absences, and suggested she *finish,* already; to Alana Conner, her amazing coauthor who saw a book and made it happen; and most of all to Robert Zajonc, who more than anyone made it apparent that culture mattered.

Alana likewise thanks her family for giving her a sense of place and past; her mentors Robert Sternberg, Avi Ben-Zeev, Mahzarin Banaji, Joan Miller, Nancy Adler, and, of course, the inimitable Hazel Rose Markus, for helping her craft a future; and her friends and colleagues Amelia, Angela, Christine, Iris, James, Lera, Lisa, Melissa, Perla, Rachel, Susan, and V for keeping her in the present.

Notes

Introduction

1. A. Chua, *Battle Hymn of the Tiger Mother* (New York: Penguin Press, 2011).
2. We use the label "West" to mean Europe, North America, Central America, South America, Australia, and New Zealand; and "East" to denote East Asia, Southeast Asia, and the Indian subcontinent. We discuss the "in-between" regions of the Middle East and Africa in chapter 9. "West" and "East" are admittedly messy categories, encompassing billions of people. But as we will reveal in chapters 1 and 2, the cultures of each hemisphere share many ideas, institutions, practices, and artifacts.
3. Chua, *Battle Hymn of the Tiger Mother*, p. 52.
4. D. Brooks, "Amy Chua Is a Wimp," *New York Times*, January 17, 2011, p. A25.
5. J. Hyun, *Breaking the Bamboo Ceiling: Career Strategies for Asians* (New York: HarperCollins, 2005).
6. The Royal Society, *Knowledge, Networks and Nations: Global Scientific Collaboration in the Twenty-First Century* (London: The Royal Society, 2011).
7. R. Atkinson, M. Shellenberger, T. Nordhaus, D. Swezey, T. Norris, J. Jenkins, . . . Y. Borofsky, *Rising Tigers, Sleeping Giant* (Oakland, CA: The Breakthrough Institute, 2009).
8. "The List: *The Art Economist*'s Top Earning 300 Artists," *The Art Economist* 1 (2011): 20.
9. S. A. Hewlett, R. Rashid, D. Forster, and C. Ho, *Asians in America: Unleashing the Potential of the "Model Minority"* (New York: Center for Work-Life Policy, 2011).

10. D. P. McAdams, *The Stories We Live By: Personal Myths and the Making of the Self* (New York: The Guilford Press, 1997).
11. N. Moray, "Attention in Dichotic Listening: Affective Cues and the Influence of Instructions," *The Quarterly Journal of Experimental Psychology* 11 (1959): 56–60.
12. H. R. Markus, "Self-Schemata and Processing Information about the Self," *Journal of Personality and Social Psychology* 35 (1977): 63–78.
13. H. R. Markus and E. Wurf, "The Dynamic Self-Concept: A Social Psychological Perspective," *Annual Review of Psychology* 38 (1987): 289–337; H. R. Markus and P. Nurius, "Possible Selves," *American Psychologist* 41 (1986): 954–69.
14. H. R. Markus and S. Kitayama, "Culture and the Self: Implications for Cognition, Emotion, and Motivation," *Psychological Review* 98 (1991): 224–53.

    We are not the first researchers to note that cultures and people come in more relational and more autonomous flavors. Harry Triandis identified the cultural syndromes of individualism and collectivism. Geert Hofstede studied these syndromes at the national and corporate level. Clifford Geertz compared egocentric selves with sociocentric selves. Within the individual, David Bakan documented the struggle between agency and communion. And long before them all, Sigmund Freud gave us the dichotomy of love and work.
15. H. R. Markus, P. R. Mullally, and S. Kitayama, "Selfways: Diversity in Modes in Cultural Participation," in U. Neisser and D. A. Jopling, eds., *The Conceptual Self in Context: Culture, Experience, Self-Understanding* (Cambridge, UK: Cambridge University Press, 1997).
16. T. Sugimoto and J. A. Levin, "Multiple Literacies and Multimedia: A Comparison of Japanese and American Uses of the Internet," in G. E. Hawisher and C. L. Selfe, eds., *Global Literacies and the World Wide Web* (London: Routledge, 2000), pp. 133–53.
17. N. Stephens, H. R. Markus, and S. S. M. Townsend, "Choice as an Act of Meaning: The Case of Social Class," *Journal of Personality and Social Psychology* 93 (2007): 814–30.
18. Chua, *Battle Hymn of the Tiger Mother*, p. 212.
19. Like Jim Crow laws for African Americans, Juan Crow laws systematically discriminate against Latinos in the United States.
20. L. Ross and A. Ward, "Naive Realism in Everyday Life: Implications for Social Conflict and Misunderstanding," in T. Brown, E. Reed, and E. Turiel, eds., *Values and Knowledge* (Hillsdale, NJ: Erlbaum, 1996), pp. 103–35.
21. M. W. Morris and K. Peng, "Culture and Cause: American and Chinese Attributions for Social and Physical Events," *Journal of Personality and Social Psychology* 67 (1994): 949–71.
22. M. D. Leinbach and B. I. Fagot, "Categorical Habituation to Male and Female Faces: Gender Schematic Processing in Infancy," *Infant Behavior and Development* 16 (1993): 317–32; G. Anzures, P. C. Quinn, O. Pascalis, A. M. Slater, and K. Lee, "Categorization, Categorical Perception, and Asymmetry in Infants' Representation of Face Race," *Developmental Science* 13 (2010): 553–64.

Chapter 1

1. S. Lubman, "Some Students Must Learn to Question," *San Jose Mercury News*, February 23, 1998, pp. 1A, 2A.
2. All quotes without references are from interviews conducted by the authors.
3. S. A. Hewlett, R. Rashid, D. Forster, C. Ho, *Asians in America: Unleashing the Potential of the "Model Minority"* (New York: Center for Work-Life Policy, 2011).
4. "East" and "West" are broad categories that include vast variability. Nevertheless, these two hemispheres host distinct overarching culture cycles, as we demonstrate.
5. H. Kim, "We Talk, Therefore We Think? A Cultural Analysis of Talking and Thinking," *Journal of Personality and Social Psychology* 83 (2002): 373–82; H. Kim and H. R. Markus, "Speech and Silence: An Analysis of the Cultural Practice of Talking," in L. Weis and M. Fine, eds., *Beyond Silenced Voices: Class, Race and Gender in U.S. Schools* (New York: SUNY Press, 2006).
6. Not his real name.
7. A. Tsai, "Equality or Propriety? A Cultural Models Approach to Understanding Social Hierarchy" (doctoral dissertation), Stanford University, Stanford, CA, 2006.
8. S. S. Iyengar and M. R. Lepper, "Rethinking the Value of Choice: A Cultural Perspective on Intrinsic Motivation," *Journal of Personality and Social Psychology* 7 (1999): 349–66.
9. T.-F. Wu, S. E. Cross, C.-W. Wu, W. Cho, and S.-H. Tey, "Cultural Values and Personal Decisions: Filial Piety in Taiwan and the U.S.," unpublished manuscript.
10. H. Kim and H. R. Markus, "Deviance or Uniqueness, Harmony or Conformity? A Cultural Analysis," *Journal of Personality and Social Psychology* 77(1999): 785–800.
11. S. J. Heine, *Cultural Psychology*, 2nd ed. (New York: W.W. Norton, 2011).
12. S. J. Heine, S. Kitayama, D. R. Lehman, T. Takata, E. Ide, C. Lueng, and H. Matsumoto, "Divergent Consequences of Success and Failure in Japan and North America: An Investigation of self-Improving Motivations and Malleable Selves," *Journal of Personality and Social Psychology* 81 (2001): 599–615.
13. H. R. Markus and S. Kitayama, "Cultural Variation in the Self-Concept," in J. Strauss and G. R. Goethals, eds. *The Self: Interdisciplinary Approaches* (New York: Springer-Verlag, 1991).
14. S. J. Heine, D. R. Lehman, H. R. Markus, and S. Kitayama, "Is There a Universal Need for Positive Self-Regard?" *Psychological Review* 106 (1999): 766–94.
15. E. Bromet, L. H. Andrade, I. Hwang, N. A. Sampson, J. Alonso, G. de Girolamo, . . . R. C. Kessler, "Cross-National Epidemiology of DSM-IV Major Depressive Episode," *BMC Medicine* 9 (2001); L. Andrade, J. J. Caraveo-Anduaga, P. Berglund, R. V. Bijl, R. D. De Graaf, W. Vollebergh, . . . H. Wittchen, "The Epidemiology of Major Depressive Episodes: Results

from the International Consortium of Psychiatric Epidemiology (ICPE) Surveys," *International Journal of Methods in Psychiatric Research* 12 (2003): 3095–105.

16. S. Kitayama, M. Karasawa, K. Curhan, C. Ryff, and H. Markus, "Independence and Interdependence Predict Health and Well-Being: Divergent Patterns in the United States and Japan," *Frontiers in Psychology* 1 (2010): 1–10.
17. Y. Uchida, S. S. M. Townsend, H. R. Markus, and H. B. Bergsieker, "Emotions as within or between People? Cultural Variation in Lay Theories of Emotion Expression and Inference," *Personality and Social Psychology Bulletin* 35 (2009): 1427–39.
18. J. Tsai, B. Knutson, and H. H. Fung, "Cultural Variation in Affect Valuation," *Journal of Personality and Social Psychology* 90 (2006): 288–307.

Chapter 2

1. For reviews of some of this work and more detailed theoretical analysis, see A. Fiske, S. Kitayama, H. R. Markus, and R. E. Nisbett, "The Cultural Matrix of Social Psychology," in D. Gilbert, S. Fiske, and G. Lindzey, eds., *The Handbook of Social Psychology*, Vol. 2, 4th ed. (San Francisco, CA: McGraw-Hill, 1998), pp. 915–81; H. R. Markus, S. Kitayama, and R. Heiman, "Culture and 'Basic' Psychological Principles," in E. T. Higgins and A. W. Kruglanski, eds., *Social Psychology: Handbook of Basic Principles* (New York: Guilford, 1997), pp. 857–913; H. R. Markus and S. Kitayama, "Models of Agency: Sociocultural Diversity in the Construction of Action," in V. Murphy-Berman and J. Berman, eds., *The 49th Annual Nebraska Symposium on Motivation: Cross-Cultural Differences in Perspectives on Self* (Lincoln: University of Nebraska Press, 2003), pp. 1–57; H. R. Markus and S. Kitayama, "Cultures and Selves: A Cycle of Mutual Constitution," *Perspectives on Psychological Science* 5 (2010): 420–30; S. Kitayama, H. Park, A. T. Sevincer, M. Karasawa, and A. K. Uskul, "A Cultural Task Analysis of Implicit Independence: Comparing North America, Western Europe, and East Asia," *Journal of Personality and Social Psychology* 97 (2009): 236–55; S. J. Heine, *Cultural Psychology* (New York: W. W. Norton, 2007); S. Kitayama and D. Cohen, *Handbook of Cultural Psychology* (New York: Guilford Press, 2007); M. G. Hamedani, H. R. Markus, and A. Fu, "In the Land of the Free Interdependent Action Undermines Motivation," *Psychological Science*, in press.
2. R. A. Shweder, *Thinking through Cultures: Expeditions in Cultural Psychology* (Cambridge, MA: Harvard University Press, 1991).
3. C. Hall, "Proud of Me" [recorded by Frank Oz], on *Let Your Feelings Show!* [LP], Sesame Street Records, 1976.
4. C. C. Lewis, *Educating Hearts and Minds: Reflections on Japanese Preschool and Elementary Education* (Cambridge, UK: Cambridge University Press, 1995).
5. R. Whiting, *You Gotta Have Wa* (New York: Macmillan Publishing Company, 1989).

6. R. G. Tweed and D. R. Lehman, "Learning Considered within a Cultural Context: Confucian and Socratic Approaches," *American Psychologist* 57 (2002): 89–99.
7. L. Story, "Anywhere the Eye Can See, It's Likely to See an Ad," *New York Times*, January 15, 2007.
8. H. Kim and H. R. Markus, "Deviance or Uniqueness, Harmony or Conformity? A Cultural Analysis," *Journal of Personality and Social Psychology* 77 (1999): 785–800.
9. J. L. Tsai, J. Y. Louie, E. E. Chen, and Y. Uchida, "Learning What Feelings to Desire: Socialization of Ideal Affect through Children's Storybooks," *Personality and Social Psychology Bulletin* 33 (2007): 17–30.
10. J. L. Tsai, F. F. Miao, and E. Seppala, "Good Feelings in Christianity and Buddhism: Religious Differences in Ideal Affect," *Personality and Social Psychology Bulletin* 33 (2007): 409–21.
11. H. R. Markus, Y. Uchida, H. Omoregie, S. S. M. Townsend, and S. Kitayama, "Going for the Gold: Models of Agency in Japanese and American Culture," *Psychological Science* 17 (2006): 103–12.
12. P. L. Berger and T. Luckmann, *The Social Construction of Reality: A Treatise in the Sociology of Knowledge* (Garden City, NY: Doubleday, 1966).
13. C. Taylor, *Sources of the Self: The Making of the Modern Identity* (Cambridge, UK: Cambridge University Press, 1989).
14. V. C. Plaut and H. R. Markus, "The 'Inside' Story: A Cultural-Historical Analysis of Being Smart and Motivated, American Style," in A. J. Elliot and C. S. Dweck, eds., *Handbook of Competence and Motivation* (New York: The Guilford Press, 2005), pp. 457–88.
15. Tweed and Lehman, "Learning Considered within a Cultural Context: Confucian and Socratic Approaches"; J. Li, "Mind or Virtue: Western and Chinese Beliefs about Learning," *Current Directions in Psychological Science* 14 (2005): 190–94; J. Li, "U.S. and Chinese Cultural Beliefs about Learning," *Journal of Educational Psychology* 95 (2003): 258–67.
16. M. Weber, *The Protestant Ethic and the Spirit of Capitalism*, T. Parsons, trans. (1905; reprint New York: Charles Scribner's Sons, 1958); J. Sanchez-Burks, "Protestant Relational Ideology: The Cognitive Underpinning and Organizational Implications of an American Anomaly," in B. M. Staw and R. M. Kramer, eds., *Research in Organizational Behavior: An Annual Series of Analytical Essays and Critical Reviews* 26 (2005): 265–306.
17. R. Nisbett, *The Geography of Thought: How Asians and Westerners Think Differently . . . and Why* (New York: The Free Press, 2003).
18. For much more on East/West differences in learning and pedagogy, see J. Li, *Cultural Foundations of Learning* (Cambridge, UK: Cambridge University Press, 2012).
19. S. Suzuki, *Zen Mind, Beginner's Mind*, T. Dixon, ed. (New York: Weatherhill, Inc., 1970).

20. L. Darling-Hammond, "Race, Inequality, and Educational Accountability: The Irony of 'No Child Left Behind,'" *Race Ethnicity and Education* 10 (2007): 245–60.
21. U.S. Department of Labor, Bureau of Labor Statistics, "Job Openings and Labor Turnover, May 2010" (Washington, D.C.: Government Printing Office); N. Terrell, "STEM Occupations," *Occupational Outlook Quarterly* 51 (2007): 26–33.
22. J. M. Harackiewicz, C. S. Hulleman, and J. S. Hyde, "Helping Parents Motivate Adolescents in Mathematics and Science: An Experimental Test of a Utility-Value Intervention," *Psychological Science* 10 (2012): 1–8.
23. Plaut and Markus, "The 'Inside' Story," pp. 457–88; S. J. Heine, D. R. Lehman, E. Ide, C. Leung, S. Kitayama, T. Takata, and H. Matsumoto, "Divergent Consequences of Success and Failure in Japan and North America: An Investigation of Self-Improving Motivations and Malleable Selves," *Journal of Personality and Social Psychology* 81 (2001): 599–615; C.-Y. Chiu and Y.-Y. Hong, *Social Psychology of Culture* (New York: Psychology Press, 2006).
24. C. S. Dweck, *Mindset: The New Psychology of Success* (New York: Random House, 2006).
25. A. L. Duckworth, C. Peterson, M. D. Matthews, and D. R. Kelly, "Grit: Perseverance and Passion for Long-Term Goals," *Journal of Personality and Social Psychology* 92 (2007): 1087–101.
26. Chua, *Battle Hymn of the Tiger Mother*, p. 29.
27. S. A. Hewlett, R. Rashid, D. Roster, and C. Ho, *Asians in America: Unleashing the Potential of the "Model Minority"* (New York: Center for Work-Life Policy, 2011).
28. A. H. Eagly and J. L. Chin, "Diversity and Leadership in a Changing World," *American Psychologist* 65 (2010): 216–24.
29. H. S. Kim, "Culture and the Cognitive and Neuroendocrine Responses to Speech," *Journal of Personality and Social Psychology* 94 (2008): 32–47.
30. S. Cheryan and B. Monin, "Where Are You *Really* From? Asian Americans and Identity Denial," *Journal of Personality and Social Psychology* 89 (2005): 717–30.
31. W. James, *The Principles of Psychology* (New York: Henry Holt and Company, 1890), p. 509.

Chapter 3

1. U.S. Department of Labor, Bureau of Labor Statistics, "Table 11: Employed Persons by Detailed Occupation and Sex, 2010 Annual Averages," *Women in the Labor Force: A Databook (2011 Edition)* (Washington, D.C.: U.S. Department of Labor, December 2011). See also H. Rosin, "The End of Men," *The Atlantic* 306 (July/August 2010): 56–72.
2. J. Chung, personal communication, 08/09/12. See also B. Luscombe, "Workplace Salaries: At Last, Women on Top," *Time*, September 2010.
3. U.S. Department of Education, National Center for Education Statistics, *Digest of Education Statistics: 2011*, "Table 283: Degrees Conferred by Degree-Granting

Institutions, by Level of Degree and Sex of Student: Selected Years, 1869–70 through 2020–21," retrieved from http://nces.ed.gov/programs/digest/d11/tables/dt11_283.asp (accessed 08/09/12); and "Table 311: Degrees Conferred by Degree-Granting Institutions in Selected Professional Fields, by Sex, Race/Ethnicity, and Field of Study: 2007–08," retrieved from http://nces.ed.gov/programs/digest/d11/tables/dt11_311.asp (accessed 08/09/12).

4. Women own a majority share of 29.6 percent of U.S. businesses and a 50 percent share of 17.5 percent of businesses (a total of 47.1 percent of U.S. businesses). Men own the majority share of 52.9 percent of businesses and a 50 percent share of 17.5 percent of businesses (a total of 70.4 percent of U.S. businesses). See U.S. Department of Commerce, Economics and Statistics Administration, "Women-Owned Businesses in the Twenty-First Century" (October 2010), retrieved from www.esa.doc.gov/sites/default/files/reports/documents/women-owned-businesses.pdf (accessed 08/09/12).
5. R. Kochar, "Two Years of Economic Recovery: Women Lose Jobs, Men Find Them" (Washington, D.C.: Pew Research Center, July 2011).
6. R. Salam, "The Death of Macho," *Foreign Policy* 173 (2009): 65–70.
7. For a summary of these findings, see P. Tyre, *The Trouble with Boys* (New York: Three Rivers Press, 2008).
8. S. Hinshaw and R. Kranz, *The Triple Bind: Saving Our Teenage Girls from Today's Pressures* (New York: Ballantine, 2009).
9. Ibid., p. 25.
10. Rosin, "The End of Men."
11. In chapter 5, we will also document how classrooms, despite their interdependent tone, are still too independent to support the selves of working-class children.
12. Center for American Women and Politics, "Women in the U.S. Congress 2012" (New Brunswick, NJ: National Information Bank on Women in Public Office, Eagleton Institute of Politics, Rutgers University, February 2012).
13. Catalyst, "Women CEOs of the Fortune 1000," *Pyramids*, May 7, 2012.
14. A. Hegewisch, C. Williams, and A. Zhang, "The Gender Wage Gap: 2011" (Washington, D.C.: Institute for Women's Policy Research, March 2012).
15. In this chapter, we focus on research about Western heterosexuals who are both sexed and gendered male or female. Sex is a biological category that has to do with which body parts you were born with; gender is a psychological category that has to do with which sex you view yourself as. Although the examples of lesbian, gay, bisexual, transgender, and intersex people and cultures offer great insights into gender, high-quality research on these groups is scant. In addition, although all cultures—hemispheres, nations, races, classes, religions, regions, etc.—draw lines between women and men, we limit ourselves to discussions of gender in the wealthy industrialized nations of the West.
16. J. Allmendinger and J. R. Hackman, "The More, the Better? A Four-Nation Study of the Inclusion of Women in Symphony Orchestras," *Social Forces* 74 (1995): 423–60.

17. R. M. Kanter, "Some Effects of Proportions on Group Life: Skewed Sex Ratios and Responses to Token Women," *American Journal of Sociology* 82 (1977): 965–90.
18. J. K. Hellerstein, D. Neumark, and K. R. Troske, "Market Forces and Sex Discrimination," *The Journal of Human Resources* 37 (2002): 353–80.
19. B. R. Reskin, D. B. McBrier, and J. A. Kmec, "The Determinants and Consequences of Workplace Sex and Race Composition," *Annual Review of Sociology* 25 (1999): 335–61.
20. M. Inzlicht and A. Ben-Zeev, "A Threatening Intellectual Environment: Why Females Are Susceptible to Experiencing Problem-Solving Deficits in the Presence of Males," *Psychological Science* 11 (2000): 365–71. See also A. Ben-Zeev, S. Fein, and M. Inzlicht, "Arousal and Stereotype Threat," *Journal of Experimental Social Psychology* 41 (2005): 174–81.
21. C. M. Steele, *Whistling Vivaldi* (New York: W. W. Norton, 2010).
22. A. W. Woolley, C. F. Chabris, A. Pentaland, N. Hashmi, and T. W. Malone, "Evidence for a Collective Intelligence Factor in the Performance of Human Groups," *Science* 330 (2010): 686–88.
23. Hellerstein, Neumark, and Troske, "Market Forces and Sex Discrimination."
24. C. Herring, "Does Diversity Pay? Race, Gender, and the Business Case for Diversity," *American Sociological Review* 74 (2009): 208–24.
25. C. L. Williams, "The Glass Escalator: Hidden Advantages for Men in the 'Female' Professions," *Social Problems* 39 (1992): 253–67.
26. J. S. Hyde, "The Gender Similarities Hypothesis," *American Psychologist* 60 (2005): 581–92.
27. Aggression can be used for both independent and interdependent ends. For instance, as we will discuss in chapter 6, U.S. Southerners use aggression to maintain honor—an interdependent motivation. In this chapter, however, we connect men's aggression to more independent sources, including the desires to individuate and influence.
28. Y. Kashima, S. Yamaguchi, U. Kim, S. Choi, M. J. Gelfand, and M. Yuki, "Culture, Gender, and Self: A Perspective from Individualism-Collectivism Research," *Journal of Personality and Social Psychology* 69 (1995): 925–37.
29. S. E. Cross, P. L. Bacon, and M. L. Morris, "The Relational-Interdependent Self-Construal and Relationships," *Journal of Personality and Social Psychology* 78 (2000): 791–808.
30. L. Madson and D. Trafimow, "Gender Comparisons in the Private, Collective, and Allocentric Selves," *The Journal of Social Psychology* 141 (2001): 551–59.
31. J. A. Hall, "Gender Effects in Decoding Nonverbal Cues," *Psychological Bulletin* 85 (1978): 845–57.
32. W. Ickes, T. Tooke, L. Stinson, V. L. Baker, and V. Bissonnette, "Naturalistic Social Cognition: Intersubjectivity in Same-Sex Dyads," *Journal of Nonverbal Behavior* 12 (1988): 58–82.

33. M. S. Mast and J. A. Hall, "Women's Advantage at Remembering Others' Appearances: A Systematic Look at the Why and When of a Gender Difference," *Personality and Social Psychology Bulletin* 32 (2006): 353–64; T. G. Horgan, M. S. Mast, J. A. Hall, and J. D. Carter, "Gender Differences in Memory for the Appearance of Others," *Personality and Social Psychology Bulletin* 30 (2004): 185–96; H. P. Bahrick, P. Q. Bahrick, and R. P. Wittlinger, "Fifty Years of Memory for Names and Faces: A Cross-Sectional Approach," *Journal of Experimental Psychology: General* 104 (1975): 54–75; S. E. Cross and L. Madson, "Models of the Self: Self-Construals and Gender," *Psychological Bulletin* 122 (1997): 5–37.
34. M. Ross and D. Holmberg, "Are Wives' Memories for Events in Relationships More Vivid Than Their Husbands' Memories?" *Journal of Social and Personal Relationships* 9 (1992): 585–604.
35. J. K. Kiecolt-Glaser and T. L. Newton, "Marriage and Health: His and Hers," *Psychological Bulletin* 127 (2001): 472–503; K. S. Kendler, L. M. Thornton, and C. A. Prescott, "Gender Differences in the Rates of Exposure to Stressful Life Events and Sensitivity to Their Depressogenic Effects," *American Journal of Psychiatry* 158 (2001): 587–93.
36. K. Schumann and M. Ross, "Why Women Apologize More Than Men: Gender Differences in Thresholds for Perceiving Offensive Behavior," *Psychological Science* 21 (2010): 1649–55.
37. S. E. Taylor, L. C. Klein, B. P. Lewis, T. L. Gruenewald, R. A. R. Gurung, and J. A. Updegraff, "Biobehavioral Responses to Stress in Females: Tend-and-Befriend, Not Fight-or-Flight," *Psychological Review* 107 (2000): 411–29.
38. A. Reid, "Gender and Sources of Subjective Well-Being," *Sex Roles* 51 (2004): 617–29.
39. A. H. Eagly, M. C. Johannesen-Schmidt, and M. L. van Engen, "Transformational, Transactional, and Laissez-Faire Leadership Styles: A Meta-Analysis Comparing Women and Men," *Psychological Bulletin* 129 (2003): 569–91.
40. N. A. Card, B. D. Stucky, G. M. Sawalani, and T. D. Little, "Direct and Indirect Aggression during Childhood and Adolescence: A Meta-Analytic Review of Gender Differences, Intercorrelations, and Relations to Maladjustment," *Child Development* 79 (2008): 1185–229; J. Archer, "Sex Differences in Aggression in Real-World Settings: A Meta-Analytic Review," *Review of General Psychology* 8 (2004): 291–322; R. F. Diekstra and W. Gulbinat, "The Epidemiology of Suicidal Behaviour: A Review of Three Continents," *World Health Statistics Quarterly* 46 (1993): 52–68.
1. S. Rosenfield, J. Vertefuille, and D. D. Mcalpine, "Gender Stratification and Mental Health: An Exploration of Dimensions of the Self," *Social Psychology Quarterly* 63 (2002): 208–23.
2. S. Guimond, A. Chatard, D. Martinot, R. J. Crisp, and S. Redersdorff, "Social Comparison, Self-Stereotyping, and Gender Differences in Self-Construals," *Journal of Personality and Social Psychology* 90 (2006): 221–42.

43. R. F. Baumeister, L. Smart, and J. M. Boden, "Relation of Threatened Egotism to Violence and Aggression: The Dark Side of High Self-Esteem," *Psychological Review* 103 (1996): 5–33.
44. R. W. Simon and L. E. Nath, "Gender and Emotion in the United States: Do Men and Women Differ in Self-Reports of Feelings and Expressive Behavior?" *American Journal of Sociology* 109 (2004): 1137–76.
45. K. D. O'Leary, J. Barling, I. Arias, A. Rosenbaum, J. Malone, and A. Tyree, "Prevalence and Stability of Physical Aggression between Spouses: A Longitudinal Analysis," *Journal of Consulting and Clinical Psychology* 57 (1989): 263–68.
46. J. P. Byrnes, D. C. Miller, and W. D. Schafer, "Gender Differences in Risk Taking: A Meta-Analysis," *Psychological Bulletin* 125 (1999): 367–83.
47. B. Barber and T. Odean, "Boys Will Be Boys: Gender, Overconfidence, and Common Stock Investment," *Quarterly Journal of Economics* 116 (2001): 261–92.
48. S. J. Heine, D. R. Lehman, H. R. Markus, and S. Kitayama, "Is There a Universal Need for Positive Self-Regard?" *Psychological Review* 106 (1999): 766–94.
49. E. M. Maccoby and C. N. Jacklin, *The Psychology of Sex Differences* (Stanford, CA: Stanford University Press, 1974).
50. S. J. Correll, "Gender and the Career Choice Process: The Role of Biased Self-Assessment," *American Journal of Sociology* 106 (2001): 1691–730.
51. A. H. Mezulis, L. Y. Abramson, J. S. Hyde, and B. L. Hankin, "Is There a Universal Positivity Bias in Attributions? A Meta-Analytic Review of Individual, Developmental, and Cultural Differences in the Self-Serving Attributional Bias," *Psychological Bulletin* 130 (2004): 711–47.
52. J. T. Jost and A. C. Kay, "Exposure to Benevolent Sexism and Complementary Gender Stereotypes: Consequences for Specific and Diffuse Forms of System Justification," *Journal of Personality and Social Psychology* 88 (2005): 498–509.
53. C. Fine. *Delusions of Gender: How Our Minds, Society, and Neurosexism Create Difference* (New York: W. W. Norton, 2010).
54. B. Rothman, *The Tentative Pregnancy: Prenatal Diagnosis and the Future of Motherhood* (London: Pandora, 1988).
55. J. Condry and S. Condry, "Sex Differences: A Study of the Eye of the Beholder," *Child Development* 47 (1976): 812–19.
56. S. M. Condry, J. C. Condry, and L. W. Pogatshnik, "Sex Differences: A Study of the Ear of the Beholder," *Sex Roles* 9 (1983): 697–704.
57. M. W. Clearfield and N. M. Nelson, "Sex Differences in Mothers' Speech and Play Behavior with 6-, 9-, and 14-Month-Old Infants," *Sex Roles* 5[illegible] (2006): 127–37.
58. J. Dunn, I. Bretherton, and P. Munn, "Conversations about Feeling States between Mothers and Their Young Children," *Developmental Psychology* 2[illegible] (1987): 132–39.
59. A. Nash and R. Krawczyk, "Boys' and Girls' Rooms Revisited: The Contents of Boys' and Girls' Rooms in the 1990s," paper presented at the Conference on Human Development, Pittsburgh, PA, 1994.

60. H. Lytton and D. M. Romney, "Parents' Differential Socialization of Boys and Girls: A Meta-Analysis," *Psychological Bulletin* 109 (1991): 267–96.
61. P. Orenstein, *Cinderella Ate My Daughter: Dispatches from the Front Lines of the New Girlie-Girl Culture* (New York: HarperCollins, 2011).
62. See, for example, S. N. Davis, "Sex Stereotypes in Commercials Targeted toward Children: A Content Analysis," *Sociological Spectrum* 23 (2003): 407–24; Orenstein, *Cinderella Ate My Daughter*; S. Lamb and L. Brown, *Packaging Girlhood: Rescuing Our Daughters from Marketers' Schemes* (New York: St. Martin's Press, 2006); J. Sheldon, "Gender Stereotypes in Educational Software for Young Children," *Sex Roles* 51 (2004): 433–44.
63. C. Good, J. Aronson, and J. A. Harder, "Problems in the Pipeline: Stereotype Threat and Women's Acheivement in High-Level Math Courses," *Journal of Applied Developmental Psychology* 29 (2008): 17–28.
64. S. Cheryan, V. C. Plaut, P. G. Davies, and C. M. Steele, "Ambient Belonging: How Stereotypical Cues Impact Gender Participation in Computer Science," *Journal of Personality and Social Psychology* 97 (2009): 1045–60.
65. V. K. Gupta, D. B. Turban, and N. B. Bhawe, "The Effect of Gender Stereotype Activation on Entrepreneurial Intentions," *Journal of Applied Psychology* 93 (2008): 1053–61.
66. M. E. Heilman, "Description and Prescription: How Gender Stereotypes Prevent Women's Ascent up the Organizational Ladder," *Journal of Social Issues* 57 (2001): 657–74.
67. J. L. Berdahl, "The Sexual Harassment of Uppity Women," *Journal of Applied Psychology* 92 (2007): 425–37.
68. Tyre, *The Trouble with Boys*, p. 130.
69. Ibid., p. 151.
70. R. R. Banks, *Is Marriage for White People? How the African American Marriage Decline Affects Everyone* (New York: Dutton, 2011); K. Bolick, "All the Single Ladies," *The Atlantic* 308 (November 2011): 116–36.
71. B. Nosek, F. L. Smyth, N. Sriram, N. M. Lindner, T. Devos, A. Ayala, . . . A. G. Greenwald, "National Differences in Gender-Science Stereotypes Predict National Sex Differences in Science and Math Achievement," *Proceedings of the National Academy of Sciences of the United States of America* 106 (2009): 10593–97.
72. A. F. Alesina, P. Giuliano, and N. Nunn, "On the Origins of Gender Roles: Women and the Plough" NBER Working Paper 17098, Cambridge, MA: National Bureau of Economic Research, 2011, retrieved from www.nber.org/papers/w17098 (accessed 09/22/2011).
73. A. Kalev, F. Dobbin, and E. Kelly, "Best Practices or Best Guesses? Assessing the Efficacy of Corporate Affirmative Action and Diversity Policies," *American Sociological Review* 71 (2006): 589–617.
74. M. Bittman, P. England, L. Sayer, N. Folbre, and G. Matheson, "When Does Gender Trump Money? Bargaining and Time in Household Work," *American Journal of Sociology* 109 (2003): 186–214.

75. L. Babcock and S. Laschever, *Women Don't Ask: Negotiation and the Gender Divide* (Princeton, NJ: Princeton University Press, 2003).
76. H. R. Bowles, L. Babcock, and L. Lei, "Social Incentives for Gender Differences in the Propensity to Initiate Negotiations: Sometimes It Does Hurt to Ask," *Organizational Behavior and Human Decision Processes* 103 (2007): 84–103.
77. E. T. Amanatullah and M. W. Morris, "Negotiating Gender Roles: Gender Differences in Assertive Negotiating Are Mediated by Women's Fear of Backlash and Attenuated When Negotiating on Behalf of Others," *Journal of Personality and Social Psychology* 98 (2010): 256–67.
78. A. Ben-Zeev, personal communication, 03/03/11.
79. D. F. Halpern, L. Eliot, R. S. Bigler, R. A. Fabes, L. D. Hanish, J. Hyde, L. S. Liben, and C. L. Martin, "The Pseudoscience of Single Sex Schooling," *Science* 333 (2011): 1706–7.
80. U.S. Department of Education, "Single-Sex versus Coeducational Schooling: A Systematic Review" (Doc # 2005-01), 2005, retrieved from www2.ed.gov/rschstat/eval/other/single-sex/single-sex.pdf (accessed 08/11/12).
81. C. L. Martin and R. A. Fabes, "The Stability and Consequences of Young Children's Same-Sex Peer Interactions," *Developmental Psychology* 37 (2001): 431–46.
82. D. M. Leonard, *Single-Sex and Co-Educational Secondary Schooling: Life Course Consequences?* ESRC End of Award Report, RES-000-22-1085, 2007, retrieved from www.esrc.ac.uk/my-esrc/grants/RES-000-22-1085/read (accessed 08/11/12).
83. A. D. Galinsky, D. H. Gruenfeld, and J. C. Magee, "From Power to Action," *Journal of Personality and Social Psychology* 85 (2003): 453–66.
84. S. Chen, C. A. Langner, and R. Mendoza-Denton, "When Dispositional and Role Power Fit: Implications for Self-Expression and Self-Other Congruence," *Journal of Personality and Social Psychology* 96 (2009): 710–27.
85. C. L. Dezső and D. G. Ross, "Does Female Representation in Top Management Improve Firm Performance? A Panel Data Investigation," *Strategic Management Journal 33* (2012): 1072–89.
86. F. Kaplan, "Obama's 'Sputnik Moment,'" *Slate*, January 2011, retrieved from www.slate.com/articles/news_and_politics/war_stories/2011/01/obamas_sputnik_moment.html (accessed 08/11/12).

Chapter 4

1. In this chapter, we use the terms *Black* and *White* instead of *African American* and *European American* because people usually link the former terms with the concepts of *race* and *ethnicity*. As we will soon discuss, many people historically considered *White* and *Black* to be biological traits that were associated with distinct behaviors. Here, we aim to reclaim these terms and show that

Blacks and Whites sometimes do have different thoughts, feelings, and actions, but for cultural reasons, not biological ones.

2. Races allegedly have a biological basis and ethnicities allegedly have historical, linguistic, or otherwise cultural bases. Yet *race* and *ethnicity* are used interchangeably because they usually belie a third variable: power. People often use race or ethnicity to assign more or less power or privilege and to justify the resulting inequality. For more on the definition of race and ethnicity, see H. R. Markus and P. M. L. Moya, eds., *Doing Race: 21 Essays for the 21st Century* (New York: W. W. Norton, 2010).
3. R. A. Wooden, "40 Years after Civil Rights Act, We Haven't Crossed the Finish Line," *USA Today*, June 30, 2004, retrieved from www.usatoday.com/news/opinion/editorials/2004-06-30-opcom_x.htm (accessed 08/08/12); J. M. Jones, "Blacks More Pessimistic Than Whites about Economic Opportunities," Gallup News Service, July 9, 2004, retrieved from www.gallup.com/poll/12307/blacks-more-pessimistic-than-whites-about-economic-opportunities.aspx (accessed 08/08/12).
4. M. I. Norton and S. R. Sommers, "Whites See Racism as a Zero-Sum Game That They Are Now Losing," *Perspectives in Psychological Science* 6 (2011): 215–18.
5. *Latino*, *Hispanic*, and *Chicano* are often used interchangeably, although each has a specific meaning. Reflecting a preference common in California, we use the term *Latino* to refer to people of Latin American descent living in the United States.
6. V. C. Plaut, "Diversity Science: Why and How Difference Makes a Difference," *Psychological Inquiry* 21 (2010): 77–99; W. J. Wilson, *More Than Just Race* (New York: W. W. Norton, 2009).
7. Markus and Moya, eds., *Doing Race*.
8. V. C. Plaut, "Diversity Science," in. G. Orfield, *Reviving the Goal of an Integrated Society: A Twenty-First Century Challenge* (Los Angeles, CA: The Civil Rights Project/Proyecto Derechos Civiles at UCLA, 2009): 77–99.
9. For an extended discussion of this idea, see S. Colbert, *The Word: Neutral Man's Burden* (television broadcast), Comedy Central, broadcast July 16, 2009.
10. U.S. Census Bureau, "Most Children Younger Than Age 1 Are Minorities, Census Bureau Reports" (Washington, D.C.: Government Printing Office, 2012); U.S. Census Bureau, "2008 National Population Projections" (Washington, D.C.: Government Printing Office, 2008).
11. J. D. Vorauer, A. Gagnon, and S. J. Sasaki, "Salient Intergroup Ideology and Intergroup Interaction," *Psychological Science* 20 (2009): 838–45.
12. For a discussion of race and ethnicity around the world, see H. Winant, *The Whole World Is a Ghetto: Race and Democracy since World War II* (New York: Basic Books, 2001); P. L. Carter, *Stubborn Roots: Race, Culture, and Inequality in U.S. and South African Schools* (New York: Oxford University Press, 2012).

13. J. N. Shelton and J. A. Richeson, "Interracial Interactions: A Relational Approach," *Advances in Experimental Social Psychology* 38 (2006): 121–81.
14. J. A. Richeson and J. N. Shelton, "When Prejudice Does Not Pay: Effects of Interracial Contact on Executive Function," *Psychological Science* 14 (2003): 287–90.
15. S. Trawalter and J. A. Richeson, "Let's Talk about Race, Baby! When Whites' and Blacks' Interracial Contact Experiences Diverge," *Journal of Experimental Social Psychology* 44 (2008): 1214–17.
16. N. R. Toosi, L. G. Babbitt, N. Ambady, and S. R. Sommers, "Dyadic Interracial Interactions: A Meta-Analysis," *Psychological Bulletin* 138 (2012): 1–27.
17. J. Blascovich, W. B. Mendes, S. B. Hunter, B. Lickel, and N. Kowai-Bell, "Perceiver Threat in Social Interactions with Stigmatized Others," *Journal of Personality and Social Psychology* 80: (2011): 253–67.
18. B. Tatum, "The Complexity of Identity: "Who Am I?" in *Why Are All the Black Kids Sitting Together in the Cafeteria?* rev. ed. (New York: Basic Books, 2002); D. Oyserman, "Racial-Ethnic Self-Schemas: Multidimensional Identity-Based Motivation," *Journal of Research in Personality* 42 (2008): 1186–98.
19. T. Forman, "Racial Apathy and the Myth of a Post-Racial America," paper presented at the Research Institute of Comparative Studies in Race and Ethnicity, Stanford, CA, April 2012.
20. Colbert, *The Word.*
21. D. Sekaquaptewa, A. Waldman, and M. Thompson, "Solo Status and Self-Construal: Being Distinctive Influences Racial Self-Construal and Performance Apprehension in African American Women," *Cultural Diversity and Ethnic Minority Psychology* 13 (2007): 321–27.
22. H. R. Markus, "Ratings of Own and Peers' Abilities," unpublished data, Stanford University, Stanford, CA, 2012.
23. J. S. Phinney, C. L. Cantu, and D. A. Kurtz, "Ethnic and American Identity as Predictors of Self-Esteem among African American, Latino, and White Adolescents, *Journal of Youth and Adolescence* 26 (1997): 165–85.
24. L. Stankov, J. Lee, and I. Paek, "Realism of Confidence Judgments," *European Journal of Psychological Assessment* 25 (2009): 123–30.
25. Touré, *Who's Afraid of Post-Blackness? What It Means to Be Black Now* (New York: Free Press, 2011), p. 88.
26. Walt Disney, *Dumbo* (motion picture), RKO Radio Pictures, 1941.
27. By 1967, Disney understood that hiring Louis Armstrong to voice King Louie would be too controversial a move, so the studio hired the Italian American entertainer Louis Prima instead. Nevertheless, King Louie's speech and music were patterned on stereotypical Black styles.
28. "Speedy Gonzales Caged by Cartoon Network," Foxnews.com, March 28, 2002, retrieved from www.foxnews.com/story/0,2933,48872,00.html (accessed 10/1/2012).
29. A. C. Martin, "Television Media as a Potential Negative Factor in the Racial Identity Development of African American Youth," *Academic Psychiatry* 32 (2008): 338–42.

30. M. Weisbuch, K. Pauker, and N. Ambady, "The Subtle Transmission of Race Bias via Televised Nonverbal Behavior," *Science* 326 (2009): 1711–14.
31. C. M. Steele and J. Aronson, "Stereotype Threat and the Intellectual Test Performance of African Americans," *Journal of Personality and Social Psychology* 69 (1995): 797–811; C. M. Steele, *Whistling Vivaldi: How Stereotypes Affect Us and What We Can Do* (New York: W. W. Norton, 2010).
32. J. Stone, C. I. Lynch, M. Sjomeling, and J. M., Darley, "Stereotype Threat Effects on Black and White Athletic Performance," *Journal of Personality and Social Psychology* 77 (1999): 1213–27. See also J. Stone, W. Perry, and J. Darley, " 'White Men Can't Jump': Evidence for the Perceptual Confirmation of Racial Stereotypes Following a Basketball Game," *Basic and Applied Social Psychology* 19 (1997): 291–306.
33. J. Oakes and G. Guiton, "Matchmaking: The Dynamics of High School Tracking Decisions," *American Educational Research Journal* 32 (1995): 3–33; Tomás Rivera Policy Institute, *Equity in Offering Advanced Placement Courses in California High Schools*, 2006, retrieved from www.trpi.org/PDFs/ap_2006.pdf (accessed 08/09/12).
34. M. Bertrand and S. Mullainatha, "Are Emily and Greg More Employable Than Lakisha and Jamal? A Field Experiment on Labor Market Discrimination, *American Economic Review* 94 (2004): 991–1013.
35. D. Pager, "The Use of Field Experiments for Studies of Employment Discrimination: Contributions, Critiques, and Directions for the Future," *Annals of the American Academy of Political and Social Science* 609 (2007): 104–33; D. Pager, B. Western, and B. Bonikowski, "Discrimination in a Low-Wage Labor Market: A Field Experiment," *American Sociological Review* 74 (2009): 777–99.
36. E. Cose, *The Rage of a Privileged Class: Why Are Middle-Class Blacks Angry? Why Should America Care?* (New York: HarperCollins, 1993).
37. M. J. Fischer and D. S. Massey, "The Ecology of Racial Discrimination," *City and Community* 3 (2004): 221–41.
38. I. Ayres, "Fair Driving: Gender and Race Discrimination in Retail Car Negotiations," *Harvard Law Review* 104 (1991): 817–72.
39. A. R. Green, D. R. Carney, D. J. Pallin, L. H. Ngo, K. L. Raymond, L. I. Iezzoni, and M. R. Banaji, "Implicit Bias among Physicians and Its Prediction of Thrombolysis Decisions for Black and White Patients," *Journal of General Internal Medicine* 22 (2007): 1231–38.
40. C. M. Bonham, *Devaluing Black Space: Black Locations as Targets of Housing and Environmental Discrimination* (doctoral dissertation), Stanford University, Stanford, CA, 2010.
41. B. Pettit and B. Western, "Mass Imprisonment and the Life Course: Race and Class Inequality in U.S. Incarceration," *American Sociological Review* 69 (2004): 151–69; L. D. Bobo and V. Thompson, "Racialized Mass Incarceration: Poverty, Prejudice, and Punishment," in Markus and Moya, eds., *Doing Race*, pp. 322–55; J. L. Eberhardt, P. G. Davies, V. J. Purdie-Vaughns, and S. L. Johnson, "Looking Deathworthy: Perceived Stereotypicality of

Black Defendants Predicts Capital-Sentencing Outcomes," *Psychological Science* 17 (2006): 383–86.

42. J. Price and J. Wolfers, "Racial Discrimination among NBA Referees," *The Quarterly Journal of Economics* 125 (2010): 1859–87
43. D. Pager and H. Shepherd, "The Sociology of Discrimination: Racial Discrimination in Employment, Housing, Credit, and Consumer Markets," *Annual Review of Sociology* 34 (2008): 181–209.
44. H. Cain, *This Is Herman Cain! My Journey to the White House* (New York: Threshold Editions, 2011).
45. J. S. Mbiti, *African Religions and Philosophy* (Garden City, NY: Doubleday, 1970).
46. A. Daly, J. Jennings, J. O. Beckett, and B. R. Leashore, "Effective Coping Strategies of African Americans," *Social Work* 40 (1995): 240–48.
47. J. Jackson, "The Masquerade of Racial Group Differences in Psychological Sciences," Keynote Speech, Association for Psychological Science Twenty-fourth Annual Convention, May 25, 2012.
48. R. J. Taylor, L. M. Chatters, and J. S. Jackson, "Religious and Spiritual Involvement among Older African Americans, Carribean Blacks, and Non-Hispanic Whites: Findings from the National Survey of American Life," *Journal of Gerontology: Social Sciences* 62B (2007): S238–S250; R. J. Taylor, L. M. Chatters, R. Jayakody, and J. S. Levin, "Black and White Differences in Religious Participation: A Multisample Comparison," *Journal for the Scientific Study of Religion* 35 (1996): 403–10.
49. T. N. Brown, E. E. Tanner-Smith, C. L. Lesane-Brown, and M. E. Ezell, "Child, Parent, and Situational Correlates of Familial Ethnic/Race Socialization," *Journal of Marriage and Family* 69 (2007): 14–25; P. Bronson and A. Merryman, *NurtureShock: New Thinking about Children* (New York: Twelve, 2009).
50. M. O. Caughy, P. J. O'Campo, S. M. Randolph, and K. Nickerson, "The Influence of Racial Socialization Practices on the Cognitive and Behavioral Competence of African American Preschoolers," *Child Development* 73 (2002): 1611–25.
51. D. Hughes, J. Rodriguez, E. P. Smith, D. J. Johnson, H. C. Stevenson, and P. Spicer, "Parents' Racial/Ethnic Socialization Practices: A Review of Research and Agenda for Future Study," *Developmental Psychology* 42 (2006): 747–70; A. Wigfield and J. S. Eccles, "Children's Competence Beliefs, Achievement Values, and General Self-Esteem: Change across Elementary and Middle School," *Journal of Early Adolescence* 14 (1994): 107–38.
52. E. V. P. Hudley, W. Haight, and P. J. Miller, *Raise Up a Child: Human Development in an African-American Family* (Chicago: Lyceum Press, 2003).
53. J. Crocker, R. K. Luhtanen, M. L. Cooper, and A. Bouvrette, "Contingencies of Self-Worth in College Students: Theory and Measurement," *Journal of Personality and Social Psychology* 85 (2003): 894–908.
54. M. Morgan and D.-E. Fischer, "Hiphop and Race: Blackness, Language, and Creativity," in Markus and Moya, eds., *Doing Race*, pp. 509–27.

55. Akrobatik [Jared Bridgeman], "Rain," *Absolute Value* (New York: Fat Beats Records, 2008).
56. H. E. Cheatham, R. B. Slaney, and N. C. Coleman, "Institutional Effects on the Psychosocial Development of African-American College Students," *Journal of Counseling Psychology* 37 (1990): 453–58.
57. P. Bronson and A. Merryman, "Is Your Baby Racist? Exploring the Roots of Discrimination," *Newsweek*, September 14, 2009.
58. J. Mazzuca and L. Lyons, "Few Americans Feel Day-to-Day Racial Tension," Gallup, August 31, 2004, retrieved from www.gallup.com/poll/12883/few-americans-feel-daytoday-racial-tension.aspx (accessed 08/09/12).
59. A. G. Greenwald, D. E. McGhee, and J. L. K. Schwartz, "Measuring Individual Differences in Implicit Cognition: The Implicit Association Test," *Journal of Personality and Social Psychology* 74 (1998): 1464–80; B. A. Nosek, M. R. Banaji, and A. G. Greenwald, "Harvesting Implicit Group Attitudes and Beliefs from a Demonstration Web Site," *Group Dynamics: Theory, Research, and Practice* 6 (2002): 101–15.
60. J. L. Eberhardt, P. A. Goff, V. J. Purdie, and P. G. Davies, "Seeing Black: Race, Crime, and Visual Processing," *Journal of Personality and Social Psychology* 87 (2004): 876–93; P. A. Goff, J. L. Eberhardt, M. J. Williams, and M. C. Jackson, "Not Yet Human: Implicit Knowledge, Historical Dehumanization, and Contemporary Consequences," *Journal of Personality and Social Psychology* 94 (2008): 292–306.
61. Green et al., "The Presence of Implicit Bias in Physicians and Its Prediction of Thrombolysis Decisions for Black and White Patients"; D. M. Amodio and P. G. Devine, "Stereotyping and Evaluation in Implicit Race Bias: Evidence for Independent Constructs and Unique Effects on Behavior," *Journal of Personality and Social Psychology* 91 (2006): 652–61; L. A. Rudman and R. D. Ashmore, "Discrimination and the Implicit Association Test," *Group Processes and Intergroup Relations* 10 (2007): 359–72.
62. P. Bronson and A. Merryman, "See Baby Discriminate," *Newsweek*, September 2009, retrieved from www.newsweek.com/id/214989 (accessed 08/08/12).
63. B. Vittrup, *Exploring the Influences of Educational Television and Parent-Child Discussions on Improving Children's Racial Attitudes* (doctoral dissertation), 2007; B. Vittrup and G. H. Holden, "Exploring the Impact of Educational Television and Parent-Child Discussions on Childrens Racial Attitudes," *Analyses of Social Issues and Public Policy* 11 (2011): 82–104.
64. C. Linnaeus, *Systema Naturae* (Vienna: Typis Ionnis Thomae nob. De Trattern, 1767); A. Smedley, *Race in North America: Origin and Evolution of a Worldview,* 3rd ed. (Boulder, CO: Westview Press, 2007).
65. P. M. L. Moya and H. R. Markus, "Doing Race: An Introduction," in Markus and Moya, *Doing Race*, pp. 1–102; S. J. Gould, *The Mismeasure of Man* (New York: W. W. Norton, 1996).
66. U.S. Constitution, Article 1, Section 2.

67. T. Jefferson, *Notes on the State of Virginia* (Richmond, VA: J. W. Randolph, 1782).
68. R. E. Nisbett, *Intelligence and How to Get It: Why Schools and Cultures Count* (New York: W. W. Norton, 2009); Markus and Moya, eds., "Doing Race: An introduction," pp. 1–102.
69. T. N. Brannon, H. R. Markus, and V. D. Jones, "'Two Souls, Two Thoughts,' Two Self-Schemas: Positive Consequences of Double Consciousness for Self-Construal and Academic Performance," unpublished manuscript, Stanford University, 2012.
70. Pew Research Center, *Blacks See Growing Values Gap between Poor and Middle Class: Optimism about Black Progress Declines*, 2007, retrieved from http://pewsocialtrends.org/files/2010/10/Race-2007.pdf (accessed 08/09/12).
71. P. McIntosh, "White Privilege: Unpacking the Invisible Knapsack," *Independent School* (Winter 1990): 31–36.
72. J. T. Jost and B. Major, eds, *The Psychology of Legitimacy: Emerging Perspectives on Ideology, Justice, and Intergroup Relations* (New York: Cambridge University Press, 2001).
73. W. G. Bowen and D. Bok, *The Shape of the River* (Princeton, NJ: Princeton University Press, 1998).
74. N. Sorensen, B. A. Nagda, P. Gurin, and K. E. Maxwell, "Taking a 'Hands On' Approach to Diversity in Higher Education: A Critical-Dialogic Model for Effective Intergroup Interaction," *Analysis of Social Issues and Public Policies* 9 (2009): 3–35.
75. S. R. Sommers, "On Racial Diversity and Group Decision-Making: Identifying Multiple Effects of Racial Composition on Jury Deliberations," *Journal of Personality and Social Psychology* 90 (2006): 597–612.
76. O. C. Richard, "Racial Diversity, Business Strategy, and Firm Performance: A Resource-Based View," *The Academy of Management Journal* 43 (2000): 164–77; K. A. Jehn, G. B. Northcraft, and M. A. Neale, "Why Differences Make a Difference: A Field Study of Diversity, Conflict, and Performance in Workgroups," *Administrative Science Quarterly* 44 (1999): 741–63.
77. V. Purdie-Vaughns, C. M. Steele, P. G. Davies, R. Ditlmann, and J. R. Crosby, "Social Identity Contingencies: How Diversity Cues Signal Threat or Safety for African Americans in Mainstream Institutions," *Journal of Personality and Social Psychology* 94 (2008): 615–30.
78. V. C. Plaut, K. M. Thomas, and M. J. Goren, "Is Multiculturalism or Color Blindness Better for Minorities?" *Psychological Science* 20 (2009): 444–46; C. Herring, "Does Diversity Pay? Race, Gender, and the Business Case for Diversity," *American Sociological Review* 74 (2009): 208–24.
79. V. C. Plaut, F. G. Garnett, L. E. Buffardi, and J. Sanchez-Burks, "'What about Me?' Perceptions of Exclusion and Whites' Reactions to Multiculturalism," *Journal of Personality and Social Psychology* 101 (2011): 337–53.
80. D. Steele in J. Banks, *Multicultural Education: Issues and Perspectives* (New York: John Wiley and Sons, 2001); H. R. Markus, C. M. Steele, D. M. Steele, "Colorblindness as a Barrier to Inclusion: Assimilation and Nonimmigrant Minori-

ties," *Daedalus* 129 (2000): 233–59.; D. M. Steele, C. M. Steele, H. R. Markus, A. E. Lewis, F. Green, and P. G. Davies, "How Identity Safety Improves Student Achievement," unpublished manuscript, Stanford University, Stanford, CA, 2007.

81. L. Hansberry, *Les Blancs*, in R. Nemiroff, ed. *Collected Last Plays of Lorraine Hansberry* (New York: New American Library, 1969).
82. M. J. Williams and J. L. Eberhardt, "Biological Conceptions of Race and the Motivation to Cross Racial Boundaries," *Journal of Personality and Social Psychology* 94 (2008): 1033–47.
83. R. Mendoza-Denton, "This Holiday, a Toast to Cross-Race Friendship," *Psychology Today*, November 23, 2010, available at www.psychologytoday.com/blog/are-we-born-racist/201011/holiday-toast-cross-race-friendship (accessed 08/09/12); K. Davies, L. R. Tropp, A. Aron, T. F. Pettigrew, and S. C. Wright, "Cross-Group Friendships and Intergroup Attitudes: A Meta-Analytic Review," *Personality and Social Psychology Review* 15 (2011): 332–51.
84. E. Page-Gould, R. Mendoza-Denton, and L. R. Tropp, "With a Little Help from My Cross-Group Friend: Reducing Anxiety in Intergroup Contexts through Cross-Group Friendship," *Journal of Personality and Social Psychology* 95 (2008): 1080–94.
85. S. Trawalter and J. A. Richeson, "Regulatory Focus and Executive Function after Interracial Interactions," *Journal of Experimental Social Psychology* 42 (2006): 406–12; E. P. Apfelbaum, S. P. Sommers, and M. I. Norton, "Seeing Race and Seeming Racist? Evaluating Strategic Colorblindness in Social Interaction," *Journal of Personality and Social Psychology* 95 (2008): 918–32.
86. H. B. Bergsieker, J. N. Shelton, and J. A. Richeson, "To Be Liked versus Respected: Divergent Goals in Interracial Interactions," *Journal of Personaltiy and Social Psychology* 99 (2010): 248–64.
87. L. A. Rudman, R. D. Ashmore, and M. L. Gary, "'Unlearning' Automatic Biases: The Malleability of Implicit Prejudice and Stereotypes," *Journal of Personality and Social Psychology* 81 (2001): 856–68.
88. d. ayo, "LIVE: How to Rent a Negro (self-published audiobook, 2007).
89. d. ayo, *I Can Fix It! Vol. 1: Racism*, retrieved from http://www.damaliayo.com/pdfs/I%20CAN%20FIX%20IT_racism.pdf (accessed 08/09/12).
90. Ibid.
91. J. Christensen, "FBI Tracked King's Every Move," CNN, March 31, 2008, retrieved from articles.cnn.com/2008-03-31/us/mlk.fbi.conspiracy_1_dream-speech-david-garrow-civil-rights?_s=PM:US (accessed 08/09/12).
92. DNBE Apparel, available from www.dangerousnegro.com/ (accessed 08/09/12).
93. G. L. Cohen, J. Garcia, V. Purdie-Vaughns, N. Apfel, and P. Brzustoski, "Recursive Processes in Self-Affirmation: Intervening to Close the Minority Achievement Gap," *Science* 324 (2009): 400–403.
94. G. L. Cohen, J. Garcia, N. Apfel, and A. Master, "Reducing the Racial Achievement Gap: A Social-Psychological Intervention," *Science* 313 (2006): 1307–10.

95. D. Oyserman, K. Harrison, and D. Bybee, "Can Racial Identity Be Promotive of Academic Efficacy?" *International Journal of Behavioral Development* 25 (2001): 379–85.
96. B. Thurston, *How to Be Black* (New York: HarperCollins, 2012).
97. R. Mendoza-Denton and E. Page-Gould, "Can Cross-Group Friendships Influence Minority Students' Well-Being at Historically White Universities?" *Psychological Science* 19 (2008): 933–39.
98. "Arizona Legislature Passes Bill to Curb 'Chauvanism' in Ethnic Studies Programs," Foxnews.com, April 30, 2010, retrieved from www.foxnews.com/politics/2010/04/30/arizona-legislature-passes-banning-ethnic-studies-programs/ (accessed 08/09/12).
99. *Parents Involved in Community Schools v. Seattle School District No. 1*, 551 U.S 701 (2007).
100. *Regents of the University of California v. Bakke*, 438 U.S. 265 (1978).

Chapter 5

1. T. Noah, *The Great Divergence: America's Growing Inequality Crisis and What We Can Do about It* (New York: Bloomsbury Press, 2012); G. W. Domhoff, "Who Rules America? Wealth, Income, and Power," last modified March, 2012, www2.ucsc.edu/whorulesamerica/power/wealth.html (accessed 08/10/12).
2. U.S. Census Bureau, "Table 231: Educational Attainment by Selected Characteristics: 2010" (Washington, D.C.: Government Printing Office, 2012); S. F. Reardon, "The Widening Gap between the Rich and the Poor: New Evidence and Possible Explanations," in G. J. Duncan and R. J. Murnane, eds., *Whither Opportunity? Rising Inequality, Schools, and Children's Life Chances* (New York: Russell Sage Foundation, 2011), pp. 91–116; A. Lareau and D. Conley, eds., *Social Class: How Does It Work?* (New York: Russell Sage Foundation, 2008); S. T. Fiske and H. R. Markus, eds., *Facing Social Class: How Societal Rank Influences Interaction* (New York: Russell Sage Foundation, 2012); P. Attewell and K. S. Newman, *Growing Gaps: Educational Inequality around the World* (New York: Oxford University Press, 2010).
3. N. E. Adler and D. H. Rehkopf, "U.S. Disparities in Health: Descriptions, Causes, and Mechanisms," *Annual Review of Public Health* 29 (2008): 235–52; M. Marmot and M. J. Shipley, "Do Socioeconomic Differences in Mortality Persist after Retirement? 25-Year Follow-Up of Civil Servants from the First Whitehall Study," *British Medical Journal* 313 (1996): 1177–80; I. T. Elo, "Social Class Differentials in Health and Mortality: Patterns and Explanations in Comparitive Perspective," *Annual Review of Sociology* 35 (2009): 553–72; S. Cohen, C. M. Alper, W. J. Doyle, N. Adler, J. J. Treanor, and R. B. Turner, "Objective and Subjective Socioeconomic Status and Susceptibility to the Common Cold," *Health Psychology* 27 (2008): 268–74; W. Johnson and R. F. Krueger, "How Money Buys Happiness: Genetic and Environomental

Processes Linking Finances and Life Satisfaction," *Journal of Personality and Social Psychology* 90 (2006): 680–91.

4. A. Conner Snibbe and H. R. Markus, "You Can't Always Get What You Want: Educational Attainment, Agency, and Choice," *Journal of Personality and Social Psychology* 88 (2005): 703–20; Fiske and Markus, eds., *Facing Social Class*; J. DeParle, "Two Classes, Divided by 'I Do,'" *New York Times* (July 14, 2012), pp. A1; J. Williams, "The Class Culture Gap," in Fiske and Markus, eds., *Facing Social Class*, pp. 39–57; C. L. Ridgeway and S. R. Fisk, "Class Rules, Status Dynamics, and 'Gateway' Interactions," in Fiske and Markus, eds., *Facing Social Class*, pp. 131–51.
5. Duncan and Murnane, eds., *Whither Opportunity?*; J. Brooks-Gunn and G. J. Duncan, "The Effects of Poverty on Children," *Future Child* 7 (1997): 55–71; S. R. Sirin, "Socioeconomic Status and Academic Achievement: A Meta-Analytic Review of Research," *Review of Education Research* 75 (2005): 417–53.
6. Duncan and Murnane, eds., *Whither Opportunity?*
7. A. Carnevale and S. Rose, "The Undereducated American" (Washington, D.C.: Georgetown University Center on Education and the Workforce, 2011).
8. U.S. Census Bureau, *Statistical Abstract of the United States: 2012* (Washington, D.C.: Government Printing Office, 2012).
9. As measured with the Gini coefficient for the total population, calculated after taxes and transfers using the most recent data available. Organisation for Economic Co-operation and Development, "Income Distribution—Inequality (data file), 2012," retrieved from stats.oecd.org/Index.aspx?DatasetCode=INEQUALITY (accessed 08/10/12).
10. Organisation for Economic Co-operation and Development, "A Family Affair: Intergenerational Social Mobility across OECD Countries," *Economic Policy Reforms 2010: Going for Growth* (Paris: OECD Publishing, 2010), pp. 181–97.
11. Organisation for Economic Co-operation and Development, "The Output of Educational Institutions and the Impact of Learning," *Education at a Glance 2011: OECD Indicators* (Paris: OECD Publishing, 2011), pp. 29–42.
12. I. Kawachi and B. P. Kennedy, *The Health of Nations: Why Inequality Is Harmful to Your Health* (New York: The New Press, 2002); N. E. Adler, W. T. Boyce, M. A. Chesney, S. Cohen, S. Folkman, R. L. Kahn, and S. S. Leonard, "Socioeconomic Status and Health: The Challenge of the Gradient," *The American Psychologist* 49 (1994): 15–24; M. Subramanyam, I. Kawachi, L. Berkman, and S. V. Subramanian, "Relative Deprivation in Income and Self-Rated Health in the United States," *Social Science and Medicine* 69 (2009): 327–34.
13. S. Oishi, S. Kesebir, and E. Diener, "Income Inequality and Happiness," *Psychological Science* 22 (2011): 1095–100.
14. C. Murray, *Coming Apart: The State of White America, 1960–2010* (New York: Crown Forum, 2012); see also D. Brooks, *Bobos in Paradise: The New Upper Class and How They Got There* (New York: Touchstone, 2001).

15. C. Graham, *Happiness around the World: The Paradox of Happy Peasants and Miserable Millionaires* (New York: Oxford University Press, 2009); Carnevale and Rose, "The Undereducated American"; Kawachi and Kennedy, *The Health of Nations.*
16. L. Darling-Hammond, "Structured for Failure: Race, Resources, and Student Achievement," in Markus and Moya, eds., *Doing Race: 21 Essays for the 21st Century* (New York: W. W. Norton, 2010).
17. Carnevale and Rose, "The Undereducated American."
18. Ibid.
19. See, for example, N. M. Stephens, S. A. Fryberg, and H. R. Markus, "It's Your Choice: How the Middle-Class Model of Independence Disadvantages Working-Class Americans," in Fiske and Markus, eds., *Facing Social Class*, pp. 87–106.; D. Reay, M. E. David, and S. J. Ball, *Degrees of Choice: Social Class, Race and Gender in Higher Education* (Sterling, VA: Trentham, 2005); D. Reay, G. Crozier, and D. James, *White Middle Class Identities and Urban Schooling* (London: Palgrave Macmillan, 2011); M. J. Bailey and S. Dynarski, "Gains and Gaps: Changing Inequality in U.S. College Entry and Completion," *PSC Research Report No. 11-746* (2011).
20. Bill Clinton, remarks to the Democratic Leadership Council, December 1993.
21. Not his real name.
22. Also a pseudonym.
23. C. Anderson and J. L. Berdahl, "The Experience of Power: Examining the Effects of Power on Approach and Inhibition Tendencies," *Journal of Personality and Social Psychology* 83 (2002): 1362–77; P. K. Smith and Y. Trope, "You Focus on the Forest When You're in Charge of the Trees: Power Priming and Abstract Information Processing," *Journal of Personality and Social Psychology* 90 (2006): 578–96; J. C. Magee, A. D. Galinsky, and D. H. Gruenfeld, "Power, Propensity to Negotiate, and Moving First in Competitive Interactions," *Personality and Social Psychology Bulletin* 33 (2007): 200–211; M. W. Kraus, S. Chen, and D. Keltner, "The Power to Be Me: Power Elevates Self-Concept Consistency and Authenticity," *Journal of Experimental Social Psychology* 47 (2011): 974–80; A. D. Galinsky, J. C. Magee, D. H. Gruenfeld, J. A. Whitson, and K. A. Lijenquist, "Social Power Reduces the Strength of the Situation: Implications for Creativity, Conformity, and Dissonance," *Journal of Personality and Social Psychology* 95 (2008): 1450–66.
24. Stephens, Fryberg, and Markus, "It's Your Choice"; L. Rubin, *Worlds of Pain: Life in the Working-Class Family* (New York: Basic Books, 1976); N. M. Stephens, H. R. Markus, and S. S. M. Townsend, "Choice as an Act of Meaning: The Case of Social Class," *Journal of Personality and Social Psychology* 93 (2007): 814–30; M. L. Kohn, *Class and Conformity: A Study in Value* (Homewood, IL: Dorsey, 1969).
25. K. Curhan and H. R. Markus, "Social Class, Self and Well-Being," unpublished manuscript, Stanford University, 2012.

26. Ibid.
27. Because of their keen awareness of rank and their lower place in the hierarchy, working-class Americans are more likely than middle-class Americans to mention that they do not let rank negatively impact their relations to others. For further discussion of the importance of rank and hierarchy in working-class worlds, see. M. Lamont, *The Dignity of Working Men: Morality and the Boundaries of Race, Class, and Immigration* (Cambridge, MA: Harvard University Press, 2000); A. S. Rossi, *Caring and Doing for Others: Social Responsibility in the Domains of Family, Work, and Community* (Chicago, IL: University of Chicago Press, 2001); N. A. Bowman, S. Kitayama, and R. E. Nisbett, "Social Class Differences in Self, Attribution, and Attention: Socially Expansive Individualism of Middle-Class Americans," *Personality and Social Psychology Bulletin* 35 (2009): 880–93; M. Argyle, *The Psychology of Social Class* (London: Routledge, 1994).
28. Curhan and Markus, "Social Class, Self, and Well-Being."
29. J. C. Williams, "The Class Culture Gap," in Fiske and Markus, eds., *Facing Social Class*, pp. 39–57.
30. Snibbe and Markus, "You Can't Always Get What You Want," pp. 703–20; H. R. Markus and B. Schwartz, "Does Choice Mean Freedom and Well-Being?" *Journal of Consumer Research* 37 (2010): 344–55; H. R. Markus and S. Kitayama, "Models of Agency: Sociocultural Diversity in the Construction of Action," in V. Murphy-Berman and J. J. Berman, eds., *Cross-Cultural Differences in Perspectives on the Self* (Lincoln: University of Nebraska Press, 2003).
31. Snibbe and Markus, "You Can't Always Get What You Want," pp. 703–20.
32. N. M. Stephens, S. A. Fryberg, and H. R. Markus, "When Choice Does Not Equal Freedom: A Sociocultural Analysis of Choice in Working-Class Contexts," *Social and Personality Psychology Science* 2 (2011): 33–41; K. Savani, H. R. Markus, N. V. R. Naidu, S. Kumar, and N. Berlia, "What Counts as a Choice?" *Psychological Science* 14 (3) (2010): 391–98.
33. Stephens, Fryberg, and Markus, "When Choice Does Not Equal Freedom"; Stephens, Markus, and Townsend, "Choice as an Act of Meaning"; Markus and Schwartz, "Does Choice Mean Freedom and Well-Being?" pp. 344–355; B. Schwartz, H. R. Markus, and A. Conner Snibbe, "Is Freedom Just Another Word for Many Things to Buy?" *New York Times Magazine* (February 26, 2006).
34. H. R. Markus, C. D. Ryff, K. B. Curhan, and K. A. Palmersheim, "In Their Own Words: Well-Being at Midlife among High School-Educated and College-Educated Adults," in O. G. Brim, C. D. Ryff, and R. C. Kessler, eds., *How Healthy Are We? A National Study of Well-Being at Midlife* (Chicago: University of Chicago Press, 2004), pp. 273–319; K. B. Curhan, "Well-Being Strategies in Japan and the United States: A Comparative Study of the Prevalence and Effectiveness of Strategies Used to Make Life Go Well for High School-Educated and College-Educated Midlife Adults" (doctoral dissertation), Stanford University, Stanford, CA, 2009; see also M. W. Kraus, P. K. Piff, R. Mendoza-Denton, M. L. Rheinschmidt, and D. Keltner, "Social Class, Solipsism, and Contextualism: How the Rich Are Different from the

Poor," *Psychological Review* 119 (2012): 546–72.; H. R. Markus, C. D. Ryff, A. Conner, E. K. Pudberry, and K. L. Barnett, "Themes and Variations in American Understanding of Responsibility," in A. S. Rossi, ed., *Caring and Doing for Others: Social Responsibility in the Domains of Family, Work, and Community* (Chicago: University of Chicago Press, 2001), pp. 349–99.

35. M. W. Kraus and D. Keltner, "Signs of Socioeconomic Status: A Thin-Slicing Approach," *Psychological Science* 20 (2009): 99–106.
36. M. W. Kraus, S. Côté, and D. Keltner, "Social Class, Contextualism, and Empathic Accuracy," *Psychological Science* 21 (2010): 1716–23; M. W. Kraus, E. J. Horberg, J. L. Goetz, and D. Keltner, "Social Class Rank, Threat Vigilance, and Hostile Reactivity," *Personality and Social Psychology Bulletin* 37 (2011): 1376–88.
37. Independent Sector, "Giving and Volunteering in the United States 2001" (Washington, D.C., 2002).
38. P. K. Piff, M. W. Kraus, S. Côté, H. Cheng, and D. Keltner, "Having Less, Giving More: The Influence of Social Class on Prosocial Behavior," *Journal of Personality and Social Psychology* 99 (2010): 771–84; National Public Radio, "Study: Poor Are More Charitable Than the Wealthy" (August 8, 2010), available from http://www.npr.org/templates/story/story.php?storyId=129068241.
39. P. K. Piff, D. M. Stancato, S. Côté, R. Mendoza-Denton, and D. Keltner, "Higher Social Class Predicts Increased Unethical Behavior," *Proceedings of the National Academy of Sciences of the United States of America* 109 (2012): 408b–91.
40. J. C. Magee, A. D. Galinsky, and D. H. Gruenfeld, "Power, Propensity to Negotiate, and Moving First in Competitive Interactions," *Personality and Social Psychology Bulletin* 33 (2007): 200–212. E. Chen and K. A. Matthews, "Cognitive Appraisal Biases: An Approach to Understanding the Relation between Socioeconomic Status and Cardiovascular Reactivity in Children," *Annals of Behavioral Medicine* 23 (2001): 101–11.
41. A. Kusserow, "When Hard and Soft Clash: Class-Based Individualisms in Manhattan and Queens," in Fiske and Markus, eds., *Facing Social Class*, pp. 195–215; A. S. Kusserow, *American Individualisms: Child Rearing and Social Class in Three Neighborhoods* (New York: Palgrave Macmillan, 2004).
42. Kusserow, *American Individualisms.*
43. Ibid.
44. Ibid.
45. P. J. Miller, G. E. Cho, and J. R. Bracey, "Working-Class Children's Experience through the Prism of Personal Storytelling," *Human Development* 48 (2005): 115–35.
46. Kusserow, "When Hard and Soft Clash."
47. D. K. Dickinson and M. W. Smith, "Long-Term Effects of Preschool Teachers' Book Readings on Low-Income Children's Vocabulary and Story Comprehension," *Reading Research Quarterly* 29 (1994): 105–22; R. Paige and T. Thompson (co-chairs), "The White House Summit on Early Childhood Cognitive Development, Proceedings," 2001; G. J. Whitehurst, D. S. Arnold,

J. N. Epstein, A. L. Angell, M. Smith, and J. Fischel, "A Picture Book Reading Intervention in Day Care and Home for Children from Low-Income Families," *Developmental Psychology* 30 (1994): 679–89.

48. B. Hart and T. Risley, *Meaningful Differences in the Everyday Experience of Young American Children* (Baltimore, MD: Paul H. Brook, 1995); A. Lareau and J. McCrory Calarco, "Class, Cultural Capital, and Institutions: The Case of Families and Schools," in Fiske and Markus, eds., *Facing Social Class*; A. Lareau, *Unequal Childhoods: Class, Race, and Family Life*, 2nd ed. (Berkeley: University of California Press, 2011); M. Phillips, "Parenting, Time Use, and Disparities in Academic Outcomes," in Duncan and Murnane, eds., *Whither Opportunity?* pp. 207–28.
49. K. B. Curhan and H. R. Markus, "Social Class, Self and Well-Being," unpublished paper, 2012.
50. Snibbe and Markus, "You Can't Always Get What You Want," pp. 703–20.
51. Letter from college invitation package, University of California, Berkeley.
52. *Stanford Preview*, Stanford, CA, 2011.
53. *Stanford Viewbook*, Stanford, CA, 2004.
54. F. Yeskel, "Diversity Training and Classism," in B. Leondar-Wright, *Class Matters: Cross-Class Alliance Building for Middle-Class Activists* (Gabriola Island, BC: New Society Publishers, 2005), pp. 153–54.
55. U.S. Department of Education, National Center for Education Statistics, "Students Whose Parents Did Not Go to College: Post Secondary Access, Persistence, and Attainment," NCES 2001–126 (Washington, D.C.: Government Printing Office, 2001).
56. Lamont, *The Dignity of Working Men*.
57. U.S. Department of Education, National Center for Education Statistics, "Students Whose Parents Did Not Go to College."
58. N. M. Stephens, S. A. Fryberg, H. R. Markus, C. S. Johnson, and R. Covarriubas, "Unseen Disadvantage: How American Universities' Focus on Independence Undermines the Academic Performance of First-Generation College Students," *Journal of Personality and Social Psychology* 102 (2012): 1178–97.
59. Ibid.
60. Personal communication, 2012.
61. For evidence that some early humans were likely egalitarian, see D. S. Rogers, O. Deshpande, and M. W. Feldman, "The Spread of Inequality," *PLoS ONE* 6 (2011): e24683.
62. M. Zitek and L. Z. Tiedens, "The Fluency of Social Hierarchy: The Ease with Which Hierarchical Relationships are Learned, Remembered, and Liked," *Journal of Personality and Social Psychology* 102 (2012): 98–115; D. H. Gruenfeld and L. Z. Tiedens, "Organizational Preferences and Their Consequences," in S. T. Fiske, D. T. Gilbert, and G. Lindsay, eds., *The Handbook of Social Psychology* (New York: Wiley, 2010); J. Sidanius and F. Pratto, *Social Dominance: An Intergroup Theory of Social Hierarchy and Oppression* (New York: Cambridge University Press, 1999).

63. N. E. Adler, E. Epel, G. Castellazzo, and J. Ickovics, "Relationship of Subjective and Objective Social Status with Psychological and Physical Health: Preliminary Data in Healthy White Women," *Health Psychology* 19 (2000): 586–92; D. Operario, N. E. Adler, and D. R. Williams, "Subjective Social Status: Reliability and Predictive Utility for Global Health," *Psychology and Health* 19 (2004): 237–46.
64. Darling-Hammond, "Structured for Failure."
65. Ibid.
66. L. Darling-Hammond, *The Flat World and Education: How America's Commitment to Equity Will Determine Our Future* (New York: Teachers College Press, 2010), p. 192.
67. G. Orfield and C. Lee, *Why Segregation Matters: Poverty and Educational Inequality* (Cambridge, MA: Civil Rights Project, Harvard University, 2005); D. S. Massey and N. A. Denton, *American Apartheid: Segregation and the Making of the Underclass* (Cambridge, MA: Harvard University Press, 1993).
68. Darling-Hammond, "Structured for Failure," p. 309.
69. S. M. Wilson, L. Darling-Hammond, and B. Berry, "Steady Work: The Story of Connecticut's Reform," *American Educator* 25 (2001): 34–39.
70. W. N. Grubb, *The Money Myth: School Resources, Outcomes, and Equity* (New York: Russell Sage Foundation, 2009).
71. E. Aronson, "The Jigsaw Classroom: A Cooperative Learning Technique," 2012, retreived from www.jigsaw.org (accessed 08/10/12); E. Aronson and S. Patnoe, *Cooperation in the Classroom: The Jigsaw Method,* 3rd ed. (London: Pinter and Martin, Ltd., 2011).
72. Stephens,Fryberg,Markus,Johnson,andCovarrubias,"UnseenDisadvantage."
73. N. M. Stephens, S. S. M. Townsend, H. R. Markus, and L. T. Phillips, "A Cultural Mismatch: Independent Cultural Norms Produce Greater Increases in Cortisol and More Negative Emotion among First-Generation College Students," *Journal of Experimental Social Psychology* 48 (2012): 1389–93.
74. The Posse Foundation, *Fulfilling the Promise: The Impact of Posse after 20 Years. 2012 Alumni Report* (New York: The Posse Foundation, 2012); The Posse Foundation, "Partner Colleges and Universities, 2012," retrieved from possefoundation.org (accessed 08/09/12).
75. J.-C. Croizet and T. Claire, "Extending the Concept of Stereotype Threat to Social Class: The Intellectual Underperformance of Students from Low Socioeconomic Backgrounds," *Personality and Social Psychology Bulletin* 24 (1998): 588–94.
76. KIPP Foundation, *KIPP: 2011 Report Card and Individual School Results* (San Francisco, CA: KIPP Foundation, 2011).
77. J. Marchese, "Is This the Best School in Philadelphia?" *Philadephia Magazine* (September 1, 2009); P. Tough, "What It Takes to Make a Student," *New York Times Magazine,* November 26, 2006; "Getting Young Lives in Line," *U. S. News & World Report,* March 14, 2004.

78. KIPP Foundation, *The Promise of College Completion: KIPP's Early Successes and Challenges* (San Francisco, CA: KIPP Foundation, 2011).
79. H. Markus and P. Nurius, "Possible Selves," *American Psychologist* 41 (1986): 954–69; D. Oyserman and H. Markus, "Possible Selves in Balance: Implications for Delinquency," *Journal of Social Issues* 46 (1990): 141–57.
80. D. Oyserman, D. Bybee, and K. Terry, "Possible Selves and Academic Outcomes: How and When Possible Selves Impel Action," *Journal of Personality and Social Psychology* 91 (2006): 188–204.
81. N. Stephens, M. Hamedani, and M. Destin, unpublished paper, 2012.
82. P. Sacks, *Standardized Minds: The High Price of America's Testing Culture and What We Can Do to Change It* (Cambridge, MA: Perseus Publishing, 1999).
83. B. Leondar-Wright, ed., *Class Matters: Cross-Class Alliance Building for Middle-Class Activists* (Gabriola Island, BC: New Society Publishers, 2005); B. Jensen, "Becoming versus Belonging: Psychology, Speech, and Social Class," in Leondar-Wright, ed., *Class Matters.*
84. Leondar-Wright, *Class Matters*, p. 145.
85. N. Fast, D. Gruenfeld, N. Sivanathan, and A. Galinsky, "Illusory Control: A Generative Force behind Power's Far-Reaching Effects," *Psychological Science* 20 (2009): 502–8; S. E. Taylor and J. D. Brown, "Illusion and Well-Being: A Social Psychological Perspective on Mental Health," *Psychological Bulletin* 103 (1988): 193–210; M. E. Lachman an S. L. Weaver, "The Sense of Control as a Moderator of Social Class Differences in Health and Well-being," *Journal of Personality and Social Psychology* 74 (1998): 763–73.
86. Reardon, "The Widening Gap between the Rich and the Poor," pp. 91–116.
87. P. Bourdieu, *The State Nobility* (Cambridge: Polity Press, 1997).
88. The idea that class equals money is captured in the following famous conversation:

    Scott Fitzgerald: "The rich are different from us."
    Ernest Hemingway: "Yes, they have more money."

    See F. Scott Fitzgerald, *The Crack-Up*, E. Wilson, ed. (New York: New Directions, 1945), p. 125.
89. P. Bourdieu, *In Other Words: Towards a Reflexive Sociology* (Stanford, CA: Stanford University Press, 1987).

Chapter 6

1. R. Molloy, C. L. Smith, and A. K. Wozniak, "Internal Migration in the United States," NBER working paper 17307 (Cambridge, MA: National Bureau of Economics Research, 2011).
2. E. Silver, E. P. Mulvey, and J. W. Swanson, "Neighborhood Structural Characteristics and Mental Disorder: Faris and Dunham Revisited," *Social Science and Medicine* 55 (2002): 1457–70.

3. M. Dong, R. F. Anda, V. J. Felitti, D. F. Williamson, S. R. Dube, D. W Brown, and W. H. Giles, "Childhood Residential Mobility and Multipl Health Risks during Adolescence and Adulthood," *Archives of Pediatrics an Adolescent Medicine* 159 (2005): 1104–10.
4. Although different researchers divide the United States differently, man agree that the South comprises U.S. census divisions 5, 6, and 7 (AL AR, DE, FL, GA, KY, LA, MD, MS, NC, OK, SC, TN, TX, WV, and VA the Northeast comprises census divisions 1 and 2 (CT, MA, ME, NH, N NY, PA, RI, and VT); the Midwest comprises divisions 3 and 4 (IA, IL IN, KS, MI, MN, MO, NB, ND, OH, SD, and WI); and the West comprise divisions 8 and 9 (AZ, CA, CO, ID, MT, NM, NV, OR, UT, WA, an WY). Our analysis excludes Hawaii and Alaska because the historie ecologies, and cultures of these two states are so distinct from those of th lower 48.
5. Molloy, Smith, and Wozniak, "Internal Migration in the United States."
6. V. C. Plaut, G. Adams, and S. L. Anderson, "Does Attractiveness Buy Hap piness? It Depends on Where You're From," *Personal Relationships* 16 (2009 619–30.
7. The West comprises two census divisions: the Pacific (CA, OR, and WA though excluding AK and HI) and the Mountain states (AZ, CO, ID, MT NM, NV, and WY).
8. V. C. Plaut, H. R. Markus, and M. E. Lachman, "Place Matters: Consensu Features and Regional Variation in American Well-Being and Self," *Journ of Personality and Social Psychology* 83 (2002): 160–84; P. J. Rentfrow, S. D Gosling, and J. Potter, "A Theory of the Emergence, Persistence, and Expres sion of Geographic Variation in Psychological Characteristics," *Perspectives o Psychological Science* 3 (2008): 339–69.
9. Ibid.
10. Famous Club for Growth PAC TV ad about Howard Dean (video file), Au gust 26, 2006, retrieved from www.youtube.com/watch?v=K4-vEwD_7H (accessed 08/14/12).
11. V. C. Plaut, H. R. Markus, J. R. Treadway, and A. S. Fu, "The Cultur Construction of Self and Well-Being: A Tale of Two Cities," *Journal of Person ality and Social Psychology* (2012).
12. S. Kitayama, K. Ishii, T. Imada, K. Takemura, and J. Ramaswamy, "Volun tary Settlement and the Spirit of Independence: Evidence from Japan 'Northern Frontier,'" *Journal of Personality and Social Psychology* 91 (2006 369–84.
13. S. Oishi, J. Lun, and G. D. Sherman, "Residential Mobility, Self-Concep and Positive Affect in Social Interactions," *Journal of Personality and Social Psy chology* 93 (2007): 131–41.
14. B. Berkner and C. S. Faber, *Geographical Mobility: 1995 to 2000* (Washington D.C.: U.S. Census Bureau, 2000), retrieved from www.census.gov/prod 2003pubs/c2kbr-28.pdf (accessed 08/12/12).

15. M. S. Granovetter, "The Strength of Weak Ties," *The American Journal of Sociology* 78 (1973): 1360–80.
16. These are the San Francisco, San Diego, Seattle, and Los Angeles regions; see J. Cortright and H. Mayer, *Signs of Life: The Growth of Biotechnology Centers in the U.S.*(Washington, D.C.: The Brookings Institution, Center on Urban and Metropolitan Policy, 2002).
17. R. Florida, *Who's Your City?* (New York: Basic Books, 2008).
18. Plaut, Markus, Treadway, and Fu, "The Cultural Construction of Self and Well-Being."
19. Robert D. Putnam, "Chapter 16: Introduction," *Bowling Alone: The Collapse and Revival of American Community* (New York: Simon and Schuster, 2000).
20. S. Oishi, A. J. Rothman, M. Snyder, J. Su, K. Zehm, A. W. Hertel . . . and G. D. Sherman, "The Socioecological Model of Procommunity Action: The Benefits of Residential Stability," *Journal of Personality and Social Psychology* 93 (2007): 831–44.
21. S. Oishi, F. F. Miao, M. Koo, J. Kisling, and K. A. Ratliff, "Residential Mobility Breeds Familiarity-Seeking," *Journal of Personality and Social Psychology* 102 (2012): 149–62.
22. A. Rao and P. Scaruff, *A History of Silicon Valley: The Greatest Creation of Wealth in the History of the Planet* (Palo Alto, CA: Omniware, 2011).
23. Martin Kenney, ed., *Understanding Silicon Valley: The Anatomy of an Entrepreneurial Region* (Stanford, CA: Stanford University Press, 2000).
24. R. Florida, *The Rise of the Creative Class* (New York: Basic Books, 2002), p. 119.
25. Ibid.
26. Putnam, "Chapter 16: Introduction," in *Bowling Alone.*
27. B. McGrory, "Not Your Father's Boston," *Boston Globe*, July 26, 2004.
28. B. Johnstone, "Features and Uses of Southern Style," in S. J. Nagle and S. L. Sanders, eds., *English in the Southern United States* (New York: Cambridge University Press, 2003), pp. 189–207.
29. D. Roberts, "Hospitality," in C. R. Wilson, ed., *The New Encyclopedia of Southern Culture*, Vol. 4 (Chapel Hill: University of North Carolina Press, 2006), pp. 234–36; quote appears on p. 236.
30. R. E. Nisbett and D. Cohen, *Culture of Honor: The Psychology of Violence in the South* (Boulder, CO: Westview Press, 1996).
31. For more on steel magnolias and other southern archetypes, see T. McPherson, *Reconstructing Dixie: Race, Gender, and Nostalgia in the Imagined South* (Durham, NC: Duke University Press, 2003).
32. R. V. Levine, T. S. Martinez, G. Brase, and K. Sorenson, "Helping in 36 U.S. Cities," *Journal of Personality and Social Psychology* 67 (1994): 69–82.
33. Plaut, Markus, and Lachman, "Place Matters."
34. A. K-Y. Leung and D. Cohen, "Within- and Between-Culture Variation: Individual Differences and the Cultural Logics of Honor, Face, and Dignity Cultures," *Journal of Personality and Social Psychology* 100 (2011): 507–26.

35. D. Cohen, J. Vandello, S. Puente, and A. Rantilla, "'When You Call Me That, Smile!' How Norms for Politeness, Interaction Styles, and Aggression Work Together in Southern Culture," *Social Psychology Quarterly* 62 (2012): 257–75.
36. C. P. Flynn, "Regional Differences in Attitudes toward Corporal Punishment," *Journal of Marriage and Family* 56 (1994): 314–24.
37. Mississippi (7.5 percent of students), Arkansas (4.7 percent), and Alabama (4.5 percent) chart the highest percentages of students struck by educators in the past year. See A. Farmer, A. Neier, and A. Parker, *A Violent Education: Corporal Punishment of Children in U.S. Public Schools* (New York: Human Rights Watch, 2009).
38. D. Cohen and R. E. Nisbett, "Self-Protection and the Culture of Honor: Explaining Southern Violence," *Personality and Social Psychology Bulletin* 20 (1994): 551–67.
39. S. J. Watkins and J. Sherk, *Who Serves in the U.S. Military? Demographic Characteristics of Enlisted Troops and Officers* (Washington, D.C.: The Heritage Foundation, 2008).
40. D. Cohen, "Law, Social Policy, and Violence: The Impact of Regional Cultures," *Journal of Personality and Social Psychology* 70 (1996): 961–78.
41. L. Saad, "Self-Reported Gun Ownership in U.S. Is Highest since 1993," Gallup, October 26, 2011.
42. Death Penalty Information Center, "Facts about the Death Penalty," 2012, retrieved from www.deathpenaltyinfo.org/documents/FactSheet.pdf (accessed 08/14/12).
43. D. Cohen and R. E. Nisbett, "Field Experiments Examining the Culture of Honor: The Role of Institutions in Perpetuating Norms about Violence," *Personality and Social Psychology Bulletin* 23 (1997): 1188–99.
44. J. S. Reed, "Below the Smith and Wesson line: Reflections on Southern Violence," in M. Black and J. S. Reed, eds., *Perspectives on the American South: An Annual Review of Society, Politics, and Culture* (New York: Cordon and Breach Science, 1981), pp. 9–22, 144.
45. R. A. Heinlein, *Beyond This Horizon* (New York: Gross and Dunlap, 1948).
46. M. K. L. Ching, "'Ma'am' and 'Sir': Modes of Mitigation and Politeness in the Southern United States," abstract in *Newsletter of the American Dialect Society* 19 (1987): 10.
47. Johnstone, "Features and Uses of Southern Style."
48. C. R. Wilson, "Manners," in Wilson, ed., *The New Encyclopedia of Southern Culture*, Vol. 4, pp. 96–103 and 102.
49. Roberts, "Hospitality," p. 236.
50. G. Metcalfe and C. Hays, *Being Dead Is No Excuse: The Official Southern Ladies Guide to Hosting the Perfect Funeral* (New York: Miramax, 2005).
51. Farmer, Neier, and Parker, *A Violent Education.*
52. D. Cohen, "Law, Social Policy, and Violence," pp. 961–78.

53. For more about British settlement of the United States, see D. H. Fischer, *Albion's Seed: Four British Folkways in America* (New York: Oxford University Press, 1989).
54. For more about the wild Southern frontier, see R. E. Nisbett, "Violence and U.S. Regional Culture," *American Psychologist* 48 (1993): 441–49; J. Beck, W. J. Frandsen, and A. Randall, *Southern Culture: An Introduction* (Durham, NC: Carolina Academic Press, 2009).
55. R. D. Baller, M. P. Zevenbergen, and S. F. Messner, "The Heritage of Herding and Southern Homicide: Examining the Ecological Foundations of the Code of Honor Thesis," *Journal of Research in Crime and Delinquency* 46 (2009): 275–300.
56. Nisbett and Cohen, *Culture of Honor.*
57. T. L. Meares and D. M. Kahan, "Law and (Norms of) Order in the Inner City," *Law and Society Review* 32 (1998): 805–38.
58. B. Hermann, C. Thoni, and S. Gächter, "Antisocial Punishment across Societies," *Science* 319 (2008): 1362–67.
59. As quoted in A. Conner, "Where Nice Is Naughty," *Stanford Social Innovation Review* 6 (2008): 14.
60. A. Knorr and A. Arndt, "Why Did Wal-Mart Fail in Germany?" (Bremen, Germany: Institute for World Economic and International Management, 2003).
61. K. Hamilton, "Students Plan to Form West Coast Club," *The Daily Princetonian*, November 9, 2004; E. Graham, "Pulling Pork; Pulling Together," *Princeton Alumni Weekly*, June 7, 2006.
62. M. Milian, "Zuckerberg's Hoodie a 'Mark of Immaturity,' Analyst Says," Bloomberg, May 8, 2012.
63. See, for example, W. Isaacson, *Steve Jobs* (New York: Simon and Schuster, 2011).

Chapter 7

1. For more on the relationship between science and religion in American history, see S. L. Otto, *Fool Me Twice: Fighting the Assault on Science in America* (New York: Rodale, 2011).
2. "Ron Paul: 'I Don't Accept the Theory of Evolution,'" CBS News, August 29, 2011, retrieved from www.cbsnews.com/2100-205_162-20098876.html (accessed 08/13/12).
3. C. Carnia, "Rick Perry: 'Evolution Is a "Theory" with 'Gaps,'" *USA Today*, August 18, 2011, retrieved from content.usatoday.com/communities/onpolitics/post/2011/08/rick-perry-evolution-presidential-race-/1#.T8Lp8r8hc60 (accessed 08/12/12).
4. "Republican Primary Candidates on Climate Change," *San Francisco Chronicle*, February 5, 2012, p. E-6.

5. T. Hooper, "Santorum and Gingrich Dismiss Climate Change, Vow to Dismantle the EPA," *The Colorado Independent*, February 6, 2012, retrieved from www.coloradoindependent.com/111924/santorum-and-gingrich-dismiss-climate-change-vow-to-dismantle-the-epa (accessed 08/16/12).
6. "Republican Primary Candidates on Climate Change," *San Francisco Chronicle*.
7. K. Tumulty, "Gingrich Vows to Ban Embryonic Stem Cell Research, Questions In Vitro Practices," *Washington Post*, January 29, 2012.
8. J. C. Green, J. L. Guth, C. E. Smidt, and L. A. Kellstedt, *Religion and the Culture Wars: Dispatches from the Front* (Lanham, MD: Rowman and Littlefield, 1996).
9. M. Wolraich, "Why Evangelicals Love Santorum, Hated JFK," CNN Opinion, March 1, 2012, retrieved from www.cnn.com/2012/03/01/opinion/wolraich-catholics-protestants/index.html (accessed 08/17/12).
10. Ibid.
11. The Pew Forum on Religion and Public Life, "The Religious Composition of the United States," in *U.S. Religious Landscape Survey* (Washington, D.C.: The Pew Forum on Religion and Public Life, 2008).
12. See W. B. Wilcox, "Conservative Protestant Childrearing: Authoritarian or Authoritative?" *American Sociological Review* 63 (1998): 796–809; J. P. Bartkowski and X. Xu, "Distant Patriarchs or Expressive Dads? The Discourse and Practice of Fathering in Conservative Protestant Families," *The Sociological Quarterly* 41 (2000): 465–85.
13. For an overview, see D. E. Sherkat and C. G. Ellison, "Recent Developments and Current Controversies in the Sociology of Religion," *Annual Review of Sociology* 25 (1999): 363–94.
14. C. G. Ellison and D. E. Sherkat, "Obedience and Autonomy: Religion and Parental Values Reconsidered," *Journal for the Scientific Study of Religion* 32 (1993): 313–29.
15. For a review, see R. D. Woodberry and C. S. Smith, "Fundamentalism et al.: Conservative Protestants in America," *Annual Review of Sociology* 24 (1998): 25–56.
16. T. M. Luhrmann, *When God Talks Back: Understanding the Evangelical Relationship with God* (New York: Alfred A. Knopf, 2012), p. 35.
17. Wilcox, "Conservative Protestant Childrearing"; Bartkowski and Xu, "Distant Patriarchs or Expressive Dads?"; and C. G. Ellison and D. E. Sherkat, "Conservative Protestantism and Support for Corporal Punishment," *American Sociological Review* 58 (1993): 131–44.
18. P. Froese and C. Bader, *America's Four Gods: What We Say about God—and What That Says about Us* (New York: Oxford University Press, 2010).
19. The Pew Forum on Religion and Public Life, "Religious Composition of the United States."
20. For one system that classifies Mormons as fundamentalists (and therefore conservatives), see T. W. Smith, "Classifying Protestant Denominations," *Review of Religious Research* 31(1990): 225–45. A second scheme, by B. Steensland et al.,

makes a strong case that Black and Mormon churches are distinct from conservative Protestant traditions, although they share many features; see B. Steensland, J. P. Park, M. D. Regnerus, L. D. Robinson, W. B. Wilcox, and R. D. Woodberry, "The Measure of American Religion: Toward Improving the State of the Art," *Social Forces* 79 (2000): 291–318.

21. The Pew Forum on Religion and Public Life, "Religious Composition of the United States."
22. See G. Layman, *The Great Divide: Religious and Cultural Conflict in American Party Politics* (New York: Columbia University Press, 2001).
23. J. Haidt, *The Righteous Mind: Why Good People Are Divided by Politics and Religion* (New York: Pantheon Books, 2012).
24. The Pew Forum on Religion and Public Life, "Religious Composition of the United States."
25. W. Herberg, *Protestant-Catholic-Jew: An Essay in American Religious Sociology* (Chicago: University of Chicago Press, 1955).
26. The Pew Forum on Religion and Public Life, "Religious Composition of the United States."
27. Ibid.
28. Although they were probably quite lethal to competing bands of humans. Conflicts between early human groups during the late Pleistocene claimed up to ten times more lives (as a percentage of all deaths) than did the European wars of the twentieth century. See J.-K. Choi and S. Bowles, "The Coevolution of Parochial Altruism and War," *Science* 318 (2007): 636–40. Steven Pinker expands on this finding in his book *The Better Angels of Our Nature: Why Violence Has Declined* (New York: Viking, 2004).
29. S. Atran and A. Norenzayan, "Religion's Evolutionary Landscape: Counterintuition, Commitment, Compassion, Communion," *Behavioral and Brain Sciences* 27 (2004):713–70; and A. Norenzayan and A. F. Shariff, "The Origin and Evolution of Religious Prosociality," *Science* 322 (2008): 58–62.
30. A. F. Shariff and A. Norenzayan, "God Is Watching You: Priming God Concepts Increases Prosocial Behavior in an Anonymous Economic Game," *Psychological Science* 18 (2007): 803–9.
31. V. Saroglou, "Religiousness as a Cultural Adaptation of Basic Traits: A Five-Factor Model Perspective," *Personality and Social Psychology Review* 14 (2010): 108–25.
32. For an easy-to-read summary of the large literature on religion and well-being, see R. D. Putnam and D. E. Campbell, *American Grace: How Religion Divides and Unites Us* (New York: Simon and Schuster, 2010).
33. For a summary of research on religion and altruism, see ibid.
34. Matthew 5:28, King James Bible.
35. A. B. Cohen and P. Rozin, "Religion and the Morality of Mentality," *Journal of Personality and Social Psychology* 81 (2001): 697–710.
36. A. B. Cohen and P. C. Hill, "Religion as Culture: Religious Individualism and Collectivism among American Catholics, Jews, and Protestants," *Journal of Personality* 75 (2007): 709–42.

37. E. E. Sampson, "Reinterpreting Individualism and Collectivism: Their Religious Roots and Monologic Versus Dialogic Person-Other Relationship," *American Psychologist* 55 (2000): 1425–32.
38. See K. Peng and R. E. Nisbett, "Culture, Dialectics, and Reasoning about Contradiction," *American Psychologist* 54 (1999): 741–54.
39. Ibid.
40. Sampson, "Reinterpreting Individualism and Collectivism."
41. N. Jewison (director), *Fiddler on the Roof* (motion picture), MGM, USA, 1971.
42. For more about the sociology of America's dominant religious groups, see the classic W. Herberg, *Protestant-Catholic-Jew: An Essay in American Religious Sociology* (Chicago: University of Chicago Press, 1955).
43. See J. P. Dolan, *The American Catholic Experience* (New York: Doubleday, 1985).
44. L. A. Keister, "Upward Wealth Mobility: Exploring the Roman Catholic Advantage," *Social Forces* 85 (2007): 1195–225.
45. J. Sanchez-Burks, "Protestant Relational Ideology and (in)attention to Relational Cues in Work Settings," *Journal of Personality and Social Psychology* 83 (2002): 919–29.
46. Y. J. Li, K. A. Johnson, A. B. Cohen, M. J. Williams, E. D. Knowles, and Z. Chen, "Fundamental(ist) Attribution Error: Protestants Are Dispositionally Focused," *Journal of Personality and Social Psychology* 102 (2012): 281–90, p. 282.
47. Ibid.
48. Cohen and Hill, "Religion as Culture."
49. M. Weber, *The Protestant Ethic and the Spirit of Capitalism*, T. Parsons, trans. (1905; reprint New York: Charles Scribner's Sons, 1958).
50. S. O. Becker and L. Woessmann, L., "Was Weber Wrong? A Human Capital Theory of Protestant Economic History," *The Quarterly Journal of Economics* 124 (2009): 531–96.
51. See R. K. Smith, "The Cross: Church Symbol and Contest in Nineteenth Century America," *Church History: Studies in Christianity and Culture* 70 (2001): 705–34.
52. Herberg, *Protestant-Catholic-Jew.*
53. Luhrmann, *When God Talks Back*, p. 14.
54. For more on the social forces that gave rise to conservative Protestantism, see D. E. Miller, *Reinventing American Protestantism: Christianity in the New Millennium* (Berkeley: University of California Press, 1997).
55. N. T. Feather, "Protestant Ethic, Conservatism, and Values," *Journal of Personality and Social Psychology* 46 (1984): 1132–41.
56. I. McGregor, K. Nash, and M. Prentice, "Reactive Approach Motivation (RAM) for Religion," *Journal of Personality and Social Psychology* 99 (2010): 148–61.
57. J. T. Jost, J. Glaser, A. W. Kruglanski, and F. J. Sulloway, "Political Conservatism as Motivated Social Cognition," *Psychological Bulletin* 129 (2003): 339–75.

58. I. Storm and D. S. Wilson, "Liberal and Conservative Protestant Denominations as Different Socioecological Strategies," *Human Nature* 20 (2009): 1–24.
59. Ibid.
60. Luhrmann, *When God Talks Back.*
61. L. A. Keister, "Conservative Protestants and Wealth: How Religion Perpetuates Asset Poverty," *American Journal of Sociology* 113 (2008): 1237–71.
62. Randy Alcorn, *The Law of Rewards: Giving What You Can't Keep to Gain What You Can't Lose* (Carol Stream, IL: Tyndale House Publishers, 2003).
63. As told to A. Conner, "Don't Save; Be Saved," *Stanford Social Innovation Review* 5 (2008): 17.
64. Keister, "Conservative Protestants and Wealth."
65. K. W. Giberson and F. S. Collins, *The Language of Science and Faith: Straight Answers to Genuine Questions* (Downers Grove, IL: InterVarsity Press, 2011); F. S. Collins, *The Language of God: A Scientist Presents Evidence for Belief* (New York: Free Press, 2006).
66. M. Deutsch, "Constructive Conflict Management for the World Today," *International Journal of Conflict Management* 5 (1994): 111–129, p. 305.
67. Quoted in R. Williams, "Breaking through to Climate Change Skeptics," Michigan Radio, January 24, 2012, retrieved from michiganradio.org/post/breaking-through-climate-change-skeptics (accessed 08/16/12).
68. T. M. Luhrmann, "Do as I Do, Not as I Say," *New York Times,* May 6, 2012, campaignstops.blogs.nytimes.com/2012/05/06/do-as-i-do-not-as-i-say/ (accessed 08/17/12).
69. For more about moralities of autonomy, community, and divinity, see R. A. Shweder, M. C. Much, M. Mahaptra, and L. Park, "The 'Big Three' of Morality (Autonomy, Community and Divinity) and the 'Big Three' Explanations of Suffering," in A. Brandt and P. Rozin, eds., *Morality and Health* (New York: Routledge, 1997).
70. Haidt, *The Righteous Mind.*
71. Evangelical Environmental Network, 2012, retrieved from creation-care.org (accessed 08/17/12).
72. J. Roughgarden, *Evolution's Rainbow: Diversity, Gender, and Sexuality in Nature and People* (Berkeley: University of California Press, 2004).

Chapter 8

1. T. Krazit, "OLCP Fires Back at Intel, Children Learn Nothing," *CNET News,* January 4, 2008, retrieved from news.cnet.com/8301-13579_3-9840478-37.html (accessed 08/17/12).
2. For instance, because Hurricane Katrina recovery efforts were profitable to the businesses contracted to carry them out, progress was delayed. See V. Adams, T. van Hattum, and D. English, "Chronic Disaster Syndrome: Displacement, Disaster Capitalism, and the Eviction of the Poor from New Orleans," *American Ethnologist* 36 (2009): 615–36.

3. M. J. Sandel, *What Money Can't Buy: The Moral Limits of Markets* (New York: Farrar, Straus and Giroux, 2012).
4. For example, C. Arthur, *Digital Wars: Apple, Microsoft, Google and the Battle for the Internet* (Philadelphia: Kogan Page, 2012); J. H. Gittell, *The Southwest Airlines Way: Using the Power of Relationships to Achieve High Performance* (New York: McGraw-Hill, 2003); J. K. Liker, *The Toyota Way: 14 Management Principles from the World's Greatest Manufacturer* (New York: McGraw-Hill, 2004).
5. Quoted in G. Packer, "No Death, No Taxes," *The New Yorker*, November 28, 2011, p. 44.
6. J. R. Rawls, R. A. Ullrich, and O. T. Nelson, "A Comparison of Managers Entering or Reentering the Profit and Nonprofit Sectors," *The Academy of Management Journal* 18 (1975): 616–23.
7. See, for example, J. L. Perry and L. R. Wise, "The Motivational Bases of Public Service," *Public Administration Review* 50 (1990): 367–73; and G. A. Brewer and S. C. Selden, "Whistle Blowers in the Federal Civil Service: New Evidence of the Public Service Ethic," *Journal of Public Administration Research and Theory* 8 (1998): 413–39.
8. S. T. Lyons, L. E. Duxbury and C. A. Higgins, "A Comparison of the Values and Commitment of Private Sector, Public Sector, and Parapublic Sector Employees," *Public Administration Review* 66 (2006): 605–18; J. Taylor, "Public Service Motivation, Civic Attitudes and Actions of Public, Nonprofit and Private Sector Employees," *Public Administration* 88 (2010): 1083–98; Z. Van Der Wal, G. De Graaf, and K. Lasthuizen, "What's Valued Most? Similarities and Differences between the Organizational Values of the Public and Private Sector," *Public Administration* 86 (2008): 465–82.
9. D. J. Houston, "'Walking the Walk' of Public Service Motivation: Public Employees and Charitable Gifts of Time, Blood, and Money," *Journal of Public Administration Research and Theory* 16 (2006): 67–86.
10. R. Dawkins, *The Selfish Gene*, 30th anniversary ed. (Oxford: Oxford University Press, 2006).
11. See, for example, L. Leete, "Whither the Nonprofit Wage Differential? Estimates from the 1990 Census," *Journal of Labor Economics* 19 (2001): 136–70; and F. Handy and E. Katz, "The Wage Differential between Nonprofit Institutions and Corporations: Getting More by Paying Less?" *Journal of Comparative Economics* 26 (1998): 246–61.
12. A. Amirkhanyan, H. Kim, and K. T. Lambright, "Does the Public Sector Outperform the Nonprofit and For-Profit Sectors? Evidence from a National Panel Study on Nursing Home Quality and Access," *Journal of Policy Analysis* 27 (2008): 326–53.
13. M. Benz, "Not for the Profit, but for the Satisfaction? Evidence on Worker Well-Being in Non-Profit Firms," *Kyklos* 58 (2005): 155–76.
14. See, for example, S. A. Frank and G. B. Lewis, "Government Employees: Working Hard or Hardly Working?" *The American Review of Public Administration* 34 (2004): 36–51.

15. C.-A. Chen, "Explaining the Difference of Work Attitudes between Public and Nonprofit Managers: The Views of Rule Constraints and Motivation Styles," *The American Review of Public Administration* 42 (2012): 437–60.
16. Although corporations also do not enjoy all the rights that individual, "natural" people do, they do retain the rights to sue, make contracts, exercise free speech, and make political expenditures (as upheld in *Citizens United v. Federal Election Commission* in 2010), as well as many other human rights.
17. C. L. Hays, "Ben & Jerry's to Unilever, with Attitude," *New York Times,* April 13, 2000.
18. All twenty-eight kinds of organizations in section 501(c) of the tax code are technically "nonprofits," including civic leagues (501(c)4s); labor unions (501(c)5s); and cemeteries (501(c)13s). Section 501(c)3, charitable nonprofits, comprises the bulk of U.S. nonprofits, and is the only category of organization for which donors receive tax deductions for their contributions.
19. See, for example, T. Hobbes, *Leviathan: Or the Matter, Forme, and Power of a Common-Wealth Ecclesiasticall and Civill,* I. Shapiro, ed. (New Haven, CT: Yale University Press, 2010); or J. Locke, *Two Treatises of Government,* ed. Peter Laslett (Cambridge: Cambridge University Press, 1988). For an overview, see M. Hechter and C. Horne, *Theories of Social Order: A Reader* (Stanford, CA: Stanford University Press, 2003).
20. Percentages calculated from 2009 U.S. Department of Commerce Bureau of Economic Analysis data.
21. M. Roomkin and B. A. Weisbrod, "Managerial Compensation and Incentives in For-Profit and Nonprofit Hospitals," *Journal of Law, Economics, and Organization* 15 (1999): 750–81.
22. K. Patterson, J. Grenny, R. McMillan, and A Switzler, *Crucial Conversations: Tools for Talking When Stakes Are High* (New York: McGraw-Hill, 2011).
23. As quoted in S. Silverman and L. Taliento, "What Business Execs Don't Know—but Should—about Nonprofits," *Stanford Social Innovation Review* 4 (2006): 36–43, p. 38.
24. B. Bozeman, "A Theory of Government Red Tape," *Journal of Public Administration Research and Theory* 3 (1993): 273–303; M. K. Feeney and H. G. Rainey, "Personnel Flexibility and Red Tape in Public and Nonprofit Organizations: Distinctions Due to Institutional and Political Accountability," *Journal of Public Administration Research and Theory* 20 (2010): 801–26.
25. See Chen, "Explaining the Difference of Work Attitudes between Public and Nonprofit Managers."
26. Al Gore and National Performance Review, *From Red Tape to Results: Creating a Government That Works Better and Costs Less* (Washington, D.C.: U.S. Government Printing Office, 1993), p. 12.
27. B. Bozeman and G. Kingsley, "Risk Culture in Public and Private Organizations," *Public Administration Review* 58 (1998): 109–18.

28. J. Lawrence, "Making the B List," *Stanford Social Innovation Review* 7 (2009): 65–66; B Lab, "2012 B Corporation Annual Report," available from http://www.bcorporation.net/2012-Annual-Report (accessed on 8/15/2012).
29. See D. Patnaik, *Wired to Care: How Companies Prosper When They Create Widespread Empathy* (New York: FT Press, 2009).
30. T. Hsieh, *Delivering Happiness: A Path to Profits, Passion, and Purpose* (New York: Business Plus, 2010).
31. J. A. Chatman, J. T. Polzer, S. G. Barsade, and M. A. Neale, "Being Different Yet Feeling Similar: The Influence of Demographic Composition and Organizational Culture on Work Processes and Outcomes," *Administrative Science Quarterly* 43 (1998): 749–80.
32. S. T. Bell, "Deep-Level Composition Variables as Predictors of Team Performance: A Meta-Analysis," *The Journal of Applied Psychology* 92 (2007): 595–615.
33. V. Liberman, S. M. Samuels, and L. Ross, "The Name of the Game: Predictive Power of Reputations versus Situational Labels in Determining Prisoner's Dilemma Game Moves," *Personality and Social Psychology Bulletin* 30 (2004): 1175–85.
34. A. C. Kay and L. Ross, "The Perceptual Push: The Interplay of Implicit Cues and Explicit Situational Construals on Behavioral Intentions in the Prisoner's Dilemma," *Journal of Experimental Social Psychology* 39 (2003): 634–43.
35. D. L. Kirp, "Life Way after Head Start," *New York Times Magazine*, November 21, 2004, pp. 32–38; R. Belfield, M. Nores, S. Barnett, and L. Schweinhart, "The High/Scope Perry Preschool Program: Cost-Benefit Analysis Using Data from the Age-40 Follow-Up," *Journal of Human Resources* 41 (2006): 162–90.
36. A. Conner Snibbe, "Drowning in Data," *Stanford Social Innovation Review* 4 (2006): 38–45.
37. Urban Institute's National Center for Charitable Statistics and the Center on Philanthropy at Indiana University. The researchers examined more than 220,000 IRS Form 990s and conducted 1,500 in-depth surveys of organizations with revenues of more than $100,000.
38. A. G. Gregory and D. Howard, "The Nonprofit Starvation Cycle," *Stanford Social Innovation Review* 7 (2009): 48–53.
39. For more about nonprofit advocacy, see F. Nelson, D. W. Brady, and A. Conner Snibbe, "Learn to Love Lobbying," *Stanford Social Innovation Review* 5 (2007): 56–63.
40. For more ways to break the nonprofit starvation cycle, see Gregory and Howard, "Nonprofit Starvation Cycle."
41. J. Aaker, K. D. Vohs, and C. Mogilner, "Nonprofits Are Seen as Warm and For-Profits as Competent: Firm Stereotypes Matter," *Journal of Consumer Research* 37 (2010): 224–37.

Chapter 9

1. Southern Sudan is now a separate state known as the Republic of Sudan.
2. S. Harrigan, "Relief and an Understanding of Local Knowledge: The Case of Southern Sudan," in V. Rao and M. Walton, eds., *Culture and Public Action* (Stanford, CA: Stanford University Press, 2004), pp. 307–27.
3. Ibid.
4. Some authorities also include China in the Global South; see, for example, J. Rigg, *An Everyday Geography of the Global South* (Abingdon, UK: Routledge, 2007).
5. United Nations Development Programme, "Human Development Report 2005"; Rigg, *An Everyday Geography of the Global South.*
6. V. Rao and M. Walton, "Culture and Public Action: Relationality, Equality of Agency, and Development," in V. Rao and M. Walton, eds., *Culture and Public Action* (Stanford, CA: Stanford University Press, 2004), p. 6.
7. For more on the relationship between economic development and independence, see G. Hofstede, *Culture's Consequences: International Differences in Work-Related Value* (Beverly Hills: Sage, 1980); R. Inglehart and W. E. Baker, "Modernization, Cultural Change, and the Persistance of Traditional Values," *American Sociological Review* 65 (2000): 19–51; and A. Inkeles and D. H. Smith, *Becoming Modern: Individual Change in Six Developing Countries* (New York: Universe, 1976/2000).
8. "Fear Grips Accra," *People and Places*, January 23–29, 1997, p. 2, cited in G. Adams and V. A. Dzokoto, "Genital-Shrinking Panic in Ghana: A Cultural Psychological Analysis," *Culture Psychology* 13 (2007): 83–104.
9. West Africa comprises Benin, Burkina Faso, Cape Verde, Côte d'Ivoire, Ghana, Liberia, Mali, Mauritania, Niger, Nigeria, Gambia, Guinea Bissau, Senegal, Sierra Leone, and Togolese. All of these countries, with the exception of Mauritania, are members of the Economic Community of West African States (ECOWAS). Retrieved from www.ecowas.int. See also Centers for Disease Control and Prevention, April 25, 2012, West Africa Region, retrieved from wwwnc.cdc.gov/travel/regions/west-africa.htm (accessed 08/11/12).; Adams and Dzokoto, "Genital-Shrinking Panic in Ghana"; G. Adams, "The Cultural Grounding of Personal Relationship: Enemyship in North American and West African Worlds," *Journal of Personality and Social Psychology* 88 (2005): 948–68.
10. Adams, "The Cultural Grounding of Personal Relationship."
11. Ibid.
12. Ibid.
13. Anthropologist Alan Fiske was one of the first social scientists to document that relationships are the basic unit of reality in much of the world, and that West Africans typically understand themselves in terms of relationships. See A. P. Fiske, "The Four Elementary Forms of Sociality: Framework

for a Unified Theory of Social Relations," *Psychological Review* 99 (1992): 689–723.

14. J. S. Mbiti, *African Religions and Philosophy* (Garden City, NY: Doubleday, 1970), p. 106.
15. Adams, "The Cultural Grounding of Personal Relationship," p. 956.
16. Ibid., pp. 948–68.
17. P. E. Lovejoy, *Transformations in Slavery: A History of Slavery in Africa* (Cambridge, UK: Cambridge University Press, 1983); J. C. Miller, *Way of Death: Merchant Capitalism and the Angolan Slave Trade, 1730–1830* (Madison: University of Wisconsin Press, 1996); B. Davidson, *The African Slave Trade: A Revised and Expanded Edition* (New York: Back Bay Books, 1988).
18. S. W. Koelle, *Polyglotta Africana, or a Comparative Vocabulary of Nearly Three Hundred Words and Phrases, in More Than One Hundred Distinct African Languages* (London: Church Missionary House, 1854).
19. N. Nunn and L. Wantchekon, "The Slave Trade and the Origins of Mistrust in Africa," *American Economic Review* 101 (2011): 3221–52.
20. Ibid., p. 9.
21. The World Justice Project, "The World Justice Rule of Law Index," 2011, retrieved from worldjusticeproject.org/rule-of-law-index/index-2011 (accessed 08/11/12).
22. For more on what happens when institutions are weak, see J. Robinson and D. Acemoglu, *Why Nations Fail: The Origins of Power, Prosperity, and Poverty* (New York: Crown Business, 2012).
23. P. S. Budhwa and A. Varma, *Doing Business in India: Building Research-Based Practice* (New York: Routledge, 2010).
24. E. Luce, *In Spite of the Gods: The Rise of Modern India* (New York: Anchor Books, 2008), pp. 201–3; see also Budhwa and Varma, *Doing Business in India*.
25. J. G. Miller and D. M. Bersoff, "Culture and Moral Judgment: How Are Conflicts between Justice and Interpersonal Responsibilities Resolved?" *Journal of Personality and Social Psychology* 62 (1992): 541–54.
26. Ibid.; J. G. Miller, "Cultural Psychology of Moral Development," in S. Kitayama and D. Cohen, eds., *Handbook of Cultural Psychology* (New York: Guilford Press, 2006).
27. K. Savani, H. R. Markus, and A .L. Conner, "Let Your Preferences Be Your Guide?: Preferences and Choices Are More Tightly Linked for North Americans than for Indians," *Journal of Personality and Social Psychology* 95 (2008): 861–76. See also K. Savani, H. R. Markus, N. V. R. Naidu, S. Kumar, and N. Berlia, "What Counts as a Choice? U.S. Americans Are More Likely Than Indians to Construe Actions as Choices," *Psychological Science* 14 (2010): 391–98.
28. R. A. Shweder, *Why Do Men Barbecue? Recipes for Cultural Psychology* (Cambridge, MA: Harvard University Press, 2003), p. 118.

29. J. G. Miller and D. M. Bersoff, "The Role of Liking in Perceptions of Moral Responsibility to Help: A Cultural Perspective," *Journal of Experimental Social Psychology* 34 (1998): 443–69.
30. R. Ferber, *Solve Your Child's Sleep Problems* (New York: Simon and Schuster, 1986); A. Mansbach, *Go the F**k to Sleep* (New York: Akashic Books, 2011).
31. R. A. Shweder, L. A. Jensen, and W. M. Goldstein, "Who Sleeps by Whom Revisited: A Method for Extracting the Moral Goods Implicit in Practice," *New Directions for Child Development* 67 (1995): 21–39.
32. M. Toledo, "First Comes Marriage, Then Comes Love," ABC *20/20*, January 30, 2009; D. Jones, "One of USA's Exports: Love, American Style," *USA Today*, February 13, 2006.
33. S. E. Cross and H. R. Markus, "The Cultural Constitution of Personality," in L. Pervin and O. John, eds., *Handbook of Personality Theory and Research* (New York: Guilford, 1999), pp. 378–96.
34. J. E. Myers, J. Madathil, and L. R. Tingle, "Marriage Satisfaction and Wellness in India and the United States: A Preliminary Comparison of Arranged Marriages and Marriages of Choice," *Journal of Counseling Development* 83 (2005): 183–90; P. Yelsma and K. Athappilly, "Marital Satisfaction and Communication Practices: Comparisons among Indian and American couples," *Journal of Comparative Family Studies* 19 (1988): 37–54; M. Pasupathi, "Arranged Marriages: What's Love Got to Do with It?" in M. Yalom, L. Carstensen, E. Freedman, and B. Gulpi, eds., *Inside the American Couple: New Thinking, New Challenges* (Berkeley: University of California Press, 2002).
35. Toledo, "First Comes Marriage, Then Comes Love"; R. Seth, *First Comes Marriage: Modern Relationship Advice from the Wisdom of Arranged Marriages* (New York: Simon and Schuster, 2008).
36. S. L. Bhansali (director), *Hum Dil De Chuke Sanam (I Have Given My Heart, My Love)* (motion picture), Bhansali Films and Jhamu Sughand Productions, India, 1999.
37. J. Ganapathi, *Ganesha: Ancient Tales for Modern Times* (Bangalore, India: Unisun Publications, 2005).
38. R. Clements and J. Musker (directors), *Aladdin* (motion picture), Disney, United States, 1992.
39. United Nations Development Programme, "Human Development Report for Central America 2009–2010," 2009.
40. J. W. Anderson, "Cartoons of Prophet Met with Outrage," *Washington Post*, January 21, 2006; B. N. Bonde, "How 12 Cartoons of the Prophet Mohammed Were Brought to Trigger an International Conflict," *Nordicom Review* 28 (2007): 33–48; "Embassies Torched in Cartoon Fury," CNN, February 5, 2006.
41. P. Cohen, "Danish Cartoon Controversy," *New York Times*, August 12, 2009; "Arson and Death Threats as Muhammed Caricature Controversy Escalates," *Spiegel Online*, retrieved from www.spiegel.de/international/cartoon-violence-spreads-arson-and-death-threats-as-muhammad-caricature-controversy-escalates-a-399177.html (accessed 08/10/12).

42. For more on Middle Eastern cultures of honor, see J. Schneider, "Of Vigilance and Virgins: Honor, Shame, and Access to Resources in Mediterranean Societies," *Ethnology* 10 (1971): 1–24; G. S. Gregg, *The Middle East: A Cultural Psychology* (New York: Oxford University Press, 2005); H. Barakat, *The Arab World: Society, Culture, and State* (Berkeley: University of California Press, 1993).
43. "Turkish PM Given Hero's Welcome," *BBC News*, January 30, 2009, retrieved from www.news.bbc.co.uk/2/hi/business/davos/7859815.stm (accessed 08/10/12).
44. L. Rosen, "Understanding Corruption," *The American Interest Magazine*, March–April 2010.
45. B. Mesquita, "Emotions in Collectivist and Individualist Contexts," *Journal of Personality and Social Psychology* 80 (2001): 68–74.
46. J. E. Greenberg, "Cultural Psychology of the Middle East: Three Essays" (doctoral dissertation), Stanford University, Stanford, CA, 2010.
47. Ibid.
48. Silatech and Gallup, "The Silatech Index: Voices of Young Arabs," June 2009, retrieved from sas-origin.onstreammedia.com/origin/gallupinc/media/poll/pdf/Silatech.Report.2011.Apr.pdf (accessed 08/10/12).
49. E. N. Akcinar, A. Maitreyi, and H. R. Markus, "Nepotism in European American and Middle Eastern Cultural Contexts," poster presented at the Society for Personality and Social Psychology, New Orleans, 2013.
50. L. Rosen, "Understanding Corruption," *The American Interest* 5 (2010), retrieved from www.the-american-interest.com/article.cfm?piece=792 (accessed 08/10/12); See also Gregg, *The Middle East*; D. G. Bates, *Peoples and Cultures of the Middle East* (Upper Saddle River, NJ: Prentice Hall, 2001); C. Lindholm, *The Islamic Middle East* (Hoboken, NJ: Wiley-Blackwell, 2002).
51. B. Herrmann, C. Thoni, and S. Gächter, "Antisocial Punishment across Society," *Science* 319 (2008): 1362–67. (Participants in Greece also show this punitive tendency.)
52. J. Cedar (director), *Footnote* (*Hearat Shulayim*) (motion picture), Movie Plus and United King Films, Israel, 2011.
53. A common Mexican expression reflecting a relaxed attitude toward time. For more on sources of this attitude, see J. Castañeda, *Mañana Forever? Mexico and the Mexicans* (New York: Alfred A. Knopf, 2011).
54. H. C. Triandis, G. Marín, J. Lisansky, and H. Betancourt, "*Simpatía* as a Cultural Script of Hispanics," *Journal of Personality and Social Psychology* 47 (1984): 1363–75; R. Janoff-Bulman and H. K. Leggatt, "Culture and Social Obligation: When 'Shoulds' are Perceived as 'Wants,'" *Journal of Research in Perosnality* 36 (2006): 260–70.
55. R. Holloway, A. M. Waldrip, and W. Ickes, "Evidence That a *Simpatico* Self-Schema Accounts for Differences in the Self-Concepts and Social Behavior of Latinos versus Whites (and Blacks)," *Journal of Personality and Social Psychology* 96 (2009): 1012–28.

56. K. Savani, A. Alvarez. B. Mesquita, and H. R. Markus, "Feeling Close and Doing Well: The Prevalence and Motivational Effects of Interpersonally Engaging Emotions in Mexican and European American Cultural Contexts," *International Journal of Psychology*, forthcoming.
57. M. C. Madsen, "Developmental and Cross-Cultural Differences in the Cooperative and Competitive Behavior of Young Children," *Journal of Cross-Cultural Psychology* (1971): 365–71.
58. J. C. Condon, *Good Neighbors: Communicating with the Mexicans*, 2nd ed. (Yarmouth, ME: Intercultural Press, 1997).
59. N. Ramirez-Esparza, M. R. Mehl, J. Alvarez-Bermudez, and J. W. Pennebaker, "Are Mexicans More or Less Sociable Than Americans? Insights from a Naturalistic Observation Study," *Journal of Research in Personality* 43 (2009): 1–7.
60. J. Faura, *The Whole Enchilada: Hispanic Marketing 101* (Ithaca, NY: Paramount, 2004), p. xvi.
61. H. R. Markus, C. D. Ryff, K. B. Curhan, and K. A. Palmersheim, "In Their Own Words: Well-Being among High School–Educated and College-Educated Adults," in O. G. Brim, C. D. Ryff, and R. C. Kessler, eds., *How Healthy Are We? A National Study of Well-Being at Midlife* (Chicago: University of Chicago Press, 2004), pp. 273–319.
62. H. R. Markus, unpublished data.
63. M. Delgado, *Social Work with Latinos: A Cultural Assets Paradigm* (New York: Oxford University Press, 2007); R. L. Smith and R. E. Montilla, eds., *Counseling and Family Therapy with Latino Populations: Strategies That Work* (New York: Routledge, 2006).
64. Condon, *Good Neighbors.*
65. Quoted in "Business in Mexico: Still Keeping It in the Family," *The Economist*, May 18, 2004.
66. Personal communication.
67. D. Acemoglu, S. Johnson, J. Robinson, and P. Yared, "Income and Democracy," *American Economic Review* 98 (2008): 808–42.
68. R. B. Reich, *Supercapitalism* (New York: Random House, 2007).
69. Acemoglu and Robinson, *Why Nations Fail.*
70. K. Jonker and W. M. Meehan, "Curbing Mission Creep," *Stanford Social Innovation Review* 6 (2008): 60–65.
71. A. Day, "The Answer Is on the Ground," *Stanford Social Innovation Review* 7 (2009): 63–64.
72. J. G. Shaheen, *Reel Bad Arabs: How Hollywood Vilifies a People* (Northampton, MA: Interlink Publishing Group, 2001).
73. C. R. Berg, *Latinos in Film: Stereotypes, Subversion, and Resistance* (Austin, TX: University of Austin Press, 2002).
74. D. Teng'o, "More of the Same: The Flow and Framing of African News on the Web Sites of Five Western News Organizations and an African News Aggregator" (master's thesis), Kent State University, Kent, Ohio, 2008.

75. C. Lutz and J. L. Collins, *Reading National Geographic* (Chicago: University of Chicago Press, 1993).
76. "The World According to Americans," available from sphotos.ak.fbcdn.net/hphotos-ak-ash1/hs736.ash1/162923_1601575914175_1079393167_3155781_2618452_n.jpg (accessed 8/15/2012).
77. M. Twain, *Innocents Abroad* (New York: Penguin Classics, 1869/2012).
78. J. Sanchez-Burks, R. Nisbett, F. Lee, and O. Ybarra, "Intercultural Training Based on a Theory of Relational Ideology," *Basic and Applied Social Psychology* 29, no. 3 (2007): 257–68.
79. J. Temple, "Tribe Teams with Google to Make Stand in Amazon," *San Francisco Chronicle*, October 18, 2009, retrieved from www.sfgate.com/green/article/Tribe-teams-with-Google-to-make-stand-in-Amazon-3213795.php (accessed 08/14/12).
80. C. Binns, "Smart Soaps," *Stanford Social Innovation Review* 6 (2008): 69–70.
81. "Cognitive Theory of Mass Communication," *Media Psychology* 3 (2001): 265–99; A. Bandura, "Social Cognitive Theory for Personal and Social Change by Enabling Media," in A. Singhal, M. J. Cody, E. M. Rogers, and M. Sabido, eds., *Entertainment-Education and Social Change: History, Research, and Practice* (Mahwah, NJ: Lawrence Erlbaum Associates, 2004); A. Bandura, D. Ross, and S. A. Ross, "Imitation of Film-mediated Aggressive Models," *Journal of Abnormal and Social Psychology* 66 (1963): 3–11.
82. Binns, "Smart Soaps."
83. May, "Airborne Peace," *Stanford Social Innovation Review* 7 (2010): 61–62.
84. E. Staub, *The Roots of Evil: The Origins of Genocide and Other Group Violence* (Cambridge, UK: Cambridge University Press, 1989).
85. May, "Airborne Peace," 61–62.
86. E. L. Paluck, "Reducing Intergroup Prejudice and Conflict Using the Media: A Field Experiment in Rwanda," *Journal of Personality and Social Psychology* 96 (2009): 574–87; E. L. Paluck, "What's in a Norm? Sources and Processes of Norm Change," *Journal of Personality and Social Psychology* 96 (2009): 594–600.
87. May, "Airborne Peace."
88. R. Ratnesar, "Arab Regimes' Nepotism Problem," *Bloomberg Businessweek*, March 9, 2011, retrieved from www.businessweek.com/magazine/content/11_12/b4220007540210.htm (accessed 08/12/12).
89. A. Bellow, *In Praise of Nepotism: A Natural History* (New York: Doubleday, 2003).
90. M. J. Bennett, "Overcoming the Golden Rule: Sympathy and Empathy," in M. J. Bennett, ed., *Basic Concepts of Intercultural Communication: Selected Readings* (Yarmouth, ME: Intercultural Press, 1998), p. 213.

Chapter 10

1. H. Herrera, *A Biography of Frida Kahlo* (New York: HarperCollins, 1983); A. Haynes, "Frida Kahlo: An Artist 'in Between,'" *eSharp* 6 (2006).

2. R. B. Gunderman and C. M. Hawkins, "The Self-Portraits of Frida Kahlo," *Radiology* 247 (2008): 303–6.
3. S. Saulny, "Black? White? Asian? More Young Americans Choose All of the Above," *New York Times*, January 29, 2011, p. A1; S. Saulny, "Census Data Presents Rise in Multiracial Population of Youths," *New York Times*, March 24, 2011, p. A3.
4. U.S. Census Bureau, "2010 Census Shows America's Diversity" (Washington, D.C.: Government Printing Office, 2011).
5. J. S. Passel, W. Wang, and P. Taylor, "Marrying Out: One-in-Seven New U.S. Marriages Is Interracial or Interethnic" (Washington, D.C.: Pew Research Center, 2010).
6. J. W. Berry, J. S. Phinney, D. L. Sam, and P. Vedder, eds., *Immigrant Youth in Cultural Transition: Acculturation, Identity, and Adaptation across National Contexts* (Mahwah, NJ: Lawrence Erlbaum Associates, 2006); A. Chandra, W. D. Mosher, C. Copen, and C. Sionean, "Sexual Behavior, Sexual Attraction, and Sexual Identity in the United States: Data from the 2006–2008 National Survey of Family Growth" (Hyattsville, MD: National Center for Health Statistics, 2011); B. Leondar-Wright, *Class Matters: Cross-Class Alliance Building for Middle-Class Activists* (Gabriola Island, BC: New Society Publishers, 2005).
7. C. Fuentes, C., ed., B. Crow de Toledo and R. Pohlenz, trans., *The Diary of Frida Kahlo: An Intimate Self-Portrait* (London: Bloomsbury, 1995).
8. For an analysis of how exposure shapes preferences, see R. B. Zajonc, "Attitudinal Effects of Mere Exposure," *Journal of Personality and Social Psychology* 9 (1968): 1–27; R. B. Zajonc, "Feeling and Thinking: Preferences Need No Inferences," *American Psychologist* 35 (1980): 151–75; R. B. Zajonc, "Mere Exposure: A Gateway to the Subliminal," *Current Directions in Psychological Science* 10 (2001): 224–28.
9. Cohorts do not have exact start and end dates. The tendencies of a person born on December 31, 1981, are probably not that different from those of a person born on January 1, 1982, even though the two people are technically of different generations. Partly because of these fuzzy boundaries, scholars use different start and end dates in naming generations. Here, we are applying the dates that historians William Strauss and Neil Howe use. See W. Strauss and N. Howe, *Generations: The History of America's Future, 1584 to 2069* (New York: William Morrow and Company, 1991).
10. Twenge dates the beginning of "Generation Me" as 1970. See J. Twenge, *Generation Me: Why Today's Young Americans Are More Confident, Assertive, Entitled—and More Miserable—Than Ever Before* (New York: Free Press, 2006).
11. J. M. Twenge and S. M. Campbell, "Generational Differences in Psychological Traits and Their Impact on the Workplace," *Journal of Managerial Psychology* 23 (2008): 862–77.
12. William Deresiewicz, "Generation Sell," *New York Times*, November 12, 2011, p. SR1.

13. Leung and Chiu, "Multicultural Experience, Idea Receptiveness, and Creativity." *Journal of Cross-Cultural Psychology* 31 (2010): 723–41; W. W. Maddux and A. D. Galinsky, "Cultural Borders and Mental Barriers: The Relationship between Living Abroad and Creativity," *Journal of Personality and Social Psychology* 96 (2009): 1047–61.
14. D. K. Simonton, "Foreign Influence and National Achievement: The Impact of Open Milieus on Japanese Civilization," *Journal of Personality and Social Psychology* 72 (1997): 86–94; L. A. Ricciardelli, "Creativity and Bilingualism," *Journal of Creative Behavior* 26 (1992): 242–54; J. M. Levine and R. L. Moreland, "Collaborations: The Social Context of Theory Development," *Personality and Social Psychology Review* 8 (2004): 164–72.
15. Leung and Chiu, "Multicultural Experience, Idea Receptiveness, and Creativity."
16. P. W. Linville, "Self-Complexity and Affective Extremity: Don't Put All Your Eggs in One Cognitive Basket," *Social Cognition* 3 (1985): 94–120; S. T. Hannah, R. L. Woolfolk, and R. G. Lord, "Leader Self-Structure: A Framework for Positive Leadership," *Journal of Organizational Behavior* 30 (2009): 269–90.
17. A. D. Nguyen and V. Benet-Martínez, "Biculturalism and Adjustment: A Meta-Analysis," *Journal of Cross-Cultural Psychology*, advance online publication, 2012; T. LaFramboise, H. L. Coleman, and J. Gerton, "Psychological Impact of Biculturalism: Evidence and Theory," *Psychological Bulletin* 114 (1993): 395–412.
18. For more on the power of suspending judgment, see C. Geertz, *Available Light: Anthropological Reflections on Philosophical Topics* (Princeton, NJ: Princeton University Press, 2000).
19. Although Hawaii is in the Western census region, most scholars agree that its culture is anomalous. See, for example, M. Haas, *Barack Obama, The Aloha Zen President: How a Son of the 50th State May Revitalize America Based on 12 Multicultural Principles* (Santa Barbara, CA: ABC-CLIO, 2001).
20. D. Remnick, *The Bridge: The Life and Rise of Barack Obama* (New York: Vintage Books, 2011); B. Obama, *Dreams from My Father: A Story of Race and Inheritance* (New York: Crown, 1995).
21. B. Gates, *The Road Ahead* (New York: Viking, 1995).
22. K. Spink, *Mother Teresa: An Authorized Biography*, rev. ed. (New York: HarperCollins, 2011).
23. M. Landler and J. H. Cushman, "In Graduation Speech to Women, Obama Leaps into Gender Gap," *New York Times*, May 14, 2012, p. A12.
24. Spink, *Mother Teresa: An Authorized Biography*.
25. D. Trafimow, H. C. Triandis, and S. G. Goto, "Some Tests of the Distinction between the Private Self and the Collective Self," *Journal of Personality and Social Psychology* 60 (1991): 649–55.
26. S. Spencer, unpublished data, University of Waterloo, 2012.
27. J. A. Bargh and E. Morsella, "The Unconscious Mind," *Perspectives on Psychological Science* 3 (2008): 73–39; M. Weisbuch and N. Ambady, "Non-Conscious

Routes to Building Culture: Nonverbal Components of Socialization," *Journal of Consciousness Studies* 15 (2008): 159–83.

28. W. L. Gardener, S. Gabriel, and A. Y. Lee, "'I' Value Freedom but 'We' Value Relationships: Self-Construal Priming Mirrors Cultural Differences in Judgment," *Psychological Science* 10 (1999): 321–26.
29. M. W. Morris and K. Peng, "Culture and Cause: American and Chinese Attributions for Social and Physical Events," *Journal of Personality and Social Psychology* 67 (1994): 949–71.
30. Y.-Y. Hong, M. W. Morris, C.-Y. Chiu, and V. Benet-Martínez, "Multicultural Minds: A Dynamic Constructivist Approach to Culture and Cognition," *American Psychologist* 55 (2000): 709–20.
31. M. Ross, W. G. E. Xun, and A. E. Wilson, "Language and the Bicultural Self," *Personality and Social Psychology Bulletin* 28 (2002): 1040–50.
32. D. A. Briley, "Cultural Chameleons: Biculturals, Conformity Motives, and Decision Making," *Journal of Consumer Psychology* 15 (2005): 351–62.
33. C. M. Fausey and L. Boroditsky, "Subtle Linguistic Cues Influence Perceived Blame and Financial Liability," *Psychonomic Bulletin and Review* 17 (2010): 644–50.
34. D. Oyserman and S. W. S. Lee, "Does Culture Influence What and How We Think? Effects of Priming Individualism and Collectivism," *Psychological Bulletin* 134 (2008): 311–42.
35. S. A. Fryberg, personal communication.
36. Not his real name. To protect children's identities, we do not use their real names in this section.
37. S. A. Fryberg and H. R. Markus, "Being American Indian: Current and Possible Selves," *Self and Identity* 2 (2003): 325–44.
38. S. A. Fryberg, H. R. Markus, D. Oyserman, and J. M. Stone, "Of Warrior Chiefs and Indian Princesses: The Psychological Consequences of American Indian Mascots," *Basic and Applied Social Psychology* 30 (2008): 208–18.
39. J. Henrich, A. Norenzayan, and S. Heine, "The Weirdest People in the World?" *Behavioral and Brain Sciences* 33 (2010): 61–135.
40. *Loving v. Virginia*, 388 U.S. 1 (1967).
41. Association of MultiEthnic Americans, *AMEA*, retrieved June 2, 2012, from www.ameasite.org (accessed 01/03/12).
42. Swirl, retrieved June 6, 2012 from www.swirlinc.org (accessed 01/03/12).
43. Herrera, *A Biography of Frida Kahlo.*

Index